PADRE PIO
UNDER
INVESTIGATION

Francesco Castelli

PADRE PIO
UNDER
INVESTIGATION

The Secret Vatican Files

Foreword by Vittorio Messori

Translated by Lee and Giulietta Bockhorn

IGNATIUS PRESS   SAN FRANCISCO

Original Italian edition:
Padre Pio sotto inchiesta: L' "Autobiografia" segreta
© 2008 by Edizioni Ares, Milan
http://www.ares.mi.it

Cover photograph (top): Stone Crucifix, Lisbon, Portugal.
Photograph by John Herreid

Cover photograph of Padre Pio in 1919
and also other photographs (in photo insert)
© The Voice of Padre Pio, San Giovanni Rotondo, Italy

Cover design by John Herreid

ISBN 978-1-58617-405-7
Library of Congress Control Number 2010931419
Printed in the United States of America ∞

The great saints . . . are called to withstand
the temptations of a particular time
in their own skin, . . . in their own souls,
. . . to bear them . . . for us ordinary souls,
and to help us persist on our way to the One
who took upon himself the burden of us all."

—Joseph Ratzinger

CONTENTS

Foreword: "I Am a Mystery to Myself"
    by Vittorio Messori   ix
Sources   xxvii

PART ONE: A New Starting Point

Introduction   3
Chapter 1: An Inquisitor in the Convent   9
Chapter 2: The Inquisitor's Interrogations   29
Chapter 3: Padre Pio's Stigmata before the Inquisitor   44
Conclusion   60
Notes to Part One   61

PART TWO: *Votum* on Padre Pio of Pietrelcina

Report on Padre Pio by Msgr. Raffaello Carlo Rossi   81
Compendium of the Report: Depositions
    by Padre Pio and Witnesses   134
Appendix: Report on Fr. Benedetto Nardella   238
Compendium of the Appendix: Letters to Padre
    Pio from Fr. Benedetto Nardella   241

PART THREE: Appendices

I. Msgr. Rafaello Carlo Rossi   265
II. Monsignor Rossi, Father Benedetto, and the
    Chronicle of Padre Pio   273
III. *Chronicle of Padre Pio*   276

IV. Padre Pio's Stigmatization: History and
   Testimonies   281
V. Chronology of the Life of Padre Pio   289
Notes to Part Three   296

Acknowledgments   299
Index   303

FOREWORD

"I Am a Mystery to Myself"

An exceptional document

"The future will reveal what today cannot be read in the life of Padre Pio of Pietrelcina." These words, written in January 1922 by Msgr. Raffaello Carlo Rossi, Bishop of Volterra—Inquisitor in San Giovanni Rotondo by order of the Holy Office in June 1921, when Padre Pio was just thirty-four years old—were then certainly a way to "cover his back", and avoid locking in too small a cage a man and a situation which to the prelate, sent on a reconnaissance mission to evaluate the stigmatic friar and the environment around him, had seemed—as we shall see—certainly out of the ordinary, but also substantially healthy and sincere. But those words were, at the same time, too easy a prophecy.

When we read them now—with Padre Pio having been proclaimed a saint in 2002, after many disagreements and vicissitudes—we can't help smiling. We now know very well what the future has said about that friar, rich since childhood in extraordinary charisms, but also—and I would say necessarily—subjected to a special attention on the part of the Church, and to a severity that often seemed excessive.

And we know it because, despite his humility and his reserve, the mission to which he had been called had an enormous echo, crossing all borders and channeling millions of pilgrims toward San Giovanni Rotondo. An event which, however one may have judged it, had captured the attention of everyone, believers and non-believers, helping considerably to strengthen the faith of many.

We should then know practically everything about him, since much has been written, both at a scholarly level and for the general public. But it is not so, as this volume by historian Fr. Francesco Castelli demonstrates. The book collects and analyzes what the jargon calls the *Votum* (that is, the final report of Msgr. Raffaello Carlo Rossi's inquiry, conducted, as noted, on behalf of the Holy Office), and other shorter texts like the *Chronicle of Padre Pio*, written by one of his spiritual directors, Fr. Benedetto Nardella of San Marco in Lamis.

These are almost entirely unpublished texts, and they are of remarkable documentary value: Since they were declared classified at that time, they didn't appear among the sources in the archives of San Giovanni Rotondo, and for this reason they were ignored for a long time. But in 2006, as is well known, Benedict XVI gave free access to the archives of the former Holy Office up until the year 1939, making it possible at last to examine what the archives held on the subject of the friar from Pietrelcina. The consequence of all this was the revival of the seemingly inexhaustible research on this saint, who has been long-loved and at the same time, in some circles, so discussed and looked upon with arrogant diffidence. These past few years have seen the arguments—both in favor and against the stigmatic Capuchin—rekindle, arguments that had apparently died down with the canonization.

Thus a volume by the Jewish historian Sergio Luzzatto, *Padre Pio. Miracoli e Politica nell'Italia del Novecento*, has caused great commotion. The book examines some documents kept in the former Holy Office, in particular the charge, attached to the Lemius Report, leveled by two pharmacists. The author, while briefly mentioning Monsignor Rossi's Visitation, meant to cast an ambiguous light on the stigmatic friar by relying on his detractors, first and foremost Father Gemelli. Luzzatto carries out his maneuver by insinuating doubts about the veracity of the stigmata, suggesting it would be impossible to rule out not only psychosomatic causes, but even chemical interventions to create and maintain them. According to this author, a great part of the "Padre Pio phenomenon" would actually be the fruit of the tight intertwining occurring at that time between the Church and Italian politics—in particular the phenomenon of clerical fascism, coupled with the fanaticism of the Catholic masses, which, according to Luzzatto, from the very beginning would have made the Capuchin untouchable—and with his own (at least partial) consent.

I have already noted elsewhere that Luzzatto's way of reading the events, by making use of historical and political, when not ideological, categories, is absolutely insufficient to describe and penetrate phenomena like the ones at issue, which, while belonging to history, at the same time transcend history. Only faith—which is not fanaticism or sentimentalism, as it would be sometimes convenient to portray it—grants that vision of the world, and hence of history, which allows for the hypothesis of God and accepts all of its consequences, including the one that he may work wonders in a person like Padre Pio and through him may powerfully intervene in the world.

Saverio Gaeta and Andrea Tornielli have accurately and vigorously answered Luzzatto in their volume *Padre Pio. L'ultimo sospetto*, in which they highlight not only the historian's numerous inaccuracies, but also his genuine mistakes and his frequent manipulation of the texts he uses to confirm his thesis. Gaeta and Tornielli did this by using various sources, and by quoting a few passages from the previously mentioned Holy Office inquiry, especially when countering the insinuations concerning the stigmata.

Now in this volume that very document, to which only very few had had access, is published in its entirety for the general public, revealing the many never-published texts it contains. Some of these are of primary importance: more than two-thirds of the answers Padre Pio gives to the Inquisitor's questions; the Inquisitor's accurate examination of the friar's stigmata, which provides researchers with new and essential elements; a letter Padre Pio wrote to a nun; and, various letters Father Benedetto of San Marco in Lamis sent to Padre Pio.

The exceptional value of this document did not escape Francesco Castelli, who has presented it well, and who has performed a crucial historiographical task. At the same time he has offered everyone the opportunity to read it and to experience personally its peculiarity, but also its beauty, since a distinctive characteristic of this inquiry is the simplicity of its language: The curial bureaucratic jargon is kept to a minimum—thanks no doubt to Monsignor Rossi, as well—which makes for a smooth, and in some ways fascinating, read, and for an immediate understanding of the texts.

"I unite you with my Passion"

The emerging picture is truly very interesting. The Inquisitor tries to reconstruct what pertains to Padre Pio not only by interrogating and examining the Capuchin directly, but also by sounding out the closest witnesses: the priests in San Giovanni Rotondo and the friars of the convent.

This makes it possible for the reader to listen directly to Padre Pio narrating what happened to him and describing his state of mind during the events. With humble but meaningful brevity, he relates how he received the visible stigmata—since he had had invisible ones for a long time—on that September 20, 1918 (that is, three years earlier). It happened one morning, in the choir, while he was reciting his thanksgiving prayer after the Holy Mass: "[S]uddenly I was overtaken by a powerful trembling, then calm followed, and I saw our Lord in the posture of someone who is on a cross (but it didn't strike me whether he had the Cross), lamenting the ingratitude of men, especially those consecrated to him and by him most favored. This revealed his suffering and his desire to unite souls with his Passion. He invited me to partake of his sorrows and to meditate on them: At the same time, he urged me to work for my brothers' salvation. I felt then full of compassion for the Lord's sorrows, and I asked him what I could do. I heard this voice: 'I unite you with my Passion.' Once the vision disappeared, I came to, I returned to my senses, and I saw these signs here, which were dripping blood. I didn't have anything before."

Never before had the Capuchin so explicitly described such an important event. Especially, he had never revealed before that sentence, essential to understanding everything, that "I unite you with my Passion", which is the key to enter into the mystery of Padre Pio's life, together with that other sentence: "At the same time he urged me to work for my brothers' salvation." The exterior "signs" of the Passion, after the long time of preparation during which they were hidden, are given to him so that his mission may appear more evident: Conformed to Jesus, marked by his same wounds, tightly united to him in sorrow and love, he can be an instrument, a channel through which salvation can abundantly come to men.

An extraordinary and mind-blowing event, then; and yet, the Capuchin accepts it and lives through it in peace. Padre

Pio admits he suffers much, physically: "Sometimes I cannot bear it", he confesses. He also acknowledges sometimes being frightened by the clamor that all this has provoked, even against his will: the rush to the convent of the faithful, ever more numerous; the pressure on the part of people devoted to him, especially women who later on will cause him so much trouble; and his ever-expanding correspondence, which threatens to overcome the little strength the convent of San Giovanni Rotondo still has. But he lives through it all calmly, every time realigning himself to the cross that was granted to him, trusting in God's help, and also in that of his Brothers and superiors.

And so, with great humility, he who is at the center of such exceptional charisms reveals the simplicity of his spiritual life, consisting of meditation, of formal prayers, and of the Rosary, said in its entirety. Asked whether he performs particular forms of penance, he candidly answers: "None: I take the ones the Lord sends." And, truth be told, we know there were not a few of them. Then he talks about the long hours spent in the confessional listening to people's sins, enlightening, admonishing, absolving.

Afterward, with the same humility and docility, he shows the Inquisitor all his sores, so that he can examine them carefully and describe them, as he did, and as we can now read, in a vividly realistic description that gives all the details. Padre Pio also makes clear that the rumored sore on his right shoulder did not exist, at least at that time. He never evaded, in any way, even the most difficult questions, not even the suspicion and doubts about the products some were insinuating he used to treat the sores.

The other friars, on the other hand, fill us with interesting details about his practical life and his humble nature— reserved in the most delicate matters, and yet playful: "In conversation, Padre Pio is very pleasant; with his Brothers, he is serene, jovial, even humorous." Truly surprising details, if we think about the constant physical pain and the psychological pressure that surrounded him. And so the Brothers tell about the very little he would eat even back then, the cup of chocolate which at that time was all his dinner, the glass of beer he would drink every now and then. Sketches of a life marked by the powerful seal of God, and yet simple and limpid.

At the end of his accurate and thorough inspection, the Inquisitor can't help but conclude: "Padre Pio is a good religious, exemplary, accomplished in the practice of the virtues, given to piety and probably elevated to a higher degree of prayer than it seems from the outside; he shines especially because of his sincere humility and his remarkable simplicity, which did not fail even in the gravest moments, when these virtues were put to the test, a test truly grave and dangerous for him." A man who seemed devoid of any mendacity, and whose deposition, then, "is to be considered sincere, since imposture and perjury would be in too stark a contrast with [his] life and virtues".

Even the environment around Padre Pio makes a good impression on Monsignor Rossi, who concludes: "The religious Community in which Padre Pio lives is a good Community and one that can be trusted."

Padre Pio, the faithful, the Church

This inquiry, published in its entirety for the first time, is important because it lets us know Padre Pio firsthand, speaking as he does after taking the oath on the Gospel, and bound to full and complete obedience to the Church. But it is also a truly interesting window on a certainly not secondary portion of the history of the Church.

We know very well how our Capuchin was immediately much loved by the faithful and even by many unbelievers, who converted in great numbers. But we also know that in the course of his life he was obstructed, limited, humiliated. And this until almost the very end, until a few years from his death, which occurred, as it is well known, on September 23, 1968. In 1923, 1931, and again in 1961, the Holy Office took heavy and painful restrictive measures against him. It will not be until 1964 that Cardinal Ottaviani, then head of the Holy Office, makes known Paul VI's will that "Padre Pio perform his ministry in total freedom". Finally, John Paul II—a long-time admirer of Padre Pio—thirty-one years after his death, in 1999, will proclaim him Blessed, and three years later, in 2002, Saint.

When the archives for the years after 1939 are opened, it may be possible to say something more about the period covering the sixties, the years of the last "persecution" against Padre Pio. But what can be said even now—penetrating, through the reading of this first inquiry on the stigmatic friar, into archives secret until recently—is that the resulting image of this institution, the Holy Office, dedicated to watch over whatever in the Church may compromise the Faith, appears much less grim than it was believed until now.

The method of the inspecting Bishop is firm but serene. He investigates everything in depth, but without prejudice. His final judgment on the person of Padre Pio is largely positive. In particular, the Bishop Inquisitor was the first high-ranking representative of a Roman congregation to conduct an accurate theological examination of the Capuchin's stigmata, drawing a conclusion fully in favor of their authenticity, and, in fact, of their divine origin. From a historical point of view, this detail of Padre Pio's life is unique and of exceptional importance, since it shows how the Church, in this circumstance, formulates a precise and reliable judgment that will turn out to be correct. The friar's stigmata are not only real: they manifest themselves in a psychologically and spiritually balanced personality.

For all this, the Bishop's advice on how to handle in the future all those extraordinary events is to follow the developments—since there will certainly be developments—with prudence, and to take some collateral measures to keep the context around the friar, more than Padre Pio himself, from possible mistakes.

What was then called into question (and I think this is also true for the following years), at least on the part of the Holy Office, was never the event of the stigmata per se. On this, Monsignor Rossi's inquiry appears to be decisive, so much that the issue will not be reviewed again, as far as we know. No, it was the way the phenomenon of the stigmata was being handled: The Holy Office fears too much clamor, the excessive fanaticism of the devout, the inevitably ever-expanding flow of money, the possibility of corruption that comes with all of this, which might also reach and involve Padre Pio. Legitimate and, I would say, appropriate worries.

On the other hand, what makes an unfavorable impression—something that we know had a great influence on the disciplinary and restraining measures adopted by the Holy Office—is the pressure exerted on this institution of the Church by some clerics who acted, at least toward Padre Pio, with a harshness that was hardly justified. Among them, Fr. Agostino Gemelli and the Archbishop of Manfredonia (the diocese to which San Giovanni Rotondo belonged), Msgr. Pasquale Gagliardi.

The inquiry published in this volume was actually born of the serious reservations Father Gemelli, a preeminent psychologist and founder of the Università Cattolica [del sacro Cuore], made known to Rome. His doubts were founded, as it has been unquestionably demonstrated, on a professed acquaintance with Padre Pio that didn't actually exist, since Gemelli had only met Padre Pio once, and for just a few minutes. Gemelli is followed by Monsignor Gagliardi, who was always, since the beginning, suspicious of and hostile toward the Capuchin, and who kept repeating his accusation—which turned out to be completely groundless—until 1929, when he was practically forced to resign.

It seems that Gemelli and Gagliardi especially are at the center of that prejudice against extraordinary mystical events which, while never completely alien to the Church of all times, certainly intensified during these recent centuries because of an often exasperated rationalism. Their prejudice certainly had much influence, given the roles of these two clerics.

Rome swayed between these two poles—Padre Pio's supporters and his opponents—at times making room for the first stigmatic priest's extraordinary charisms and mission, at times applying the brake and restraining his pastoral action. This certainly didn't change Padre Pio's deep commitment to offering up everything as always, as he had done since the beginning, even for his own detractors. During those times, his apostolate was extremely limited, but—who knows—maybe even more effective. "And I, when I am lifted up from the earth, will draw all men to myself", said Jesus of himself. It was likely the same for that "other Christ", who in those moments clung even more to the Cross of his Lord, and who was even more like his Teacher, rejected especially by his own. That man whom Jesus wished to send us, marked with his same wounds, exactly in the century of the worst ideological horrors, that he may remind us, more alive and near, of the Emmanuel, God with us, and of his work of salvation.

I believe the document presented here furthers the understanding that the Church as an institution—when examined with hindsight—might at times be excessively severe, but also that the Holy Office was not, and is not, under its current name of Congregation for the Doctrine of the Faith, the place of incomprehension and inhuman dogmatism that it is too often accused of being. To be sure, prudence often trumps other considerations, to the point of heavily limiting even very important charisms. But let's be completely sincere—would it have been better to risk a worldwide scandal because of charisms that were simulated, or whose degeneration might have truly compromised the image of the Church and of the Faith, and destabilized many people? Or, in the end, wasn't it better to contain and keep in check a situation which, if true, would have emerged, in the end, in all its greatness and profundity?

After all, when we reason about these things, I believe we must not forget that, if we could have a Padre Pio, it is because, in part, the Church succeeded, despite all the limitations of her men (starting with ourselves, to be sure), to keep alive and intact her faith in Jesus, in that incarnate Man-God, who died for us and then resurrected. Indeed, it is this faith that allowed and allows us to recognize in the humble and stigmatic friar from Pietrelcina the signs of that Passion and of that Resurrection which now and forever work through the Church. It is, then, the Church as Mystery that justifies and explains a Padre Pio, who would be absolutely incomprehensible outside the Church. But it is to protect the Mystery that the Church as an institution can sometimes appear excessively distrustful and severe.

The game is worth the candle; and since history vindicates, what is true, holy, and conforming to the Faith will emerge in the end: as in fact happened on that June 16, 2002, in Saint Peter's Square, when a large crowd participated and rejoiced in the glory given to God by an extraordinary saint, image of the Son, masterpiece of the Holy

Spirit. And so, if there are a Father Gemelli and a Monsignor Gagliardi, who hold back and cause some damage, there are also always, sooner or later, a Monsignor Rossi, a Paul VI, and a John Paul II, who lead the way again.

It is only right, for the sake of historical accuracy, to make the due clarifications, to identify who—if anyone—is to blame, even in Padre Pio's case, and to evaluate the measures that were taken and their possible limits. But always with humility, since the historian knows it does not make sense to judge past events in the light of subsequent knowledge and mentality. It might have been possible, a few decades ago, to have even justified doubts and perplexities regarding the stigmatic friar that of course are now easy to judge as groundless.

The historian also knows—thanks to the experience he has acquired through the study of two thousand years of Christianity—that it is necessary to work without arrogance, since in the end even "the judges will be judged". No one, not even in our time, can have the certainty—nonexistent by definition, for a Christian—to have made no mistakes, and therefore to have understood everything of the Gospel, and to have reached completeness and perfection in translating it into practice. The truth is, we are all marching toward a destination that is not the fruit of justice alone, but one that is born especially of God's mercy. In this, we are guided by a Church that is certainly limited in her men, but is built on the rock, who is Jesus Christ. And if it is our job to criticize her in order to help her—since she is ours, too—we also have a duty to love her from the bottom of our hearts, the way a mother is loved, accepting when necessary her prudent, and in some cases perhaps excessive, severity.

After all, if it is true that, as Monsignor Rossi's inquiry also demonstrates, the faithful, with their *sensus fidei*, were since the beginning the great supporters and defenders of

Padre Pio—so much that the inquiring Bishop has to admit that moving him from San Giovanni Rotondo would cause an insurrection—it is also true that Padre Pio himself openly expresses his fears: "I was terrified. I tried to listen to everyone, as far as possible, and to work. Even in the Community we were invaded. We had to resort to the *Carabinieri*." We know, after all, that the fine line between proper devotion and fanaticism is not difficult to cross. Also, it's true there is the risk of idolatry, which would make the sign prevail over the reality behind it. Not without reason Padre Pio used to say he was only an instrument, that the extraordinary wonders were the work of God, and God alone. A valuable crowd, then, was the one looking for Padre Pio to the point of siege—a rich but also dangerous potential, which brings joy to a believer, but which must also be handled with prudence.

Alter Christus, humble Cyrenian, sign of the Resurrection

If the Holy Office investigation clarifies, as we have seen, the most visible and easy-to-assess aspects concerning the friar who had received in his flesh the Lord's wounds, it also urges us to try to find a way to penetrate the heart of the innermost secret of this man, who often said he was "a mystery to [him]self". After all, the inquiry shows how, from the very beginning, Padre Pio aroused opposite reactions in people, who either understood him joyously and flocked to him, or looked upon this religious with out-of-the-ordinary charisms with distrust, when not with annoyance and contempt. I think both these reactions are understandable.

Let's try for a moment to think about all that revolves around the stigmata: open flesh that doesn't heal; bleeding wounds; bandages that collect the blood and that the faithful try to hoard; scabs that form, then fall off, and then form again; crowds, often excited and always full of problems, that gather hoping for miracles. A set of phenomena that cannot fail to impress, but also to shake, whoever is not able to grasp the meaning beyond the appearances.

We must keep in mind that the stigmata are a phenomenon belonging only to Catholicism, since Protestants do not appreciate certain "miraculous" aspects of the Faith, while the Orthodox tend to experience different charisms, like the radiation of light—which might refer to the Resurrection—from the face of Saint Seraphim of Sarov. But even in the Catholic faith the stigmata are unknown before Saint Francis received his at La Verna—with the exception of the literal interpretation some exegetes give to Saint Paul's assertion: "I bear on my body the marks of Jesus" (Gal 6:17). After Saint Francis, there were a few other cases before Padre Pio, who, as we have said, is the first stigmatic priest. Science has much investigated the phenomenon, without reaching a precise conclusion. With the obvious exclusion of fraud, all the various psychosomatic hypotheses have not found practical confirmations. Without acknowledging a supernatural reference, then, this phenomenon remains on the whole inexplicable.

In the case of Padre Pio, moreover, further elements must be considered. First of all, we know a fragrance followed the Capuchin friar, something noted already by Monsignor Rossi. Those open sores, those wounds that normally should emanate the foul smell of coagulated blood, are instead accompanied by a pleasant and appealing scent of flowers. Also, the man who bears those wounds is subject to constant pains, has fevers that reach 118.4° F, and is ceaselessly oppressed by chronic, acute illnesses all his life. To us this poor friar seems crushed by his interior dark night of the senses, as he often reveals in his correspondence, but also oppressed by the requests for help from millions of people; and yet, he holds out all his life, spending countless hours in the confessional, with interior and exterior calm. He was supported by an extraordinary strength, just like his sores which do not heal, no, but do not get infected, either, nor do they suppurate—they will be sterile until their disappearance, just days before Padre Pio's death, with no signs of cicatrization.

It is understandable that all this may be dismaying—strongly attracting some and just as strongly repelling others.

In this second case, I think there might be, behind the mask of whoever says he is not a simpleton to be duped, a sort of fear, maybe even authentic *timor Domini.* I am actually convinced that part of Padre Pio's mission was to dismay, to raise questions, to confuse, to explode certainties of any kind, even scientific. Padre Pio was, and still is, a mystery that only finds its explanation in the eyes of faith. He is a "sign", as we were saying, that can be recognized and interpreted by whoever has already encountered Jesus Christ, or whoever is willing to humbly meet him the moment he is before Christ's image, as renewed and presented again in Padre Pio.

Then, the ever-flowing blood impresses him, but doesn't make him flee; on the contrary, it attracts him, since he recognizes in those wounds the same signs he has read about in the Gospels, the outcome of the Son of God's death on the Cross. He also recognizes that that wounded flesh is strictly connected to that Incarnation from which everything began. It is a reminder that we Christians believe in a God who is not only spirit, but who also willed, from the beginning and to the point of death, to take on our own human flesh and blood. For this reason, flesh and blood are not destined to end in a sepulcher and stay there forever: They are called instead to a destiny of transfiguration and resurrection.

At this point we understand that, in Padre Pio's sores, in his wounds surrounded by a halo of fragrances, we Christians can read something more: We can remember the apparitions of the Resurrected Jesus, especially the one to Thomas, when the Redeemer shows himself in glory, yes, but with his wounds still open, into which the doubting and incredulous apostle may put his finger. In this, the Western tradition and the Eastern tradition seem to find their unity again: The stigmata strongly point to the Passion, but they carry the mystery of the Resurrection; the light on the holy faces of Orthodoxy refers directly to the Resurrection, but obviously presupposes that Passion which led to it.

Padre Pio is all of this: He is the memorial of the sorrowful Passion of the Lord, but also, and at the same time, of his glorious Resurrection. He reminds us of the necessity of going through Calvary, but also of the Easter morning. He testifies to a redemption forever at work, in which there are pain and suffering, but not as an end to themselves. The goal is life, not death.

"I unite you with my Passion." This wonderful and terrifying sentence we read in Padre Pio's testimony also can appall whoever approaches it for the first time. It recalls Paul's powerful statement: "[I]n my flesh I complete what is lacking in Christ's afflictions." How to understand such disconcerting expressions? Certainly not by assuming that Jesus' offering and sacrifice were insufficient.

To understand, we must ponder the fact that the Resurrection earned two thousand years ago on Golgotha was not a bureaucratic event, a sort of one-time tax applied to every man forever and ever. It was certainly an act of justice, but above all it was an act of love to be reciprocated. It was a concrete opportunity, available to each man, to enter fully into the Trinitarian mystery and into the divine life, a "narrow door" to go through, accepting to follow the Teacher, carrying our share of the purifying cross.

A yoke that Christ has made light and easy to carry, but one that we have to experience nonetheless. A yoke that, in the Mystical Body, we can share with our brothers, becoming Cyrenians toward them, the way that first Cyrenian in history was toward Jesus. In this journey we will in turn be helped by the many hidden Cyrenians who in silence offer up their suffering and their lives, and by the extraordinary ones, those whom the Lord sometimes elevates on the hill, as in the case of Padre Pio—this humble and quiet friar, the great Cyrenian of our time. Only after death will we truly understand what this man consented to be done through his person, the rivers of grace that went through his stigmata and flooded and transformed the hearts of so many.

Yet, we can state even now—without fear of denial, I think—that few events have contributed, in the century that ended not long ago but that will have an everlasting echo, to save the faith of the People of God, to bring back to Jesus so many of the doubtful and the uncertain, as much as the humble and doleful presence of this friar, of this *alter Christus*, whom the divine benevolence willed to grant us.

Vittorio Messori

SOURCES

ACDF = Archive of the Congregation for the Doctrine of the Faith

Il Beato Padre Pio = Gerardo Di Flumeri, *Il Beato Padre Pio da Pietrelcina*. San Giovanni Rotondo: Edizioni "Padre Pio da Pietrelcina", 2001.

Epistolario = Padre Pio da Pietrelcina, *Epistolario, I, Corrispondenza con i direttori spirituali (1910–1922)*. San Giovanni Rotondo: Edizioni "Padre Pio da Pietrelcina", 1992.

Lemius = Archive of the Congregation for the Doctrine of the Faith, S.O., Dev. Var., 1919, I, *Cappuccini*, P. Pio da Pietrelcina, folder I, Padre Pio, document 14 [Manuscript and printed copy of the report by Father Joseph Lemius, Qualificator of the Holy Office].

Misteri di scienza = Giorgio Festa, *Misteri di scienza e luci di fede. Le stigmate del Padre Pio da Pietrelcina*. Second edition. Rome: Stabilimento Tipo-Litografico Vittorio Ferri, 1938.

Rossi = Archive of the Congregation for the Doctrine of the Faith, S.O., Dev. Var., 1919, I, *Capuchins*, Padre Pio da Pietrelcina, folder I, Padre Pio, document 21 [Manuscript and printed copy of the report by the Apostolic Visitor, Msgr. Raffaello C. Rossi].

Le stigmate = Gerardo Di Flumeri, *Le stigmate di Padre Pio da Pietrelcina. Testimonianze Relazioni*. San Giovanni Rotondo: Edizioni "Padre Pio da Pietrelcina", 1985.

Un tormentato settennio = Gerardo Saldutto, *Un tormentato settennio (1918–1925) nella vita di Padre Pio da Pietrelcina.* Doctoral dissertation, Università Gregoriana: Rome, 1974. Published edition. San Giovanni Rotondo: Edizioni "Padre Pio da Pietrelcina", 1986).

PART ONE

A New Starting Point

INTRODUCTION

1. The unpublished *Acts* of the Holy Office's first investigation

After studies, debates, and interviews, we thought we knew everything about him. Not even the recent opening of the archives of the former Holy Office up to the year 1939 portended any news. As it turns out, there was news. Buried among archived papers was a document of extraordinary importance, which now comes back from the past: the *Acts* of the first inquiry on Padre Pio ordered by the Holy Office.[1]

The document dates back to 1921, and contains the Capuchin's secret revelations—six valuable depositions, given under oath before an Inquisitor of the Holy Office. In them Padre Pio, revealing facts and phenomena never related to anyone, told his autobiography in person, and handed it over to the Church and to history.

But this is not all. The Inquisitor who obtained Padre Pio's secrets didn't limit himself to the Capuchin's words to trace his spiritual profile and his mystical identity. He tried to put his finger on a sore point and, taking the bandage off Padre Pio's hands, he rigorously examined the friar's stigmata. An unprecedented assessment ensued, with fascinating and unexpected implications.

Moreover, the Inquisitor started a rigorous investigation, interrogating witnesses and inspecting places. The material he gathered was so abundant that, though largely unknown up to now, it truly constitutes a complete and original account of the Capuchin, making it also possible to update thoroughly his existing historiography.

Kept for many years from the eyes of scholars and the faithful, the *Acts* [or *Votum*] of the first investigation of the Holy Office are now for the first time published in their entirety, thanks to Benedict XVI's decision to make available, beginning in June 2006, the documents from the period of Pius XI's pontificate (1922–1939).

The events related in these pages are also useful to write a chapter in the history of the Holy Office, whose image, so commonly vituperated, emerges renewed and free of clichés. Questionable instead is the image of those who meant to use the Holy Office as a tool for their envy and animosity, while edifying is the image of Franciscan life in Apulia, at the beginning of the twentieth century.

Now, to understand who Padre Pio was, and why the Holy Office started an investigation about him, we must go back in time. It is September 20, 1918.

2. The Holy Office under pressure

Europe is about to come out of World War I when Padre Pio of Pietrelcina receives the signs of Christ's Passion: the stigmata.[2] The news spreads quickly,[3] and faithful, pilgrims, priests, and some merely curious arrive at the convent of San Giovanni Rotondo.[4]

After the first clinical exams,[5] a lively debate arises about the nature of the wounds and the presumed holiness of the stigmatized. The discussion also reaches the Vatican, at the Inquisition, which had taken the name of Holy Office a few years before.[6] The dreaded Roman office—in charge of safeguarding the Faith and of investigating accusations of "simulated sanctity"—has received surprisingly contradictory letters.[7] Those who extol the Capuchin's holiness are countered by those accusing him of producing the stigmata with carbolic acid and veratridine![8] Among those doubting the authenticity of the stigmata is a distinguished scholar: Fr. Agostino Gemelli, O.F.M. On April 18, 1920, the learned Franciscan very briefly meets with his Brother. A few minutes,[9] a few words, no examination of the stigmata, and Padre Pio dismisses him: That is all.[10] But the next day Gemelli sends a personal letter to the Holy Office, declaring the stigmata *the fruit of suggestion*,[11] and two months later he sends a second one with specific advice on the measures to take.[12]

Under the pressure of so many denunciations, almost forced to take a stand, the Holy Office promotes more exhaustive investigations, and, toward the end of 1920, it receives from the Capuchins' general minister new and reassuring information. Two groups of documents are presented: the first, of a religious and disciplinary nature; the second, of a medical-scientific nature.[13] In the meantime, though, the Holy Office also receives the first accusations of the Archbishop of Manfredonia, Msgr. Pasquale Gagliardi.[14]

The situation is complex, and the Holy Office decides to entrust the file on Padre Pio to a man of proven experience: the Dominican Fr. Joseph Lemius, general procurator of the Oblates of Mary Immaculate.[15]

The theologian is asked a very precise question: "What measures, if any, should be adopted by the S. O. [Sanctum Officium, or Holy Office] regarding Padre Pio of Pietrelcina, Capuchin?"[16] Father Lemius studies the documentation on the friar with the "utmost diligence and application", and prepares his *Votum*—that is, the much-awaited answer.

From the very first lines Father Lemius, advancing some perplexity about the divine origin of the sores, acknowledges he cannot affirm "anything for sure about the origin of his stigmata" because of the lack of a direct examination in the field.

For this reason, he suggests an Apostolic Visitor be sent to San Giovanni Rotondo, to conduct "a thorough investigation [. . .] of Padre Pio's moral, ascetic, and mystical character [. . .], focusing especially on humility and obedience, and to test him prudently with regard to these two virtues", taking care to "watch his way of dealing with women". The Visitor should "check his use of pharmaceutical products [. . .], and for this purpose visit his cell every once in a while, [and he should verify the accusation of having caused the stigmata himself with] that carbolic acid he requested in connection with some injections to be administered to the novices. If, that is, he really had to give them injections [. . .]; [the Visitor should] keep the former provincial Fr. Benedetto away from San Giovanni for the length of the inquiry. [. . .] [He should] follow closely that chronicle ordered by the Provincial."[17]

The suggestion of the Qualificator is adopted. The Congregation looks for a suitable candidate for the Apostolic Visit,[18] a priest who is "at the same time a good theologian and a man of unique prudence, able to resist that atmosphere of suggestion that was mentioned, but who possesses the *critical* mind necessary to the investigation of the truth in such a delicate matter, and shrewd enough to conduct a careful inquiry without having the air of doing so."[19]

The choice falls on Msgr. Raffaello Carlo Rossi, Bishop of Volterra and future cardinal.[20] To him the Holy See entrusts the task of answering a difficult question: Who really is Padre Pio?[21]

3. A guide to reading

Before we delve into the investigation, it may be useful to describe the structure of this volume, its contents, and the previously unpublished materials.

The book consists of three parts.

The first one, comprising three chapters, presents the story of the Apostolic Visit of 1921; the contents of the interrogations and some historical appendices; the analysis and the originality of the examination of the stigmata conducted by the inquiring bishop, and his positive judgment on the origin of the Passion's signs.

In the second part we find the full transcript of the invaluable *Acts* of the Apostolic Visit [the *Votum*]. It is a historical source mostly unpublished before including almost the entirety of the depositions of the witnesses questioned during the inquiry, which are located in the compendium. More precisely, two-thirds of the greatly significant depositions of Padre Pio, also found in the compendium, are unpublished, while the examination of his stigmata (deposition XXI) is entirely unpublished. Document XXVI in the compendium is a letter from the Capuchin to a spiritual daughter, Sister Giovanna Longo: This too is unpublished.

In the final part of the *Votum* there is an appendix with a collection of letters sent to Padre Pio by Fr. Benedetto Nardella of San Marco in Lamis, spiritual father of the stigmatic. Some of them have been published already, others, though, had been lost, and for this reason they don't appear in the volume of the published correspondence devoted to the letters between the Capuchin and his spiritual director. Specifically, according to the numbering established by Monsignor Rossi, the letters numbered 15, 16, 18, 24, and 27 have never been published. From now on, then, they are handed back to history, and can be included in the body

of correspondence of Padre Pio, together with the aforementioned letter of the Capuchin.

The third part of the book offers to the reader's attention
five appendices. The first is a short biographical sketch of
Cardinal Rossi, followed by some historiographical considerations. The third appendix is the full transcript of a partially unpublished document, requested by the Apostolic
Visitor at the end of his inquiry: the *Chronicle of Padre Pio*
written by Fr. Benedetto Nardella. It is a source of considerable importance, not much studied so far, of which we
will soon offer a detailed historical analysis in the magazine
Parola e Storia.[22] It is followed by supplementary material
useful to the reader who may be approaching for the first
time Padre Pio's life and spirituality: a lively narration of
Padre Pio's stigmatization (which started well before September 20, 1918), and a chronology with the most important dates and events of Padre Pio's life.

As far as the unpublished materials are concerned, this
volume collects an enormous quantity of sources—some
autobiographical—on Padre Pio, and is indispensable for
knowing the Capuchin.

Finally, to make reading easier, the footnotes for this intro-
ductory essay and for the supplementary materials have been
placed at the end of the respective parts of the volume. The
footnotes related to the Apostolic Visitor's report are found
at the foot of the page, conforming to the original document.

Chapter 1

An Inquisitor in the Convent

1. "Go to Padre Pio"

In the first days of May 1921, the Most Reverend Eminence Monsignor Raffaello Carlo Rossi is in his episcopal residence when the letter arrives from the Holy Office, with the charge of a canonical visit to San Giovanni Rotondo.

A Tuscan from Pisa, now Bishop of Volterra, Monsignor Rossi probably doesn't even know where San Giovanni Rotondo is, but this is not what worries him. The content of the letter troubles him. He is ordered to conduct an inquiry concerning not simple disciplinary or doctrinal matters, but a "stigmatic". A difficult task: Monsignor Rossi knows it well, and for this reason decides to decline.

He writes to Cardinal Merry del Val[1] asking to be relieved of the task, for "it is of a considerable and arduous gravity. I am not saying arduous to perform; what is arduous, one can understand, and full of responsibility, is to reach those conclusions that the S.C. [Sacred Congregation] will have to rely on, in issuing its authoritative judgment. In this regard, therefore, if, by the benevolence of the Most Eminent Fathers, I could be excused, I would be most happy and I would immediately redouble my thanks." [2]

After a negative answer from the secretary of the Holy Office,[3] the now Apostolic Visitor accepts the task and goes to Rome to examine the friar's file.[4] It is a thick group of documents kept by the Holy Office, in which praise and criticism accumulate and contrast each other. With the papers in his hands, Monsignor Rossi brings into focus the delicate problems of this story. Then, he leaves for San Giovanni Rotondo.

Once in Apulia, he climbs the switchbacks of the Gargano Mountains and heads toward the small town where Padre Pio lives. Who is this friar, exactly? Opening his report, Monsignor Rossi writes: "Padre Pio, whose given name is Francesco Forgione, was born in Pietrelcina, the first station after Benevento along the Benevento-Campobasso railway, thirty-four years ago. In 1902 or 1903 he entered the Order of Capuchins of the Province of Foggia, and for his novitiate and his studies he went from convent to convent; however, many times the state of his health forced him to go back to breathing his native air. He was said to be suffering from bronchial pneumonia; in reality, the medical exams never confirmed this positively. To me, after frequently interacting with him for eight days, he gave the impression that he was truly suffering from said illness: It is, though, just an impression, caused above all by a light cough noticed in the Religious, a cough that generally characterizes those suffering from pulmonary ailments. During one of his frequent stays with his family, Padre Pio was ordained as a priest, around 1910. After the outbreak of the war, he enlisted as a soldier, although intermittently and briefly, actually staying as an in-patient at the hospital in Naples.[5] Afterward, he was sent to Foggia, then to San Giovanni Rotondo, where he currently resides. A set of circumstances, in which I think he had no part, brought him to San Giovanni Rotondo; perhaps he wasn't even aware of them. But it seems there was someone who was working to move him, that is, who took advantage of the 'oportunity' of Padre Pio, with the intention—which we want to think was good—of serving the Faith." [6]

2. Arrival in San Giovanni Rotondo

A desolate landscape, a dirt road, a poor convent located in a hard-to-reach place.[7] Arriving in San Giovanni Rotondo on June 14, 1921, Monsignor Rossi finds before him an unlikely stage for the presence of a mystic.

Probably reflecting on these details, he presents himself to the convent. In a simple priest's cassock? As a bishop? We have no information about this, but it is certain that as soon as he arrives at the convent he offers his "credentials" and begins the inquiry.[8] He takes the Gospels, makes the persons questioned touch it with their hands, and requires of them a solemn oath: to tell the truth and maintain silence.

Did they maintain silence? There is no doubt. In the sources of Capuchin origin there is no trace of these interrogations, and the memory of the inquiry has faded in time,[9] except for the *Acts* now available for consultation.

From the convent chronicle we only know that on June 25, 1921, due to the suspect conduct of an out-of-town priest, the rumor spread in San Giovanni Rotondo of a transfer of Padre Pio.[10]

Could that out-of-town priest have been Monsignor Rossi? It is likely.

At any rate, to know what Monsignor Rossi sees, whom he questions, and which conclusions he reaches, we can only follow attentively his report, which now enters the heart of the narration.

3. The stigmatic's appearance

Going into the convent, Monsignor Rossi wants to see him above all: Padre Pio. Therefore, once in the presence of the subject of his investigation, he observes him with attention, and notes the main features of his physiognomy. This is what he writes [quoting from a previous description and bracketing his own impressions]: "Padre Pio has a 'pale complexion [but I wouldn't say *too* pale], sickly, suffering aspect [*not too much*, though]; droopy bearing [I'd rather say [. . .] slow and sometimes uncertain gait].[11] The demeanor of the person [. . .] modest and solemn [better, *composed*]'".[12]

Then the Visitor notes in his report some aspects of Padre Pio's nature [still quoting from another source]: " '[T]he high and serene forehead; the look in his eyes, which is lively, sweet and sometimes wandering [but sometimes *vibrant*, too [. . .]]; the expression on his face, which speaks of goodness and sincerity:[13] They all inspire sympathy.' " "It is true", writes Monsignor Rossi, expressing his pleasure at Padre Pio's nature.[14] The "gruff Capuchin" seems to him good, sincere, even pleasant. A completely unexpected finding![15]

The questioning has yet to start. As it appears from his report, Monsignor Rossi doesn't go immediately into the matter of his investigation. He first checks on a rumor. It is said that the stigmatic friar doesn't touch food. Monsignor Rossi investigates and notes: "Truth be told, Padre Pio has been presented as somebody who almost lives off air: There may be some exaggeration. He doesn't eat much, no; and especially when the 'pilgrims' were most numerous, it was truly amazing how he could bear up in the confessional for so many hours without adequate nourishment. In fact, he doesn't take anything in the morning [. . .]; his lunch certainly isn't lavish; he eats very little in the evening: some hot chocolate, sometimes not even that, thus reducing all the meals of the day to just one [. . .]; but everyone says he does eat."[16]

Monsignor Rossi draws conclusions from these observations and denies that Padre Pio totally lacks nourishment: "Clearly, then, his nutrition is not abundant, but I don't think we are at the point of making of Padre Pio a 'phenomenon' in this regard, too."[17]

So Padre Pio doesn't eat enough, considering the amount of his work. But, at least until 1921, it is incorrect to say he doesn't eat at all. He eats a bit of vegetables, sometimes an apple or two; he doesn't drink coffee, but beer brewed by a lay brother. Nevertheless, it is obvious that something extraordinary is going on because of the disproportion between his incessant work and his scarce nourishment. The Visitor himself, in fact, will soon ask: "How can it be explained, so much work with so little nourishment?"[18] Nobody will give him an answer.[19]

4. Let the inquiry begin

After observing Padre Pio's physical appearance and examining the nourishment issue, Monsignor Rossi tries to discover the "moral" and "spiritual" traits of the Capuchin friar, one of the most important tasks of his investigation.

In order to "study" the subject of his investigation, he proceeds systematically. Starting on June 14, he summons and interrogates nine witnesses—to be specific, two diocesan priests and seven Capuchin Brothers.

"Tell me about Padre Pio, tell me everything you know!" This is how we could summarize the barrage of questions to which Monsignor Rossi subjects them for eight days. Those questioned feel free to talk and, not intimidated by the importance of their interlocutor, they give answers rich with details.

On the whole, their answer is univocal: "Padre Pio has always been a very good religious."[20] It almost seems a firm enunciation of principle, one that the Bishop, surprised, clearly emphasizes: "They all proclaim it in unison, both priests and Brothers."

"A chorus of approval and praises",[21] declares Monsignor Rossi, that are especially credible because "they are not exaggerations: Padre Pio's piety, at least judging from the outside, is thought to be common, ordinary, not much different from that of his Brothers."[22] The authenticity of the depositions, moreover, stands out for another reason: "[T]he 'good' Religious is not spared even small reproaches." Free of emotional influences, the witnesses report the positive aspects, but also acknowledge their Brother's limitations.

All in all, the witnesses' declarations turn out to be something original. For the first time, nobody speaks really ill of a future saint![23] We will discuss this in the next chapter.

5. The Inquisitor's doubts

How did Padre Pio welcome the news of a Holy Office inquiry concerning him? What did he feel upon seeing his Inquisitor? What kind of attitude did he assume during the interrogations? It would be interesting to know, but not a sentence, not a line alluding to these circumstances is recorded in the Capuchin's letters. Not a word left his mouth, and on this subject the sources are silent.

As for Monsignor Rossi, by his own admission he arrived in San Giovanni Rotondo prejudiced against Padre Pio.[24]

Still, in his report he writes: "I must admit Padre Pio made a rather favorable impression on me." The reason for this change of mind is easily explained.[25] The Inquisitor starts to shadow Padre Pio: at the altar, in the refectory, in the convent. Monsignor Rossi doesn't miss anything. He observes him talking to others, he interrogates him personally, he questions him about problems and accusations. He finds that "in conversation, Padre Pio is very pleasant; with his Brothers, he is serene, jovial, even humorous".[26]

In conversation, he "is [. . .] polite and respectful", even though it is surprising that he says "*per Bacco*" [by Jove]. It is also surprising, continues Monsignor Rossi, to hear him "use as an interjection [. . .] the Holy Name of God, with habitual 'my God', 'my Jesus' [or] to comment easily, I won't say on specific persons, [. . .] but on townsfolk".

On the whole, declares the Visitor, Padre Pio emerges as a "serious religious, distinguished, dignified, but also frank and casual in the convent. In church he assumes a measured gravity, as is only appropriate, after all. He doesn't have [. . .] the abandoned, careless manner of not a few of his Brothers (apart from the less-than-perfect way of staying in the choir): half-sitting down, half-genuflecting, with the arms on the pew and the head on the forearms".[27]

Monsignor Rossi continues his observations and adds without reticence: "Imperfections can therefore be observed in him, yes; but, after all . . . he is walking toward perfection; why declare he has already reached it?"

After this thought, the Inquisitor Bishop prepares to get to the heart of the matter and examine the most important aspects of the stigmatic friar's spiritual life: the virtues.

6. Three counts: poverty, chastity, obedience

Perhaps Padre Pio doesn't expect this. To verify his poverty, the Inquisitor asks to see his room. The door flings open, and there it is: modest, narrow; "the various drawers are somewhat disordered: sheets of paper, gloves, quinine,[28]

candies for the boys, images, everything rather muddled".[29] On the whole, a very plain cell, with no noteworthy elements.

Another issue to be scrutinized is the use of the donations Padre Pio receives.[30] Initially the Capuchin, with the
permission of his superior, would manage money[31] received
with letters coming from all over, even from the United
States of America. After the new provincial's instructions,
however, he doesn't manage donations anymore, but desires
the proceeds to be used "according to the benefactors' aims
and intentions". With regard to this matter, a touching fact
emerges: To his own family, which is poor, Padre Pio doesn't
give anything, using everything for other people in need.

If Padre Pio's poverty is beyond dispute, can the same be
said about his simplicity and purity of heart?[32]

Among many rumors, some doubts have been raised about
his familiarity with his spiritual daughters, since Padre Pio
addresses some women as *tu*, for some too familiar a ges-
ture. The Visitor, instead, clarifies this circumstance and suggests one need not be surprised: "[L]et's not dwell on it too
much: We are in southern Italy. He told me 'I hardly ever
use *lei*: I use *tu* and *voi* indifferently.' "[33]

Regarding other accusations, Monsignor Rossi proves to
be a good investigator, discerning rumors, insinuations, and
calumnies. Padre Pio, whose purity is acknowledged and
praised by all the witnesses, was seen in the guest quarters
of the friary with a woman: so far, nothing strange. But
somebody fantasized on the circumstance, without actually
producing any proof or arguments. Rumors spread, and a
scandal was born. Monsignor Rossi finds out who spread
the news, and figures out his intentions: it was "the young
lady's former fiancé!"

In another instance it was said that "some women would
touch the ill Religious [while he was assisted by a man and

by the superior's sister] 'to take hold of his holiness'". In this case, too, Monsignor Rossi checks the facts and concludes: "It was all the product of deluded minds and small brains, and the occasion had been imprudently created, alas, by the superior. But Padre Pio, who out of obedience and necessity had submitted to living outside the cloister, was never aware of what was going on and never had doubts, as is clear from the questioning that was prudently conducted on this matter."

After confronting possible objections about purity, the Visitor declares: "[W]e can rest assured that even with regard to this most important Christian, religious, and priestly virtue, Padre Pio is unassailable—as all witnesses, after all, attest." [34]

What remains is the examination of the most important virtue: obedience. Padre Pio, the Visitor observes, lives in "profound humility" [35] and in the "utmost simplicity and indifference" to the praises of which he is the protagonist. It is "as if nothing had ever occurred around his person, and he wasn't still the object of so much attention and of an admiration that on the part of many is absolute veneration." His humility manifests itself especially in his submission to the Church. [36] Questioned on this topic, [37] Padre Pio declared he intends always to obey, since "[f]or the Holy Church it is God himself who speaks." [38] Strong words, but can they be trusted? Monsignor Rossi thinks so, because the friar gave him a shining testimony of his obedience. The Inquisitor asked to examine the correspondence with his spiritual director—an unusual request [39]—and the Capuchin didn't blink: He accepted. Admiring and amazed, Monsignor Rossi writes: "[H]e gave me an outstanding proof of obedience [40] by putting in my hands, upon my first hint and without the slightest objection, all the letters he received from the former provincial, Father Benedetto. [. . .] Moreover, once back in Volterra, when I expressed the desire to

see the letters again, he promptly sent them with renewed
feelings of submission, and since it occurred to him, while
sending the letters, that he had by an oversight kept some
that he hadn't found right away, he hurried to send me
these, too, separately." [41]

Before concluding his assessment, Monsignor Rossi inspects
the friar's prayer life. He observes him while he is meditating, when he is on his knees, with the Rosary in his hands:
"[N]othing extraordinary", he observes, "appears from the
outside in Padre Pio, besides that *special recollection* that the
superior noted." [42] But the Capuchin friar admits to being
favored with apparitions and intellectual visions and, more
or less, "with a spirit of elevation".

The inquiry goes on even during the Holy Mass. While
Padre Pio is putting on the sacred vestments, the Inquisitor enters the little church and, sitting in the wooden pews,
waits. The bell rings. Monsignor Rossi observes and notes:
Padre Pio celebrates with "too much devotion: five minutes for the *Memento* of the living; four or five for the
Memento of the dead; two minutes for the consecration of
the chalice—measured with watch in hand". Liturgical mistakes or flaws are not lacking: "I didn't see him bow his
head at the name of the Holy Father in the Collect; he
doesn't open and close his hands well at the *Oremus*; he
doesn't incline toward the crucifix at the *Per D.[ominum]
N.[ostrum] Iesum Christum*; when turning the pages of the
missal with one hand, he also keeps the other hand up in
the air; he doesn't bow perfectly toward the altar at the
Munda and at the *Te Igitur*—maybe because of the pain in
his ribs; he is not entirely precise in the ceremonies of
Communion ... All things to which ... a *saint* should pay
attention." [43]

But Monsignor Rossi immediately notes: These are not
imperfections stemming from Padre Pio himself, but "from

his formation, from the instructions imperfectly received at the time of his priestly ordination".[44] So Monsignor Rossi keeps track of the times and observes the gestures. In short, nothing escapes him. Then he can be a thoughtful interpreter of all he has seen and recorded, as he reaches his first conclusion: Regarding these issues, Padre Pio is unassailable from any point of view.

7. The second degree of judgment

"A miracle, a miracle!" Monsignor Rossi knows that miracles and episodes of bilocation are attributed to Padre Pio. The Visitor is neither a credulous person nor a skeptic, and, after examining Padre Pio's spiritual life, he wants to see things clearly. Now begins the second degree of judgment, focused on Padre Pio's extraordinary phenomena.

The Visitor interrogates some Capuchins, and at night, in his room, he reads by candlelight the letters sent to the convent. Of the alleged healings, many are unconfirmed or nonexistent. In Padre Pio's correspondence, however, there are some credible declarations[45] that attribute miracles to his intercession.[46] But without medical confirmation it is difficult to reach a conclusion, and the issue remains open.

Even more complex is the case of bilocation. It is impossible to verify the phenomenon, and there is nothing else to do but to ask Padre Pio himself. Shy, little inclined to talk about himself, Padre Pio cannot deny it under oath, and, even though embarrassed, he gives his confirmation—a confirmation, observes Monsignor Rossi, that "until proven otherwise, is to be considered sincere, since imposture and perjury would be in too stark a contrast with [his] life and virtues." [47]

More precisely, the stigmatic friar acknowledges only a few cases of bilocation, and he does so with such simplicity and candor as to leave his interlocutor amazed. What's more, Padre Pio talks to him about his own behavior, confirmed by his Brothers, meant to hush up and hide everything.

It's not pleasant to read about these events. The accusations against this man and the many interrogations to which he is subjected don't do justice to his evangelical life. Monsignor Rossi understands that; and grasping the resounding contradiction between the accusations about the "cunning friar" and the evidence of the facts, which show him to be humble and inclined to self-effacement, he writes: "To think that so many idle words had cast such an unfavorable light on this poor Capuchin! I'll take the liberty then to call to the attention of the Most Eminent [Fathers] his genuine and honest depositions, since they reveal him to be not at all like an unscrupulous miracle worker or an enthusiastic instigator of mobs. He is a poor friar who, as far as I know, keeps his place and unwittingly has become the center of such attraction. These past years many things have been attributed to him which, had they even been true, he wouldn't have liked to see talked about. Whenever he was able, he never failed to raise his voice: *After all*— these are his own words—*of many of these things that were said to be true or made up, the last one to know, or the one who knew the least, was* [*Padre Pio himself*]." [48]

8. The Inquisitor, the defendant, and the stigmata

On the afternoon of June 17, the Apostolic Visitation has its most dramatic moment.

The inquiry is well under way. Three days have passed; Monsignor Rossi has interrogated many witnesses—and also Padre Pio, three times. In his first interrogation, the Capuchin talked to him about the stigmata, and revealed to him facts that dumbfounded the Visitor. Padre Pio told him: "[The day I received the stigmata] I saw our Lord in the posture of someone who is on a cross. [. . .] He invited me to partake of his sorrows [and he told me,] 'I unite you with my Passion.' Once the vision disappeared, I came to, [. . .] and I saw these signs here, which were dripping blood." [49]

Since then, the Capuchin hides them jealously: He has covered the wounds on his hands with half-gloves, while on his feet he wears socks and shoes. But what is he hiding?

Monsignor Rossi decides to unveil the mystery: It is 4:30 p.m. He heads to the stigmatic's cell, crosses the hallway, comes to the door, knocks on it resolutely, and the young Capuchin, modestly, opens it for him. "Let me see your stigmata", Monsignor Rossi orders him.

For Padre Pio it is like a bolt in the blue. Monsignor Rossi sees this, and notes: "Padre Pio [. . .] *resigned himself* to endure the examination: His face betrayed his interior suffering—it didn't escape me. Then that evening he told me: 'How much I have felt the burden of obedience today!'" [50]

The resigned Capuchin uncovers his hands. Some blood has stuck on the gloves and it is obviously painful to take them off. Here now are the stigmata, under the eyes of the Inquisitor, who observes and writes: "The stigmata *are there*: We are before a real fact—it is impossible to deny it."

He explains what he sees: "The 'stigmata' *on the hands* are very visible, and caused, I think, by a bloody exudation: There is absolutely no opening or breaking up of the tissues, at least on his palms. It might be said there is on the back of the hands, even though I don't think there is, but then it must be agreed that the hypothetical opening doesn't penetrate through the hand cavity and doesn't come out on the palm." [51]

These stigmata, therefore, are different from those on Saint Francis, which had the look of fleshy excrescences.

Monsignor Rossi observes with attention, takes a tape measure, measures the size of the sores—it is a matter of a few centimeters—notes the presence of scabs, asks Padre Pio to remove them and tries to remove them himself. At this point Padre Pio must already feel burdened. Moments of silence alternate with questions. His Inquisitor now invites him to sit down. The inspection seems to be over, but it is not so: "Take off your socks and shoes", Monsignor Rossi asks. Padre Pio's shoes are those of a poor Capuchin friar. Once he has taken them off and put them aside, the Visitor, intrigued, bends down and looks.

The sores on the feet "were about to disappear: What was possible to observe resembled two buttons with whiter and more delicate skin". The changeability of the appearance of the stigmata is something bewildering. Monsignor Rossi expected them to be bleeding, like the ones on the hands, and asks for clarification. The defendant answers that the stigmata "at times [...] are more noticeable, at times less so; sometimes they look like they are about to disappear, but they don't, and then come back, flourishing again". It may be the case, concludes Monsignor Rossi, that those on the feet "could now be open again".

Monsignor Rossi is still pondering this phenomenon when he asks Padre Pio to take off his habit and his undershirt, and to uncover the wound in his side. The Inquisitor, who already knows the shape of that sore from the descriptions of the doctors who have preceded him, goes close to Padre Pio's chest and looks at the wound: unbelievable! Though expecting a cross or a cut, vertical or horizontal, Monsignor Rossi observes: "*In his side*, the sign is represented by a triangular spot, the color of red wine, and by other smaller ones, not anymore, then, by a sort of upside-down cross."[52]

Without hiding his surprise, the Inquisitor asks Padre Pio whether there are other "signs" or other "changes" on his body, but Padre Pio assures him that "nothing like that is on his person."[52] Until 1921, therefore, Padre Pio has no other stigmatic signs on his body. The Capuchin's torment is nearly over. He composes himself and puts the habit back on. The test is finished.

9. The Inquisitor's night

It is evening. Perhaps Monsignor Rossi is in his room. He is thinking of all he has seen and heard during that day. Padre Pio has revealed to him that the author of the stigmata has a very precise identity. Also, according to the Capuchin, he spoke words to the friar, and he entrusted a mission to him: "I unite you with my Passion."[53] Then, the stigmatization.

But is it all true? With this question Monsignor Rossi begins the trial of Padre Pio's stigmata. The sores are now in the dock. The prosecutor will take the floor. In dealing with Padre Pio's case, the Dominican Father Lemius had advanced four possible hypotheses of the causes of the phenomenon:

1. hypothesis of self-inflicted stigmata *ab intrinseco*, through a morbid condition of a pathological nature;
2. hypothesis of self-inflicted stigmata *ab estrinseco*, through suggestion or voluntary application of artificial means;
3. hypothesis of stigmata of divine origin;
4. hypothesis of stigmata of diabolic origin.

In his report, the Inquisitor observes that the last hypothesis has no possibility, especially in light of Padre Pio's spirituality. So he discards it.

As for the other hypotheses, Padre Pio's way of life, his commitment to a spiritual life, his dedication to the pastoral life, the strong but polite nature of his temperament, his smile and his jokes, rule out a pathological state of auto-suggestion produced by meditations on the crucifix. On this subject Monsignor Rossi writes: "Father Lemius [...] upon meeting him, could not understand how someone suffering from a neuropathic disorder could endure the hard work of the ministry, and how it was that phenomena resulting from such a condition—for example, inflammation, etc.—never appeared on him." [54]

The previous considerations also rule out auto-suggestion caused by the spiritual direction of Father Benedetto. On this point Monsignor Rossi demonstrates he is a shrewd investigator. He examines the letters exchanged between the two of them and notes that, unlike what Father Gemelli hypothesized, it is Padre Pio who first introduced, and who talked most about, the theme of sharing in Christ's suffering. [55]

The only remaining hypothesis is the one of stigmata self-inflicted by external means, physical and chemical.

Monsignor Rossi considers the accusation concerning carbolic acid and veratridine. Then he asks himself: "Were the stigmata a sham, a vulgar fraud? Did Padre Pio, at the cost of suffering pain, cause them, did he cultivate them, did he make them grow artificially, so as to increase the fame of his 'holiness'...?" [56] After a careful review, the Inquisitor concludes: "[Padre Pio] requested carbolic acid to disinfect syringes needed for shots, and veratridine for . . . a prank to be played during recreation!! Padre Pio had experienced the effects of this powder mixed, in an imperceptible dose, in the tobacco offered to him by a Brother. Without knowing anything about poisons, without even considering what veratridine was (and that is why he asked for four grams), he requested it to repeat the joke and laugh at the expense of some Brothers! That's all. Instead of malice, what is revealed here is Padre Pio's simplicity, and his playful spirit."[57]

Ruling out the preceding hypotheses, Monsignor Rossi analyzes the one linking the sores to a divine origin. "[N]ot an easy analysis, and a very difficult judgment", the Visitor immediately concedes, deciding to suspend any final judgment. But, he admits, "there seem to be enough reasons to lean toward the presence of a supernatural gift".

The Bishop then begins a series of subtle arguments, from which it emerges "[t]hat Padre Pio's 'stigmata' do present the supernatural character of the outpouring of blood", and that the characteristics of the true stigmata can be observed in those of the Capuchin. Before dealing with the next issue, the Visitor asks himself an inevitable question: "Are we then really before Saint Francis of Assisi's marvel, renewed somehow in one of his sons?" He prudently answers, "I do not know."

10. A scent of violets in a furnace

The Inquisitor thought he had concluded his investigation. But during his stay in San Giovanni Rotondo he encounters two exceptional phenomena that amaze him and which he, as a representative of the Holy Office, has the duty to explain. While he is staying at the convent, he notices a very pleasant and vivid fragrance, "similar to the scent of the violet".[58] They say it comes from Padre Pio, and that all his fanatics sense it. But "I am not [. . .] an admirer of the Padre", Monsignor Rossi writes in his report, "I feel complete indifference [toward Padre Pio]."

Where does this inexplicable fragrance come from, then? It's hard to tell. In his cell Padre Pio has nothing but soap;[59] the smell, moreover, is sensed at times, in waves, from a distance. Time passes, even years, and clothes that have been worn—Padre Pio's hair, too—"keep this scent".[60]

Monsignor Rossi is still reflecting on this mystery when he learns about a second inexplicable fact. Padre Pio is affected by very strong episodes of hyperthermia: normal thermometers break, and those for horses show his temperature reaches 118.4°F. Many attest to this, even the incredulous who, despite themselves, have observed it.

Monsignor Rossi wants to understand, and asks Padre Pio what causes the phenomenon. "Internal feelings", he answers, "the consideration, or some representation, of the Lord." It is, writes the Visitor, a moral illness, not a physical one, in which Padre Pio finds himself, by his own admission, as in a furnace. The phenomenon is so peculiar that "under the strain of this fever, Padre Pio is not knocked down, but gets up, moves about, and can do everything." In this instance also the phenomenon can only have one origin: the divine one. Monsignor Rossi, however, is prudent and doesn't lean one way or the other. He thinks about it, and in his report he writes: "Whether this phenomenon, besides being exceptional, is also miraculous, the Lord will reveal when he thinks the time is right."[61]

11. Who are you, Padre Pio?

Eight days have passed. Monsignor Rossi has interrogated, inquired, observed. After an analytical inquiry, precise to the point of exasperation, without making allowance or considering extenuating circumstances, the Bishop Inquisitor sums up the information gathered and with quick brushstrokes outlines Padre Pio's human and spiritual sides. The account is of historic importance because of the clarity of its conclusions. We would like to see them engraved in eternal memory: "Padre Pio is a good religious, exemplary, accomplished in the practice of the virtues, given to piety and probably elevated to a higher degree of prayer than it seems from the outside; he shines especially because of his sincere humility and his remarkable simplicity, which did not fail even in the gravest moments, when these virtues were put to the test, a test truly grave and dangerous for him." [62]

12. The return

The moral, spiritual, and mystical examination of Padre Pio concluded, [63] Monsignor Rossi may already be back in Volterra when he asks himself one last question: "What is going on around Padre Pio today, in the convent and in the town?" [64]

After eight days in San Giovanni Rotondo, the Visitor acknowledges that "things have now a different look compared to that in the past: more serious, calmer. The popular enthusiasm has waned", [65] even though episodes of "ridiculous flaunting", of which Padre Pio disapproves, are not lacking.

To transfer Padre Pio, observes the Visitor, would cause "fierce opposition on the part of the people of San Giovanni Rotondo".

And Padre Pio's Brothers? "In the convent all is well", adds Monsignor Rossi. "The religious who make up the Community of San Giovanni Rotondo are serious, reserved, prudent: No measure regarding them is necessary." [66]

Later in his report, after some brief observations and after dealing with a specific issue concerning the spiritual direction of a Brigittine nun, the Visitor notes the essential components of the results of his inquiry, before sending them to the Holy Office:

1. "Padre Pio is a good religious."
2. "[O]f the 'graces' beseeched, as it is said, through his prayers, many do not hold true—many are only asserted, but lack a legal proof."
3. "[W]hatever is extraordinary in what happens to the person of Padre Pio cannot be explained, but it certainly does not happen either by diabolical intervention, or through deception, or with fraud."
4. "The popular enthusiasm has greatly waned."
5. "[T]he religious Community in which Padre Pio lives is a good Community and one that can be trusted." [67]

Finally, Monsignor Rossi gives some advice on the decisions the Holy Office must take upon itself; in particular, he offers some indications regarding spiritual direction to be communicated to Father Benedetto. At the same time, he asks that the Holy Office acquire, "to consult it, the *Chronicle of Padre Pio*, which Father Benedetto is said to be composing, or at least to acquire whatever he is gathering to write someday on the life of Padre Pio". [68]

Monsignor Rossi ends his report on October 4, 1921, the Feast of Saint Francis of Assisi. Then he sends it to the Holy Office, [69] taking care to add an attachment rich in further elements to be observed with attention: the compendium, that is, the transcripts of the witnesses' depositions.

Chapter 2

The Inquisitor's Interrogations

1. The witnesses' depositions

Leaving his room, Monsignor Rossi always carries with him three small objects: a book with the Holy Gospel, to request the solemn oath not to lie and to tell the whole truth; some paper; and an inkwell to write down the depositions of the persons he will interrogate: These he will later re-read, correct, and have signed.

In his investigation the Visitor doesn't follow a set plan: He calls and interrogates the witnesses to his liking. He doesn't start with Padre Pio, but he does finish with him. He listens to some of them just once, but decides to hear others two or three times. He asks just a few questions to some, but with others he insists on topics already addressed. The pace of the interrogations is furious. Monsignor Rossi is ready to start at 7:30 A.M., and keeps going until the evening. In two cases the interrogations even start after dinner, at 9 P.M., ending late at night.

On the whole, the Inquisitor collects twenty-four depositions, and he organizes them according to a specific order.

First are the declarations of two people from outside the convent: the sly archpriest pastor of San Giovanni Rotondo,

Canon Giuseppe Prencipe, and the young Canon Domenico Palladino, bursar of the same parish.[1] Subjected to three interrogations, the former, by insinuating rather than clearly stating, laments the climate of religious fanaticism surrounding Padre Pio, and criticizes the conduct of his Brothers. He advances some doubts about the Capuchin and his demeanor toward women, but, all in all, he doesn't express a negative opinion on Padre Pio.[2]

The latter, that is, D. Domenico Palladino, might have pre-arranged with his pastor the tone and the contents of his depositions. Before the Inquisitor, in fact, he reports some doubts about Padre Pio's purity and accuses the friars of spreading news of nonexistent miracles. But in the second deposition he adjusts the target and, while censoring the atmosphere surrounding the Capuchin, he praises the friar and his spirituality.

Even though they don't contain actual accusations, Prencipe and Palladino's depositions turn out to be unreliable. Toward the end of his life Palladino will admit to having lied and will confess openly the untruthfulness of his declarations.[3]

With the curtain dropped on the two outside witnesses, the scene now opens inside the convent: Padre Pio's Brothers are called to testify. Monsignor Rossi summons seven of them.

The superior of the convent, Father Lorenzo of San Marco in Lamis, is heard first.

Talking before the Inquisitor about the first years lived with Padre Pio, the Religious recalls the jealousies that arose among the Brothers because of the consideration the superiors had for him. Monsignor Rossi asks for elucidations, and Father Lorenzo answers frankly: They "found him to be most exemplary, not a grumbler".[4]

The Inquisitor presses on and asks him to continue. Father Lorenzo talks about two exceptional phenomena: the episodes of hyperthermia and the mysterious scent. About the very high fevers, he declares that, even though at first he was skeptical, he personally witnessed three temperature measurements. The first one was 109.4°F, then 113°F, finally 118.4°F: This is what the mercury inside the thermometer showed!

On the origin of the mysterious scent of violet, he recognizes he can't give any explanations. Then he gives some details on Padre Pio's character, the time he spends in the confessional, and how he prays.

The Inquisitor re-reads the deposition, and, dissatisfied, he again summons the convent's superior. Father Lorenzo offers the requested information about the human and spiritual traits of the friar under investigation, then addresses an unexplored topic: the conversions[5] inspired by Padre Pio.

"I must remark", he observes, "how the name of Padre Pio has brought here some non-baptized and Protestants who received here the sacraments and entered the Church."[6]

Then he lists them: a Florentine Jew; a Dutch Protestant who had never been baptized; a Protestant born to German parents; a young Protestant woman from Holland; a young lady from Estonia, daughter of Protestant pastors. But there is more. Padre Pio also converts intellectuals far from the faith. Such is the case of a man from Milan, a follower of theosophy,[7] who "recognized his errors; he stayed here for about a month, receiving Communion every day". A British woman, "also a follower of theosophical doctrines, [. . .] mended her ways. She remained here almost two months, and still comes back every five or six months."[8]

There are also cases of young, and not so young, people who decide to consecrate their lives to God after meeting the stigmatic friar.[9]

At this point Monsignor Rossi dismisses Father Lorenzo and summons other friars who, one after the other, appear before the Inquisitor.

Father Ignazio of Jelsi relates how, until recently, the mailman would deliver to the poor convent in San Giovanni Rotondo up to six or seven hundred letters a day for Padre Pio. An exceptional number for the 1920s! In the past, each convent kept its own healing herbs and medicines. Regarding this topic, Father Ignazio declares that he keeps a little veratridine powder, and that he uses it for pranks: "One evening, joking with the Brothers, I made them try the effects it produces when it is drawn close to the nose. Padre Pio, too, took some, and he had to go back to his cell because he couldn't stop sneezing." [10]

After taking the oath, Father Luigi of Serracapriola reports some information about the atmosphere in the convent. The friars, says the Religious, have contained the devotion surrounding Padre Pio. Monsignor Rossi, though, is interested in the defendant's attitude in the face of the people's enthusiasm, and Father Luigi confides: "Simplicity, always indifferent before any honor, etc. We have never seen him abandon his simplicity." [11]

Before the Inquisitor, Father Lodovico of San Giovanni Rotondo talks about the stigmatic Capuchin's prayer life. He says candidly that Padre Pio "protracts [his prayer], and one tires of waiting for him, especially if he is meditating"! [12]

Father Cherubino of San Marco in Lamis, instead, talks about the sensationalism, but declares it a fact of the past.

Finally, the Inquisitor summons Father Pietro of Ischitella, at the time the provincial of the Foggia Province. The Religious describes some aspects of his "subject", whom he has known since the years of his formation in Sant'Elia a Pianisi. Rossi takes notes, and after the witness's signature he dismisses him.

2. Padre Pio's interrogations

One day has passed since the Inquisitor's arrival, and, on June 15, 1921, at 5 P.M., he decides to summon him: Padre Pio. Slowly and with an unsteady gait, the young Capuchin arrives before him, takes the solemn oath and gives his personal details. So begins the first of six very rigorous interrogations in which Padre Pio is subjected to a heap of questions. In the minutes of the depositions, there are one hundred forty-two of them, covering a wide range of topics, from the smallest details of everyday life to the greatest mysteries of the spiritual life.

After a few words about his life, the friar, then thirty-four years old, tells about his priestly ministry, says that he administers the sacrament of penance, but unexpectedly declares: "As for preaching, I have never preached." [13]

Then he starts talking about a delicate issue: mystical occurrences. Padre Pio tells of the "malicious external visions, now under human shape, now under beastly shapes", and adds: "I haven't heard noises or had visions in years." [14] Apparitions of the Lord, of our Lady, and of Saint Francis, instead, still occur, but more rarely. [15] Regarding them, Padre Pio declares: "I would receive exhortations regarding myself, as well as others, and even reproaches, always about the spiritual life." [16]

After these words, Monsignor Rossi changes the subject and asks Padre Pio the question that matters most to him: "Tell me about your stigmata!"

It would be interesting to have a picture of the Inquisitor's face while he listens to Padre Pio. The Capuchin reveals now—he will never do it again in his life—the touching dialogue with the mysterious person, the author of the stigmata, and the words that will forever mark his spiritual identity: "I unite you with my Passion." [17]

After more questions, the interrogation stops; perhaps Padre
Pio and Monsignor Rossi are tired. A one-hour break, then
a second interrogation begins. It is 7 P.M.

The Inquisitor wants to see the defendant's cell: He inspects
it, but doesn't find medicines, or anything else noteworthy.[18]

He asks him to talk about the fragrance that apparently
emanates from the stigmata. But Padre Pio doesn't get into
the matter of its source and says he cannot explain the phenomenon: "In my cell", he declares, "I have nothing but
soap." [19]

The Visitor goes back to the subject of the stigmata, and
asks: "Padre Pio, what do you feel?" He answers: "Pain, always,
especially on those days when they bleed. The pain is more
or less intense: Sometimes I cannot bear it." [20] Monsignor
Rossi then asks him to explain how his body temperature
could "sometimes reach 118.4° F". Padre Pio doesn't like
talking about the extraordinary events that happen to him,
but being under oath he can't refuse, and so admits he suffers this phenomenon when he is thinking of the Lord and
feels as if he were in a furnace. The deposition ends, and
Monsignor Rossi gives Padre Pio an appointment for the
next day, at 4:30 P.M. The third interrogation begins.

The Inquisitor asks some questions about his relationship
with his spiritual director, Father Benedetto. He then broaches
two topics about the supernatural: the ability—which Padre
Pio admits to possessing—to see into people's hearts, and
episodes of bilocation. "I don't know how it is", says the
Capuchin [about bilocation], "or the nature of this phenomenon, and I certainly don't give it much thought, but it did
happen to me to be in the presence of this or that person, to
be in this or that place; I do not know whether my mind
was transported there, or what I saw was some sort of representation of the place or the person; I do not know whether
I was there with my body or without it." [21]

But how does this phenomenon happen? Padre Pio recounts: "Usually it has happened while I was praying. At first my attention was turned to prayer, then to this representation; and then I would find myself exactly as I was before."

The Visitor wants to understand clearly, and asks Padre Pio about specific episodes. The Capuchin describes the one involving a sick woman, Maria of San Giovanni Rotondo: "I spoke words of comfort; she begged me to pray for her healing. This is the substance." Yet another case involves a bilocation to urge a conversion: "A man [Padre Pio doesn't mention the name out of discretion] presented himself to me, or I presented myself to him, in Torre Maggiore—I was in the convent—and I rebuked him and reproached him for his vices, urging him to convert, and then later on this man came here, too." [22]

Dissatisfied with the information he has received, Monsignor Rossi wants to know who spread the news of these phenomena. Padre Pio explains he has never talked to anyone about his bilocating, then adds: "These people talked to me about it, but I was discreet; I neither denied it, nor confirmed it."

After further analyzing the existence of alleged miracles, [23] the Inquisitor changes subject completely, and directs his questions toward a delicate topic: Padre Pio's relationship with women. The stigmatic friar clarifies the episodes that are held against him, and explains his staying in the guest quarters during his illness.

With this topic completed, Monsignor Rossi interrogates him about his prayer life. Two hours of meditation every day; "fifteen minutes, half an hour, depending on the circumstances" for the thanksgiving prayer after the Holy Mass. [24] In particular, Padre Pio loves the Rosary, which he says in full as his "habitual prayer". Then the ejaculations".

One of the Visitor's questions is very interesting for the understanding of Padre Pio's spirituality: "Which penitential practices, if any, besides the ones prescribed [...] he performs"? With simplicity Padre Pio answers: "None: I take the ones the Lord sends."

As far as studying, Padre Pio declares: "Excellency, I am always hearing confessions. For this reason I am always keeping up to date with the necessary studies." Other important questions follow, about discernment criteria and spiritual direction. Padre Pio affirms he leads souls "along the way of virtue and the accomplishment of one's duties", while he guides them along extraordinary ways only "when the Lord calls them to it".[25]

The next day the Visitor interrogates his Brothers, then, at 7 P.M., he summons the Capuchin again. Monsignor Rossi asks once more about his prayer life. Regarding the stigmata, Padre Pio adds that the pains that started in 1911 were not continuous: "They generally happened from Thursday evening through Saturday morning, and occasionally on Tuesdays, too."

The fifth deposition happens after the dinner of June 17, more precisely at 9 P.M. Padre Pio attests he has never "suffered from nervous disorders, hysteria", that he hasn't applied iodine on the sores in "two years; less for the starch glycerolate: Once it was applied by the Father Provincial himself, because I was bleeding." [26]

Then, a hammering series of sworn statements begins. Padre Pio puts his hand on the Gospel and Monsignor Rossi asks: "Does Y.P. [hereafter Your Paternity] swear on the Holy Gospel that he has never made use of perfumes, and that he is not using them now on his person?" And "Padre Pio swears, adding that, even regardless of his being a religious, he has always found their use revolting." [27]

Monsignor Rossi insists: "Does Your Paternity swear on the Holy Gospel that he has not, directly or indirectly, produced, nurtured, cultivated, grown, or preserved the signs he bears on his hands, his feet, and his chest?" Padre Pio answers: "I swear." It is not over yet. At a cracking pace, Monsignor Rossi asks: "Does Your Paternity swear on the Holy Gospel that he has never made use of dermatography on his person, that is, that you have never, on account of a sort of autosuggestion, made signs that could then appear visible depending on fixations or obsessions?" Padre Pio answers, frankly, demonstrating further his humility: "I swear, for goodness' sake, for goodness' sake! Quite the contrary, if the Lord relieved me of them, how grateful I would be!"

The series of interrogations seems finished. But it is not so. After three days, after he has heard other witnesses, Monsignor Rossi decides to summon Padre Pio one last time. It is 4:30 p.m. on June 20.

Monsignor Rossi is well informed about events in the life of the defendant. He knows, for example, that Padre Pio and Father Agostino of San Marco in Lamis have exchanged letters in French. He asks whether "without knowing [Greek] sufficiently well, you once wrote a letter using it?" Padre Pio denies: "I don't think so: at most, some greetings, fruit of the kind of knowledge I had." [28]

The Inquisitor keeps asking a great number of questions. One of them is fundamental to understand the reason for the difference, morphological and phenomenological, between the stigmata on the hands and those on the feet. "Could Your Paternity explain to me why there is a difference between the signs he has on his hands and those on his feet, which seem cicatrized?" Padre Pio answers: "They don't always keep the same appearance: At times they are more visible, at times less so; sometimes they look like they are about to disappear, but they don't, and then come back,

flourishing again. And this happens to all the signs, including the one on the side.'"

"All of this having been read and approved", concludes
the Visitor, "Padre Pio was dismissed after the oath *de secreto
servando* [of secrecy] taken on the Holy Gospels. In confirmation of everything, it was signed." [29]

3. The identity of the "mysterious person"

Until today, it was believed Padre Pio had never revealed to
anyone what happened on September 20, 1918, the day he
received the stigmata.

A brief mention was made in a letter to his spiritual director, Father Benedetto, but on this point the Capuchin
revealed almost no detail.[30] He had only talked about a
"mysterious person" who had given him the stigmata.

According to some scholars, Padre Pio didn't know his
identity. Speaking about this issue during a conference, Ottaviano Schmucki declared: "It seems to me an obvious, albeit
involuntary, transposition, influenced by the considerable distance in time from the event, if in 1966 Padre Pio identified the mysterious person [. . .] with Christ Crucified,[31]
while merely a month after the event (October 22, 1918)
this person seemed to him "mysterious", that is, not recognizable. Perhaps this phenomenon is explained by the over-
lapping, in the mystic's memory, of recollections of various
interior experiences, occurring at different times and under
different circumstances, which imperceptibly fuse into a com-
posite image. On the other hand, it is likely that, after the
central experience—that is, the vision of the 'mysterious
person' who produced the stigmata—other prior visions may
have lost their psychological relevance and may have caused
a partial amnesia in him." [32]

In reality, a source did exist[33]—we will examine it shortly—which should have prompted more caution when advancing the hypothesis of Padre Pio's amnesia. Nevertheless, at that time no one advanced doubts. Padre Pio's first deposition before Monsignor Rossi now casts a definitive light on this subject.

In answering the Visitor who asks him to talk about the stigmata, Padre Pio, less than three years after the event, reveals to him: "On September 20, 1918, after celebrating the Mass, I stayed in the choir for the due thanksgiving prayer, when suddenly I was overtaken by a powerful trembling, then calm followed, and I saw our Lord in the posture of someone who is on a cross." [34]

After three years, then, Padre Pio is perfectly able to identify whom he saw: *Our Lord in the posture of someone who is on a cross.* The hypothesis of amnesia caused by the "considerable distance in time" is then proven wrong, since Padre Pio claims to know who gave him the stigmata.

From now on, in the light of Padre Pio's own words, the "mysterious person" has a precise and sure identity: He is Jesus Crucified.

4. The conversation with the Crucified

The second original aspect of Padre Pio's account of the stigmatization contained in the deposition concerns the conversation with Jesus Crucified. Also on this point the situation was anything but clear.

In his aforementioned paper, Ottaviano Schmucki quoted a deposition by Fr. Giuseppe Orlando, according to whom the friar denied receiving during the stigmatization "a verbal communication from the mysterious person".[35]

But actually, on this very subject another deposition had been published in 1986: the one by Fr. Raffaele D'Addario. D'Addario, recalling the conversation he had with Padre Pio in 1967, had written: "I then asked him whether there had been a conversation with Jesus, and he answered candidly and with simplicity: 'Of course there was, because it was exactly during the conversation that I received them.' "[36]

Until today, therefore, contradicting sources made it impossible to know with certainty whether or not there had been a conversation with our Lord.

Padre Pio's deposition clears up the uncertainty.

Continuing the narration of his stigmatization, the Capuchin friar mentions the conversation and its contents. Here is the text to which I am referring:

"[I]t didn't strike me whether he had the Cross, [while] lamenting the ingratitude of men, especially those consecrated to him and by him most favored. This revealed his suffering and his desire to unite souls with his Passion. He invited me to partake of his sorrows and to meditate on them: At the same time he invited me to work for my brothers' salvation. I felt then full of compassion for the Lord's sorrows, and I asked him what I could do. I heard this voice: 'I unite you with my Passion.' Once the vision disappeared, I came to, I returned to my senses, and I saw these signs here, which were dripping blood. I didn't have anything before."[37]

From Padre Pio's testimony, then, we learn two new, important elements.

First of all, Padre Pio clearly knew the identity of the "mysterious person", author of the stigmata: "our Lord in the posture of someone who is on a cross".

Secondly, the stigmatization occurs at the end of a conversation.

Other elements worthy of attention emerge from this conversation.

Padre Pio reveals that the stigmatization was not the result of a personal request of his own, but of an invitation by our Lord, who "invited me to partake of his sorrows".[38] Jesus Crucified, in fact, lamented the ingratitude of men, especially of consecrated persons. Following these premises, invited to unite himself to the pains of the Cross, Padre Pio didn't ask to receive the stigmata, but simply "what he could do" for the Lord and for the salvation of his brethren. The stigmatization, therefore, came at the end of an interior mystical preparation in which the Capuchin had the role not of an initiator, but of a recipient of an invitation and a mission.

5. Padre Pio's mission

What was the mission entrusted to Padre Pio? Regarding this question, the document we are examining is clear: Padre Pio was united with the Passion of our Lord to remedy men's ingratitude. This, then, is the sense and the character of his mission as a stigmatic: to share in Christ's Passion for the sake of his brothers' salvation.[39]

On the same subject, we would like to highlight another peculiar aspect. The theme of ingratitude on the part of men, especially of those who are most favored by God, is not new in the private revelations of the Capuchin. A similar apparition occurred a few years before, on April 7, 1913. Padre Pio wrote to Father Agostino: "On Friday morning I was still in bed, when Jesus appeared to me. He looked all battered and disfigured. He showed to me a great multitude of priests, regular and secular, among whom many ecclesiastical dignitaries; some of them were celebrating, some were putting on the sacred paraments, and others were taking them off.

"The sight of Jesus in distress was very painful to me, so I asked him why he was suffering so much. He didn't give me any answer. Then his glance turned to those priests; but soon, almost horrified and as if he tired of looking, he glanced down, and when he looked back up at me, with great horror I saw two tears running down his cheeks. He moved away from that throng of priests with an expression of great disgust on his face, crying: 'Butchers!' And looking at me he said: 'My son, do not think that my agony only lasted three hours, no; I will be in agony until the end of the world, on account of the souls whom I have most blessed. During the time of my agony, my son, it is necessary not to sleep. My soul keeps looking for a drop of human compassion, but, oh, they leave me alone under the weight of their indifference. The ingratitude and the sleep of my ministers make my agony even more burdensome. Oh, how badly they return my love! What torments me most is that, to their indifference, those people add their contempt, their incredulity. How many times I was about to strike them, if the angels and the souls who love me had not stopped me'" [40]

It is an interesting text, one accused of being the product of plagiarism because of the consonance, of language and theme, with a private apparition to Saint Gemma Galgani. [41]

However, in the light of his deposition, the return, in the apparition preceding the stigmata, of the theme of offering himself as a victim proves that the theme and the communication really belong to Padre Pio. It also highlights how his offering for the salvation of his brothers is the main feature of his life and of his mission as a stigmatic priest.

In conclusion, there is nothing left to say but repeat the established fact. Padre Pio's first deposition sheds light on many issues, and is by far the most clear and important autobiographical source to define the nature and spirit of the Capuchin's mission: that of a priest united with Christ's Passion.

Chapter 3

Padre Pio's Stigmata before the Inquisitor

1. The doctors' examinations

Before analyzing Padre Pio's sores, Monsignor Rossi must certainly put in order the papers he has received from the Holy Office. In the bulky file about Padre Pio, in fact, there are the descriptions by the doctors and experts who have preceded him.

The first, in chronological order, is the one by Dr. Luigi Romanelli (May 15–16, 1919); the second, by Prof. Amico Bignami (July 26, 1919); the third and fourth, by Dr. Giorgio Festa (on October 28, 1919, and on August 31, 1920). Dr. Festa will also draft a fifth report, following his visit of April 7, 1925, after the events related in this book.[1]

They are interesting descriptions, but not without problems. The sores on the feet did not appear the same way to everyone: To some they looked like stab wounds, to others like "exudations", that is, bleeding, but without any cut. It even appears that the sore on the side often changed position and even shape.

Aware of these difficulties, the Inquisitor begins his painstaking examination, in search of a solution.

2. The examination of the stigmata

It is 4:30 P.M. on June 17, 1921, when Monsignor Rossi begins the examination of the stigmata. The Apostolic Visitor immediately realizes and notes that Padre Pio "wears woolen half-gloves on his hands".[2] He asks him to take them off, then examines the right hand.

3. The examination of the right hand and of the left hand

On the palm of the right hand "a large round spot can be observed, two inches in diameter".[3] Obviously, the spot is caused by the leakage of coagulated blood.

The Visitor immediately notices an important element: On Padre Pio's palms there is "no lesion of the skin, no hole, either central or lateral". From this he draws a very precise conclusion: The blood that is on the palms and coagulates comes out of the skin through "exudation".

Continuing, the Visitor asks the Capuchin whether he feels pain: "My whole hand is aching; the pain is stronger in the middle, inside."

He asks the friar to close his hand: Padre Pio does it; he can close his fist, but not tightly. The Visitor is a careful observer: he sees it, and asks for the reason. Padre Pio explains it is because of "the pain, which intensifies when I clench".

After examining the palm of the right hand, Monsignor Rossi observes the back, and ascertains the absence of lesions.

As far as the pain, Padre Pio attests: "Just like on the palm." [4]

At this point the Visitor verifies the correspondence, or lack thereof, between the wound on the back and the one on the palm.

From the reports by Bignami and Romanelli we knew that the stigmata on the palms were symmetrical to the ones on the back.[5] Monsignor Rossi, instead, observes that, in a straight line, the center of the sore on the palm corresponds with the upper edge of the sore on the back. He then confirms the description that Dr. Festa[6] had made in his first report, in contrast with the one of his colleagues Romanelli and Bignami.

As for the left hand, "the spot on the palm has a diameter of two inches; the one on the back 1.6 inches."[7] The Visitor doesn't dwell on the description, since "the characteristics are identical to those of the right hand".[8]

The examination of the hands completed, the Inquisitor turns to the examination of the feet.

4. The stigmata on the feet: a changeable appearance

As soon as he sees them, Monsignor Rossi immediately observes that the sores on the feet present a different phenomenology from those on the hands: "On the inferior extremities the 'stigmata' were about to disappear: What was possible to observe resembled two buttons[9] with whiter and more delicate skin." Surprising!

Intrigued by this phenomenon, Monsignor Rossi questions the Capuchin. Padre Pio explains to him that the stigmata, at least those on his feet, are not always perfectly the same: Both their appearance and the bleeding are changeable. "Padre Pio assures that the 'stigmata' 'at times [...] are more noticeable, at times less so; sometimes they look like they are about to disappear, but they don't, and then come back, flourishing again': So it may be the case that those on the feet, too, could now be open again."[10]

The fact is relevant. From Padre Pio's own mouth we learn that the examination of the stigmata doesn't always produce the same results, since they are changeable.[11] The findings of the previous medical descriptions, then, were different not because of the observer or his mistakes, but because of an objective difference in the stigmata being observed. The first issue is then resolved.

5. The examination of the right and left feet

Observing the right foot, Monsignor Rossi writes: "On the upper side there is something like a rosette, of about one inch in diameter, with no trace of blood, neither recently flowed, nor long ago."[12] To clarify what he has observed, the Visitor writes: "Let's imagine a closed wound, fully healed, over which a more delicate and whiter skin has grown: Such is the sign that appears on the upper side of this right foot."

Monsignor Rossi asks Padre Pio whether there are bleeding and scabs. The friar answers: "Sometimes there are droplets of blood; sometimes there are very small scabs that have never even turned black."

In the central area of the sole, the appearance of the lesion is on an even smaller scale. Monsignor Rossi observes "a rosette of a 0.6-inch diameter. Here, too, no trace of blood. Actually, it is covered with a thin layer of almost callous skin about to come off, since its edge is turned up all around."

Looking at the traces of the stigmata on the upper side of the foot, it seems to him that "once that callous skin that is now visible falls off, it seems that there should remain no trace of special signs."

The Visitor then gets meticulous; he uses his own fingers as a pair of calipers and verifies the correspondence between the superior sore and the inferior one. "The 'calipers' with two fingers cannot be done well," he notes, "but it seems that the center of the rosette on the upper side of the foot corresponds directly to the center of the one on the sole."

Questioned about the pain, Padre Pio is very clear: "Just like in the hands." [13]

Turning to the left foot, Monsignor Rossi observes that on the upper side "there is a rosette just like on the right foot. It looks like a healed wound over which new skin has formed, slightly colored, under the epidermis, in a light shade of purple." Under the sole, the same things as on the right foot can be observed, but "the callous film is almost completely fallen off, so the outline isn't perfectly recognizable anymore, and once it will have come off completely, it seems that no trace of special signs will remain."

Finally, Monsignor Rossi aptly asks Padre Pio if he can walk easily. The friar answers: "I don't always experience the same fatigue. I cannot stand up for long because of the internal pain." The weariness, then, is variable—likely because of the different phenomenology of the sores on his feet. The strain, though, remains constant because of the "internal pain".

6. The stigmata on the side: previous observations

The sore on the side is the most problematic, one that has had scholars arguing for a long time,[14] since, to the eyes of the observers, it has always assumed a different shape and different positions.

In May 1919, Dr. Romanelli saw "on the left hemithorax, precisely between the nipple line and the anterior axillary line, almost in correspondence with the sixth left intercostal space, [. . .] a lacerated wound, linear, following the direction of the ribs, around 2.8 inches long, with definite, slightly wrinkled margins, involving soft tissues."[15] "The characteristics of the wound are those of a stab wound."[16] Romanelli then saw a wound, no exudation.

Two months later, in July 1919, it was Professor Bignami's turn: The wound on the chest had changed. Now it had the shape of a cross, and had moved more toward the side. Here's what Bignami tells: "On the left side of the thorax, between the anterior axillary line and the mid-axillary line, a cross-like shape can be observed, whose longer arm—situated obliquely—goes from the 5th to the 9th rib, reaching the costal border, while the short arm is about half the length [. . .]. In no place is the lesion deep. The derma is not damaged at all."[17] The wound is now superficial.

Bignami, moreover, doesn't say anything about the direction of the cross, so the question of its orientation remains.

Further information about the appearance of the chest sore comes from Father Paolino of Casacalenda. The Religious reports that the wound has "almost the shape of an X"[18] and is deep.

Judging it superficial, like Bignami, and of the shape of an upside-down cross, Dr. Festa so describes in his first report the wound he examined: "In the anterior region of the left thorax, situated the distance of about two fingers held horizontally under the mammary papilla, presents one last and more interesting lesion, in the shape of an upside-down cross. Its longitudinal arm measures about 2.8 inches: it starts from the anterior axillary line at the level of the 5th intercostal space, and goes down obliquely almost until the cartilaginous costal border, going through the skin in an area that is, as I have already pointed out, at a distance of about two fingers held horizontally below the mammary papilla. The horizontal arm of the cross is about 1.4 inches long, intersects the longitudinal arm not with a right angle, but slightly obliquely, at about 2 inches from its starting point, and looks wider and somewhat round at its lower extremity. This cross-like shape is very superficial." [19]

During the second visit, on July 16, 1920, Dr. Festa repeats the examination with Dr. Romanelli. The result is nearly identical to Dr. Festa's first report, with one difference: The transversal is "probably much wider and longer".[20]

In 1925 Padre Pio had hernia surgery performed by Dr. Festa, and while the patient was unconscious, the surgeon analyzed the sore, which appeared in "the shape of a cross, and with short, but clearly visible *bright radiations* bursting from its outline".[21]

Until today, it was believed that "the stigmata on the side [remained] practically unchanged until July 5, 1964, when it was seen by Father Eusebio Notte, who so describes it: 'It was a cross-like wound, [. . .]. The vertical arm was 2.4–2.8 inches long, slightly oblique, with the lower part more toward the left side. The horizontal arm was much shorter.' " [22]

Finally, there is another testimony, among those regarding the stigmata on the side, that has been surprisingly neglected by the studies on Padre Pio: the witness of Father Nazareno, superior of the convent in San Giovanni Rotondo from November 11, 1910, until July 1, 1914.[23]

The Religious had asked to see the stigmata of the side, and Padre Pio, after an initial refusal, "showed to me his ripped chest. [On the] left side [one could see] a vertical wound of about 2.4 inches. The two sides were far from each other." [24] Another different shape, then!

7. "A triangular spot on the chest"

Monsignor Rossi's description of the stigmata on the chest is definitely different from the ones of those who preceded him and of those who followed him, and compels a revision of the whole issue.

The Bishop Inquisitor, having uncovered Padre Pio's chest, observes a "triangular spot", even though he expected an upside-down cross, or an oblique one. In the minutes of the examination, with more precision than in the final report, he notes: "On the left side, 1.2 inches from the last rib, there is a triangular spot [. . .] whose side measures about 0.8 inches, the color of red wine. There are no openings, cuts, wounds. About 2.8 inches above it, there are other small, scattered spots, as shown in the drawing, but small: the last one, on top, slightly bigger." [25]

The Visitor continues his examination. He likely establishes that the lesion is superficial: "Considering the absence of wounds, it can be justifiably supposed that the blood comes out through exudation."

Then he asks Padre Pio an important question: "Has this sign always looked like this?" Padre Pio's answer is vague: "More or less the same [. . .]: I've never really observed it." [26]

The examination is over, and Monsignor Rossi understands the reason for the different reports about the chest stigmata. This sore, more than any other, is changeable not only in relation to the bleeding, but also in its shape: Now it has taken a triangular shape!

8. The authenticity of the signs of the Passion

According to insinuations, the carbolic acid and the veratridine used by Padre Pio were anything but tools to sterilize or to play pranks: They actually were, in all likelihood, the artificial cause of the stigmata. Monsignor Rossi, therefore, naively believed in Padre Pio's oath, and he much too easily considered as plausible the sores' divine origin. [27]

This opinion offers the occasion to explain the reason for Monsignor Rossi's positive evaluation of the origin of the stigmata, evaluation founded not simply on the Capuchin's sworn statements.

But let's proceed with order. The close examination of Padre Pio's sores performed by Monsignor Rossi revealed at least three important elements:

1. The "signs of the Passion" on Padre Pio's body were not open wounds; they didn't consist of lesioned tissues. They were bloody exudations—that is, bloody matter oozed out by way of a hyper-permeability of the vein walls. Now, a constant, continuous, heavy exudation—only in specific body areas and with a clear outline, that can even assume very precise shapes in different positions—was in itself a fact that, being scientifically very strange, testifies in favor of a non-human origin of the stigmata. These exudations, moreover, didn't cause inflammation or suppuration. This, too, was an indication in favor of the sores' supernatural origin.

2. The application of carbolic acid causes a very different effect than the one observed in the stigmatic's sores, and ends up consuming the tissues, causing the inflammation of the surrounding area. This was not the case with the examined stigmata.

3. Padre Pio's "sores" and the coagulated blood emitted a strong scent of violets, not a foul odor, as would normally happen in the presence of bleeding wounds. This scent, moreover, showed an exceptionally strong power of penetration of smells and spaces![28] This fact, too, was decidedly in favor of the supernatural origin of the stigmata. It was insufficient to formulate the hypothesis that Padre Pio made heavy use of fragrances. The scent, in fact, was sensed at times, not continuously, sometimes at a great distance from Padre Pio.

Also, the accusation of using medications to cause the stigmata was easily denied by a blatantly obvious fact. Padre Pio was a friar who never moved from the convent, and was now a celebrity "under strict surveillance". How could he ask for and obtain heavy quantities of veratridine or carbolic acid for years, without the news leaking?

As far as Padre Pio's sworn statement regarding the stigmata, it was credible because of some of his attitudes and answers, which we can summarize as follows:

1. Padre Pio's stigmata didn't appear to the Visitor the same way they did to Dr. Romanelli, Professor Bignami, and Dr. Festa. The ones on the upper side of the feet seemed close to disappearing. This fact, obviously, was in favor of the authenticity of the stigmata and of the stigmatic himself. If, in fact, the sores had been caused through the use of medications, Padre Pio should have tried to revive them before the Visitor's examination.

2. Asked about the phenomenology of the stigmata, with no difficulty Padre Pio quickly admits a fluctuating evolution. Now, if he had been in bad faith, he would have tried to deny such evolution. And if he had been under the influence of suggestion, he would have been displeased by the reduced visibility of the signs of the Passion. Instead, not only does Padre Pio readily tell the Visitor that sometimes the signs seem close to disappearing, but he also adds that he would be glad if these "exterior signs" disappeared completely.

3. From his conversations with Padre Pio, from the friar's correspondence, from the witnesses, and from his own inquiry, Monsignor Rossi finds out something: Padre Pio doesn't like having these visible "signs of the Passion". He doesn't want to let anybody see them, he hides them, he even suffers when he is forced to show them. Seeing this, Monsignor Rossi, addressing the cardinals of the Supreme Congregation, notes: "As for Padre Pio, he resigned himself

to endure the examination: His face betrayed his interior suffering—it didn't escape me. Then that evening he told me: 'How much I have felt the burden of obedience today!' " [29] How could the friar desire or cause the stigmata, then, when he himself was trying to hide them? What's more, when asked about the origin of the scent of his stigmata, the stigmatic humbly declares: "I don't know, I can't smell anything. I only have soap in my cell." Padre Pio almost seems to ascribe the problem to the soap, eschewing the hypothesis that is more reliable and interesting. Here, too, Monsignor Rossi notices in Padre Pio an attitude averse to any sensationalism and exaltation.

9. The information acquired

Monsignor Rossi's description of Padre Pio's stigmata offers important new knowledge.

First of all, we learn that the stigmata on the feet had a less marked shape than those on the hands, and that, most importantly, their phenomenology was not stable. It is Padre Pio himself who declares it unambiguously. This, then, explains the reason for the different findings of the previous medical examinations.

Secondly, we learn new information about the stigmata on the side, particularly its morphology. Historically, it has appeared in different shapes: a horizontal lesion, a vertical lesion, a cross-like shape with the cross arm longer, a cross-like shape with the cross arm shorter, an upside-down cross, a more or less oblique cross. Now it appears to Monsignor Rossi like a triangular spot with more, smaller scattered spots above it—one of them, on top, bigger.

In light of this changeability, a question arises: What is the meaning of this changeability, and what is the meaning of the different shapes the sore assumes? This question remains, for now, without an answer. We also gain important confirmations about the authenticity of the sores. The constant bloody exudation with specific shapes; the scent emanating in place of a foul odor (usually caused by bacterial infections and by the necrosis of the tissues); the absence of tissue degeneration processes and of any kind of cicatrization; the changing shape of the sore on the side; the disappearing of the stigmata at the end of Padre Pio's life, with no trace of scars—these are all facts that cannot be scientifically explained, proving the non-human origin of these signs. Moreover, Padre Pio's self-effacement observed by Monsignor Rossi; his desire that the supernatural signs belonging to him not be seen and examined; his willingness to share in the Lord's Passion, but without those "exterior signs"; his propensity for smiles and jokes; his profound communion with the Lord—all these prove the sincerity of his statements on the origin of his sores.

All things considered, with this inquiry on the stigmata the Holy Office offered a great opportunity to Padre Pio. Against the dismissive chorus of the detractors, the Bishop of Volterra enabled Padre Pio to deny thoroughly his accusers' insinuations regarding the origins of the stigmata.

10. A question about other hypothetical sores

Before concluding the examination of the stigmata, Monsignor Rossi asks Padre Pio a very interesting question: "Whether anywhere on his person, on the chest, on the back he may have other similar signs, eczema, etc." He needs to understand whether there might be other sores, and if there is the famous sore on the shoulder mentioned in a prayer attributed to Saint Bernard.

Padre Pio answers: "No, I never had." [30]

After receiving the stigmata, then, up until 1921, Padre Pio never had visible wounds other than those on his hands, feet, and side.

In order to understand better this issue, especially with reference to the news of a sore on the shoulder, we will now offer the essential elements of the topic and the established facts.

11. The problem

During the conference on the stigmata of the Servant of God Padre Pio of Pietrelcina, Fr. Gaetano Intrigillo, delegate for the Apulia region at the Centro Internazionale di Sindonologia in Turin, raised an issue. He wondered whether Padre Pio might have had "signs" on his shoulders, proof of his participation in the carrying of the *patibulum Domini* [the Lord's Cross].

From his research, though, almost nothing had emerged. This was for two reasons: On one hand, because of his natural reserve, Padre Pio had never hinted at the existence of this hypothetical sore; on the other hand, "nobody, under the obligation of obedience, [had ever asked Padre Pio] whether he had any 'sign' [. . .] on his shoulders." [31]

The only trace that could be found was a shirt of Padre Pio's that showed bleeding on the upper right side. [32] For the scholar this was "the sign of lesions on the right shoulder, to be ascribed to the traditional way of carrying a whole cross".

A comparison with other shirts that didn't present a similar bloody spot, and the absence of any confirmation to be found in the medical examinations conducted on the stigmatic friar, led the expert to a specific conclusion: "The lesion caused by the carrying of the cross [had] not been continuous." [33]

12. What we know about the wound on the shoulder

The certain knowledge of the existence of a wound on Padre Pio's shoulder seemed to come a few years later. In an interview, Cardinal Deskur revealed the content of the conversation between Fr. Karol Wojtiła and Padre Pio, in the distant year of 1948. The young Polish priest allegedly asked the stigmatic friar which sore was the most painful: "The one on the shoulder", Padre Pio allegedly replied, "which nobody knows about, and which isn't even treated." [34]

It was an unexpected and unforeseen discovery. In fact, Cleonice Morcaldi, too, had asked Padre Pio the same question, and the Father had told her: "My head and my heart." [35] The fact, then, that Padre Pio said "treated" was surprising, since it had never been seen by anybody.

In the light of this development, in fact, the issue was far from resolved.

On one hand there was a testimony by Mrs. Morcaldi and many medical examinations, which had never documented a lesion on the shoulder; on the other hand, a single shirt with a very visible bloody spot, and Cardinal Deskur's memory of Father Wojtyła's conversation with Padre Pio.

The historical data, therefore, were contradictory and not sufficient to provide a historically documented solution.

To this we might add that John Paul II's autobiographical memoir—dated April 5, 2002, and sent to Father Cocomazzi, superior of San Giovanni Rotondo—didn't make any mention of the content of the conversation with Padre Pio. [36] Moreover, other shirts belonging to Padre Pio did have blood

on them, although not in a spot similar to the one mentioned above, but in spots scattered all over.

13. A certain historical datum, a new starting point

From Monsignor Rossi's Apostolic Visitation something new
emerges now: Before 1921, even though he had already
received the stigmata, the saint of the Gargano [region] didn't
have any visible wounds other than those on his hands, feet,
and chest.

Monsignor Rossi, in fact, after a very scrupulous inquiry
on the signs of the Passion, their origin and their phenomenology, asks the friar if he has other sores or "similar signs".
On the subject, Padre Pio is categorical: "No, I never
had." Monsignor Rossi notes the importance of this detail
and, in his report, he doesn't neglect to present it to the
cardinals of the Holy Office: "Padre Pio assured me that
nothing like that [i.e., like the marks on the hands, feet,
and chest] is on his person." [37]

This is very important: Padre Pio, talking to the Visitor,
doesn't say, "I don't have similar signs", but affirms he has
"never" had any other sign akin to the stigmata.

This way he denies he has ever had other sores that might
have appeared, even just once or intermittently, as it happened on the occasion of the first apparition of the invisible stigmata, which he talks about in his depositions. [38]

It is clear, then, that the wound Cardinal Deskur's testimony hints at could not have appeared before 1921. Padre
Pio, in fact, supposedly told Father Wojtyła that it was a
sore that was "not treated". Now, if it had appeared before
1921, it would have been seen by the doctors, and if it was
intermittent, Padre Pio wouldn't have said "I never had"
[other similar signs]!

From now on, therefore, 1921 is the year one can't go past in order to attribute to Padre Pio the existence of any further sign of the Passion. And this by virtue of what Padre Pio himself declared under oath!

CONCLUSION

Forty years have passed since Padre Pio's death, and until today many have tried to reveal the secrets of his life. The *Acts* of the Holy Office Apostolic Visit, now published for the first time, conclusively shed light on his mystery and become the key to understanding in depth his person and his mission. In his depositions, in fact, Padre Pio explains the reason for his stigmata and the identity of the mysterious person who appeared to him on September 20, 1918. Furthermore, Padre Pio himself relates unknown episodes and lets us "observe" him while he performs the deeds of a simple Capuchin as well as those of a great mystic. The miracles, the episodes of bilocation, the hyperthermia, his reading into people's hearts, the mysterious scent, his prayer life, and his jokes are marvelously told and explained.

Likewise, by taking his gloves, socks, and shoes off, and even lifting his habit, Padre Pio lets every reader look and observe his stigmata, in an unprecedented way. In the *Acts* of the Apostolic Visitation the figure of the Bishop Inquisitor, later Cardinal, also shines: His Most Reverend Excellency Monsignor Raffaello Carlo Rossi. For him, too, the source under consideration provides reason for study and appreciation, on account of the prudence and independent judgment that distinguished him in such a complex and delicate episode.

Now it is the turn of the reader, who, going through the document, will be able with joy to see once again the living face of Padre Pio.

NOTES TO PART ONE

Notes to the Introduction

[1] The *Votum*—this is the technical name of the document—is a type-written text of 141 pages, kept in the Archive of the Congregation for the Doctrine of the Faith. Drafted in 1921 by the Inquisitor of the Holy Office, it is divided into two parts: a report and the minutes of the depositions. The report includes biographical information regarding Padre Pio, the reason for the investigation, a "moral and religious" portrait of its subject, and the analysis of extraordinary phenomena concerning him. Advice on Padre Pio's case and the final evaluation follow. The minutes of the depositions contain the complete transcripts of the witnesses' testimonies, and an examination of the stigmata. They are followed by a further appendix of documents and interrogations.

[2] Regarding Padre Pio's stigmatization, see appendix IV. As we shall see, from now on the first deposition Padre Pio gave in this Apostolic Visitation is to be considered the most important source for knowing that decisive moment in the life of the Capuchin.

[3] The first newspaper article about Padre Pio's stigmata dates back to May 9, 1919. See *Il Beato Padre Pio*, p. 19.

[4] For an example, see the testimony of the Bishop of Melfi and Rampolla, Msgr. Alberto Costa, in appendix IV.

[5] For a complete picture of the medical examinations, see *Un tormentato settennio*, pp. 111–18.

[6] Until June 29, 1908, the date of the promulgation of Pius X's *Sapienti Consilio*, the Sacred Congregation of the Holy Office [now the Congregation for the Doctrine of the Faith] was called the Sacred Congregation of the Roman and Universal Inquisition, instituted by Paul III with the Apostolic Constitution *Licet ab initio* of July 21, 1542. It is to be distinguished from the tribunals of the medieval Inquisition and from the Spanish Inquisition, which had different origins and purposes. With the *motu proprio Alloquentes* of March 25, 1917, Benedict XV appended to the

Holy Office, as a section of it, the Congregation of the Index. After the 1908 reform, the Holy Office became the most prominent Roman congregation on account of the importance of the topics and the issues entrusted to it; as for the qualification of Supreme, it appears for the first time in the Pontifical Yearbook of 1927.

Members of the Holy Office were some cardinals—General Inquisitors—who met in plenary assembly every Wednesday, chaired by a cardinal secretary. The latter, despite the appellation "secretary", functioned as prefect, even though the Holy Father formally held that title, according to Canon 247, ¶ I of the Pio-Benedictine Code. There was then the assessor, with the function and rank of secretary of the dicastery. Head of the section of preliminary investigation of criminal causes was the Father Commissioner, who, like the assessor, was a major official. The others were all minor officials.

As far as the appointment of the members, the majority was reserved to the Holy Father. Among these was the appointment of the Qualificators, to be consulted for the examination and proscription of books.

On this topic, a useful book is Andrea Del Col, *L'Inquisizione in Italia. Dal XII al XXI secolo* (Milan: Mondadori, 2006), pp. 819–22.

The literature on the theme of simulated sanctity increases by the day. For an effective introduction to the issue, of paramount importance is the volume Gabriella Zarri (ed.), *Finzione e santità tra medioevo ed età moderna* (Turin: Rosenberg e Sellier, 1991).

[7] The first negative report dates back to June 6, 1919. See ACDF, S.O., Dev. Var., 1919, I, *Cappuccini*, Padre Pio da Pietrelcina, folder 1, Padre Pio, document 1.

For a complete and effective evaluation of Luzzatto's work, a useful read is the article by Prof. Carmelo Pellegrino, whose introduction includes: "Professor Luzzatto should not be offended, but his 'padrepio' really disappointed us. It was heralded as the first historical study on the saint—but first historical study it was not. It was announced as full of great new findings; but these turned out to be well-known documents, sometimes even already published, as well as pieces of information that had little or nothing to do with the friar. In vain we have tried to find in it the immense effort of scientific objectivity, which parses all the elements, which grasps human dynamics beyond the papers, which formulates well-grounded hypotheses, which can perceptively tell the center from the periphery. We got constantly lost in the labyrinth of preconceptions—political, religious, social, etc.—of the Inquisitor, who splits humanity in two and sees the devil everywhere, invariably wearing a black habit. For this reason we think it is just another fool's 'padrepio'—surreal because it only exists in those who interpret him—certainly far from the 'Vernacoliere' or irreverent one (not praised, but mentioned colorfully without veils, pp. 17–18), but not much closer to reality, since the real story of Padre Pio of Pietrelcina remains unexplored territory in Luzzatto's book." In Carmelo Pellegrino, *Il surreale "padrepio" di Luzzatto*, in "Studi su Padre Pio", vol. VIII, issue 3 (2007), p. 431. The article ends on page 456 with an accurate denial of Luzzatto's most important assertions.

[8] Toward the end of June 1920, in fact, Monsignor Bella, Bishop of Foggia, takes to the Holy Office the depositions of two pharmacists who fear Padre Pio is artificially causing the stigmata with the use of the aforementioned drugs. The depositions are found in *Lemius*, enclosure 2, p. 23.

[9] On the subject of Gemelli's visit, see *Un tormentato settennio*, pp. 118–23.

Luzzatto, with a mistake that is relevant to the formulation of a precise historical evaluation of this story, misremembers the length of this meeting, and writes: "[Agostino Gemelli] spent a few hours with Padre Pio in person", in Sergio Luzzatto, *Padre Pio. Miracoli e politica nell'Italia del Novecento* (Turin: Einaudi, 2007), p. 78. Luzzatto's book, which has provoked an impressive array of criticism, received a first response from Professor Carmelo Pellegrino and Professor Luciano Lotti, in two essays we will quote later on. Later, in a more extensive discussion of the subject, Andrea Tornielli and Saverio Gaeta have countered many of Luzzatto's assertions in S. Gaeta and A. Tornielli, *Padre Pio. L'ultimo sospetto* (Milan: Edizioni Piemme, 2008).

[10] Father Benedetto of San Marco in Lamis, who was present at the meeting, wrote: "Fr. Gemelli, then not yet a university chancellor (1919–1920), wrote to the Provincial Fr. Pietro, that he wanted to come visit San Giovanni. Father Pietro wrote back that, if he meant to go as a scientist to observe Padre Pio, he should obtain permission to do so from the Superiors in Rome, knowing Padre Pio's great reluctance to subject himself to such examinations. Gemelli answered that he would only come for personal and spiritual reasons. [. . .] Gemelli arrived in the evening and didn't even verbally express to Fr. Pietro his desire to observe Padre Pio. The next day we were there with the Vicar general, the Secretary from Foggia, the Lenten preacher Fr. Gerardi, and the Friars Minor's Guardian with Ms. Barelli. Ms. Barelli asked to talk with Padre Pio, and, with me present, she also asked him whether the Lord would bless the planned Institution (the Catholic University [being founded by Gemelli]).

Padre Pio answered with a monosyllable: 'Yes.' Then evening came, and the next day Ms. Barelli started pleading with me to authorize Gemelli to observe Padre Pio. I answered that I couldn't do anything because the Provincial had expressly told me not to force such grave embarrassment on Padre Pio, since Fr. Gemelli had not asked for an authorization [. . .] Having abandoned the idea of an examination, Gemelli asked for an informal talk with Padre Pio, which happened in the sacristy. It lasted a few minutes. I was far in a corner and I had the impression Padre Pio dismissed him almost with annoyance. That's all." In *Un tormentato settennio*, p. 324.

[11] Gemelli's letter has been published in *Il Beato Padre Pio*, pp. 421–24.

[12] Ibid., pp. 426–27.

[13] In the first group is a letter from the provincial of the Capuchins in Foggia, Father Pietro of Ischitella. Wisely, the superior doesn't offer a personal judgment of Padre Pio, but reports those of authoritative personalities, in the Church and outside. Among them, the very flattering opinion of the Bishop of Melfi and Rapolla, Monsignor Costa, the report of the scrutiny of Dr. Romanelli's heart—which happened in the presence of other witnesses—the news of the bandaging of Padre Pio's sores and of the removal of all medicines from his room.

In the second group there are four medical reports about Padre Pio's stigmata: one by Dr. Bignami, one by Dr. Romanelli, and two by Dr. Festa. See ACDF, S.O., Dev. Var., 1919, I, *Cappuccini*, Padre Pio da Pietrelcina, folder 1, Padre Pio, documents 10–14. Monsignor Costa's testimony has been published in *Un tormentato settennio*, pp. 332–33.

[14] He was an opponent of Padre Pio, involved in many issues faced by the stigmatic friar and the Capuchins in the 1920s. He will be invited to renounce the direction of the diocese in 1929.

[15] The charge was given by the secretary of the Holy Office, Cardinal Rafael Merry Del Val. As for Lemius, he is a well-known theologian on account of his drafting the doctrinal section of the encyclical *Pascendi*. The rest was the work of Cardinal Calasanz Vives y Tuto.

[16] *Lemius*, p. 1.

[17] Ibid., p. 15. Bracketed ellipses indicate omitted text. Unbracketed spaced periods are suspension of thought points that exist in the original documents.

[18] The Apostolic Visitation is, in the former code of canon law, a particular form of Canonical Visitation.

By Canonical Visitation is meant an investigation [*investigatio seu inquisitio forma solemniore*] of people, things or places, that gives the Visitor the power to proceed to the correction, through legal measures, of the abuses he has verified [*cum iure corrigendi et reformandi si quos abusus visitator invenient*]. Depending on the circumstances, a Canonical Visitation can be ordinary or extraordinary; with regard to the Visitor's authority, it can be jurisdictional or disciplinary. A particular form of Visitation is the one *occasionaliter decretata*, that is, occasionally mandated by direct order of the Apostolic See. Since it is promoted by the Holy See, it takes the name of *Apostolic Visitation*. Authority and power for the Visitor, in this case, differ according to the mandate he has received. See Pio Paschini, "*Visita canonica*", in *Enciclopedia Cattolica*, vol. XII (1954) (Vatican City: Ente per l'Enciclopedia Cattolica e per il Libro Cattolico, 1948–1954), p. 1494.

[19] *Lemius*, p. 15.

[20] For a complete, in-depth study of Raffaello C. Rossi, see appendix I. Born in Pisa on October 28, 1876, Rossi, after enrolling in his hometown college to obtain a BA in Literature, enters the Order of Discalced Carmelites on October 3, 1897, and receives the Carmelite habit on December 19, 1898. In 1899 he makes his perpetual profession, and two years later he is ordained as a priest. For his human and spiritual traits, he is named coadjutor. In 1919 he becomes the Apostolic Visitor to the Apulia seminary and takes charge of the Venerable English College in Rome. He is appointed Bishop of Volterra on April 22, 1920, though he continues his work of Visitor. On June 30, 1930, Pius XI names him a cardinal, entrusting to him the charge of secretary of the Sacred Consistorial Congregation [now Congregation for Bishops]. He dies the night of September 16, 1948, in Crescano del Grappa. The process of his beatification is currently underway.

There are many publications about Cardinal Rossi, although the analysis of his role as Visitor is only at its beginning. In particular, the absence of a study of his canonical inquiry regarding Padre Pio calls for an update of the scientific contributions about his mission and his personality. For some useful in-depth analysis, see Valentino and Vito Bondani (editors), *Pastore e maestro* (Milan: Ancora, 1971); id. (editors), *Come lo conobbero* (Rome: Edizioni Saggi ed Esperienze, 1973); id. (editors), *Carisma della paternità*. Epistolario I (Rome: Edizioni del Teresianum, 1974); id. (editors), "*Riempite le idrie*": *Note di spiritualità* (Rome: Edizioni del Teresianum, 1976); id., *Raffaello Carlo card. Rossi: A servizio della Chiesa* (Rome: OCD, 1977); id., *Paternità di servizio. Raffaello Carlo card. Rossi e gli Scalabriniani* (Rome, OCD, 1981); Valentino Bondani and Maria Zalum Papasogli, *Attuazione delle norme concordatarie lateranensi* (Rome: Edizioni del

Teresianum, 1978); Maria Zalum Papasogli, *Il Cardinale del silenzio. Raffaello Carlo Rossi* (Rome: OCD, 1983). Very useful for understanding the Visitor's qualities and his experience in this field are two recent articles, in which are published, as appendices, the acts of Rossi's Apostolic Visitations to the Pontificio Seminario Regionale Pugliese: F. Sportelli, *Le visite apostoliche di Raffaello Carlo Rossi al Pontificio Seminario Regionale Pugliese (Lecce, 1911–Molfetta, 1919) (Parte prima)*, in "Rivista di Scienze Religiose" 15 (2001) pp. 259–99; id., *Le visite apostoliche di Raffaello Carlo Rossi al Pontificio Seminario Regionale Pugliese (Lecce, 1911–Molfetta, 1919) (Parte seconda)*, in "Rivista di Scienze Religiose" 16 (2002), pp. 59–100.

[21] Saldutto asserts that, before 1921, other Apostolic Visitations took place. However, there is no trace of them in the body of documents kept in the Archive of the Congregation for the Doctrine of the Faith. For Saldutto's statements, see *Un tormentato settennio*, pp. 139–41.

[22] This article was published in the fall of 2008.—TRANS.

Notes to Chapter 1

[1] The missive is dated May 30, 1921.

[2] ACDF, S.O., Dev. Var., 1919, I, *Cappuccini*, Padre Pio da Pietrelcina, folder I, Padre Pio, document 17.

[3] The charge of conducting a canonical inquiry was signed by Cardinal Merry del Val on June 11, 1921. See ACDF, S.O., Dev. Var., 1919, I, *Cappuccini*, Padre Pio da Pietrelcina, folder I, Padre Pio, document 18.

[4] In fact, Rossi must have arrived in Rome on June 10 or June 11 to receive the "opportune instructions". See ACDF, S.O., Dev. Var., 1919, I, *Cappuccini*, Padre Pio da Pietrelcina, folder I, Padre Pio, document 17.

[5] The main facts about the period of his military service come from the letters in which Padre Pio gives his spiritual directors information about this difficult period of 182 days, after which he will be declared unfit for military service. See *Epistolario*, p. 12.

[6] *Rossi*, pp. 2–3. According to the information acquired from the declarations of one of the witnesses, San Giovanni Rotondo's archpriest Giuseppe Prencipe, the transfer of Padre Pio to San Giovanni Rotondo would have been desired and planned by one of the friar's Brothers, Father Paolino of Casacalenda. Alas, on the whole, one cannot much trust Prencipe's declarations, as subsequent facts will reveal.

For a detailed chronology of Padre Pio's life, see *Il Beato Padre Pio*, pp. 17–70.

[7] The convent in San Giovanni Rotondo, the oldest among those in Apulia, was less than a mile from the town. San Giovanni Rotondo itself was a town with a population of about 10,000. See *Un tormentato settennio*, p. 334.

[8] The appointing document, dated June 11, 1921, is a letter that reads: "With the present it is made known that the Most Honorable and Most Reverend Msgr. Raffaele Carlo Rossi, Bishop of Volterra, is charged by this Supreme Sacred Congregation of the Holy Office with conducting a canonical inquiry concerning the Rev. P. PIO [*sic*] of Petralcina [*sic*], Capuchin. It is therefore ordered to whomever is concerned, to let him act freely, to comply with what he may require, and to cooperate with him in any way in the accomplishment of the mission entrusted to him. R. Card. Merry del Val." in ACDF, S.O., Dev. Var., 1919, I, *Cappuccini*, Padre Pio da Pietrelcina, folder 1, Padre Pio, document 18.

[9] Evidence of this is the doctoral dissertation of Gerardo Saldutto, *Un tormentato settennio*. The essay makes no mention of Rossi's Apostolic Visitation. This can be explained inasmuch as obviously no trace was left of the apostolic inquiry.

[10] See Padre Pio Archive, *Cronistoria*, ms. f. 30.

[11] *Lemius*, p. 49.

[12] Further information on the young Padre Pio can be acquired through the army matriculation roll, kept in the State Archive in Benevento, in which are recorded some physical characteristics of Private Francesco Forgione: "Height: 1.66 meters; chest: 0.82 m.; hair: color: brown, appearance: straight; eyes: brown; complexion: rosy; set of teeth: healthy", in *Il Beato Padre Pio*, p. 311. Cf. *Epistolario*, pp. 21–50.

[13] As to this aspect of Padre Pio, see *Il Beato Padre Pio*, pp. 316–18.

[14] The historical sources of this period, including those of the detractors, are unanimous in sketching the figure of Padre Pio as one of a cheerful, frail Capuchin. About this, see the testimony of an important Capuchin, Father Roberto of Nove, on September 4, 1920: "Padre Pio came toward me with a cheerful face, glancing down modestly, and he hugged me the way friars do. I was struck by the clear beauty of his face, the composure, the serenity, the simplicity, combined with a natural joviality, of his countenance", in *Un tormentato settennio*, p. 335.

[15] That Padre Pio's nature was anything but gruff is documented by various testimonies. Among these, allow me to refer to an article of mine with an unpublished testimony of 1922, written by the Venerable

Giocondo Lorgna. In it, the sweetness of the Capuchin's nature is hinted at in a very meaningful way: "Back from Padre Pio—[. . .] He's most affable—very humble—very cordial—two luminous eyes—a more-than-angelic smile—divine—most obedient—always ill since he was 16—he has healed others, asking to bear the infirmity himself—for lunch he only eats a bit of boiled vegetables, and some light soup in the morning and in the evening; a raw apple, if there is one—he received the stigmata 3 years ago [in reality, more than four years have passed] after a forty-day fast [information completely unknown until now], only receiving the Eucharist [. . .]", in Francesco Castelli, *Una lettera inedita di P. Pio*, "Servi della Sofferenza," XVII, no. 4 (April 2008), p. 23.

The Venerable Giocondo Lorgna was born on September 27, 1870, in Popetto di Tresana (in the Province of Massa Carrara). Sensing a special call toward consecration to God, in 1889 he entered the Dominican Order of Preachers, and took the name of Pio. After his perpetual profession he was ordained a priest on December 23, 1893, and in 1905 he became a pastor in Venice. The spiritual director of some Dominican tertiaries, in 1909 he decided to found the Pia Unione Adoratori-Adoratrici and a day-care service for poor children in the parish. In spite of numerous difficulties, his work strengthened and on October 30, 1922, his Eucharistic and educational community became a religious foundation: the The Dominican Sisters of the Blessed Imelda. This foundation was then followed by the Pia Unione delle Ancelle Missionarie del Santissimo Sacramento.

[16] *Rossi*, pp. 6–7.

[17] Ibid., p. 7.

[18] Ibid., p. 64.

[19] To learn about Padre Pio's typical day, the information provided by the witnesses of the Apostolic Visitation turns out to be particularly important. We will see that later. Here I will quote, because of its relevance to what is reported above, the testimony, dating back to 1920, of the philosopher and theologian of the Capuchin family, Father Roberto of Nove, southwest of Bassano del Grappa: "His habits. Padre Pio gets up at the same time as the community, 5:30 A.M. (Standard Time: here Daylight Saving Time does not exist). He hears confessions until 10 A.M., when he celebrates Holy Mass. After Mass, he returns to his cell for the thanksgiving prayer. He then goes down to the sacristy to listen to all those who wish to talk to him and be blessed: They are many and come from all the regions of Italy and from abroad. It takes great patience to listen to so many miseries and to welcome so many sick and desperate souls,

who ask for help, confidence, faith, peace. At noon he has lunch in the refectory of the small minor seminary of which he is the spiritual director: his menu consists of boiled vegetables, fruit (when in season), with sometimes an egg. And this is all he eats in one day, since neither in the morning nor in the evening does he take anything else. Actually, it was observed that, if at dinner he had some pasta or a bowl of milk, his stomach would not tolerate it. In the evening, after dinner, he stays a while to converse with the community." In Giuseppe Pagnossin, *Il calvario di Padre Pio* (Conselve, Padua: Tipografia Maffeo Suman, 1978), vol. II, pp. 414–416.

To eat very little will be a constant in Padre Pio's life. About thirty years later, a relevant and very significant episode happens in the presence of one of the witnesses of the beatification process:

"He would eat very little. One afternoon Padre Pio was in the hallway of the convent with his nephew Mario, who had around him his little children: the Padre was looking at them with tenderness. Pointing his finger to one of them, Mario jokingly accused him: 'Uncle, this one is a big eater.' 'Why?' asked Padre Pio. 'Today he ate up a loaf of bread this long and this big', explained Mario. Padre Pio smiled. Then he asked: 'How heavy was it?' 'A pound, at least', answered the nephew. Padre Pio thought about it a little, then said: 'In forty years'—Padre Pio was then over 60 years old—'I haven't been able to eat even half of that loaf of bread.' I was at Mario's side; we looked at each other as if to say: 'But how can he live without eating?'" In Pierino Galeone, *Padre Pio, mio padre* (Cinisello Balsamo: Edizioni San Paolo, 2005), p. 46.

[20] *Rossi*, p. 8.

[21] Ibid., p. 10.

[22] Ibid., p. 10.

[23] In order to know Padre Pio's human and mystical personality, the depositions given during the beatification process are particularly valuable. According to Cardinal Saraiva Martinis, current Prefect of the Sacred Congregation for the Causes of Saints, among the many depositions a prominent place belongs to the one of Msgr. Pierino Galeone, now published in Pierino Galeone, *Padre Pio, mio padre* (Cinisello Balsamo: Edizioni San Paolo, 2005).

[24] *Rossi*, p. 11.

[25] With the exception of Padre Pio's own statements, this account represents the most important and analytical source of this period for knowing the inner life and the story of the Capuchin.

[26] *Rossi*, p. 12.

[27] Ibid., p. 11.

[28] Drug used in the first half of the twentieth century to prevent and cure malaria.

[29] *Rossi*, p. 12. Rossi continues: "Few books: a commentary on the Holy Scriptures by Father Sales; Scaramelli, Sardou, something by Fr. Ventura, various booklets. By the bed, a terracotta image of the Nazarene; one of the B.V. [Blessed Virgin] on paper, with a hanging calendar attached to it."

[30] See *Il Beato Padre Pio*, pp. 253–58; pp. 322–23.

[31] *Rossi*, p. 16.

[32] *Il Beato Padre Pio*, pp. 261–71; p. 323.

[33] *Rossi*, p. 15. *Lei* is the formal "you" in Italian. *Tu* and *voi* are informal.

[34] Ibid., p. 14. "'His demeanor toward women *is proper, religious*', testified Father Lorenzo, the superior: '*With regard to chastity, I believe him to be angelic.*' '*As far as chastity is concerned,*' declared Father Romolo, '*his tact is extraordinary: as to this, nobody doubts he is an angel.*' The Father Provincial says he admires *his purity and modesty*; Father Lodovico attests that, when relating to women, *he shows politeness, reserve, and at times has even been austere*; Father Cherubino, finally, testifies that Padre Pio treats all women *with affability and sweetness, but is always most reserved.*"

[35] Ibid., p. 13.

[36] On this subject, cf. *Il Beato Padre Pio*, pp. 245–50, 321–22.

[37] *Rossi*, p. 14.

[38] Ibid., p. 106.

[39] Adriano Prosperi, *L'inquisizione Romana. Letture e ricerche* (Rome: Edizioni di Storia e Letteratura, 2003), pp. 229ff.

[40] The first theologian consultor of the Theological Congress that examined, at the Sacred Congregation for the Causes of Saints, the Capuchin's virtues, called the Servant of God's obedience to the Church authority "super-heroic". *Relatio et Vota*, p. 25.

[41] *Rossi*, p. 14.

[42] Ibid., p. 16.

[43] Ibid., pp. 16–17. Among the most significant testimonies about Holy Mass as celebrated by Padre Pio, the one provided by John Paul II is of particular value. The future pontiff and the stigmatic friar met after the end of World War II. The year of the meeting, as John Paul II himself remembers in a memoir he wrote, is "1948 [. . .], in the evening of a day in April".

On that date, with one of his "fellow students, Stanislaw Starowieyski", from Kraków, a little younger than he and not yet a priest, Father

Karol arrives at San Giovanni Rotondo to see Padre Pio "to attend Holy Mass and, possibly, to have him hear my confession". The next day, Father Karol attends Padre Pio's Mass: "It was long [. . .], one could see from his face that he was suffering profoundly. I saw his hands celebrating the Eucharist; the places of the stigmata were covered with a black wrap. We were aware that here on the altar, in San Giovanni Rotondo, the sacrifice of Christ himself, the bloodless sacrifice, was taking place, and at the same time, the bloody wounds on the hands made us think of the whole sacrifice, of Jesus crucified."

For the future Pope this "vision" is an exceptional fact: "Such event stayed with me as an unforgettable experience." Then he adds: "This memory lasts until today and somehow, today I have before my eyes what I myself saw then."

At the end of the Mass Father Karol made his confession to Padre Pio. Some journalists have spread the rumor of a prediction of the pontificate by the stigmatic friar. But things went differently. John Paul II has said Padre Pio was a very simple confessor, clear and concise, but has denied many times the rumor about the prophecy of his pontificate. After that, Karol Wojtyła never saw Padre Pio's face again. The memoir written by John Paul II about his encounter with Padre Pio has been published in Stefano Campanella, *Il Papa e il frate* (San Giovanni Rotondo: Edizioni "Padre Pio da Pietrelcina", 2005), p. 34.

During the historical research for the beatification and canonization of the Servant of God John Paul II, one last letter surfaced—the third, according to the number known as of today—which the future pontiff, then a bishop, wrote to Padre Pio. I have published it with a critical commentary in Francesco Castelli, *La terza lettera di Msgr. Wojtyła a Padre Pio*, "Servi della Sofferenza", XVII, no. 1 (January 2008), pp. 6–11. Cf. also id., *Monsignor Wojtyła e Padre Pio: il rapporto si intensifica*, "Studi su Padre Pio", IX, no. 1 (2008), pp. 131–43.

[44] *Rossi*, p. 17.

[45] Ibid., p. 20.

[46] Ibid., "To be sure, these, shall we say, prodigious facts have neither been subjected to formal examinations, nor expounded with due documentation and in the proper legal form, but they nevertheless make us ponder, in general and since they confirm each other, whether the Lord truly is availing himself of this pious Religious in order to once again manifest his goodness and his might."

[47] *Rossi*, p. 22.

[48] Ibid., p. 19.

[49] Ibid., p. 97. Cf. compendium, deposition 18.

[50] *Rossi*, p. 23.

[51] Ibid. In this, Rossi agrees with Dr. Festa, rather than with Dr. Romanelli, who asserted the existence of a wound from one side to the other, and even believed the metacarpus ruptured.

[52] *Rossi*, p. 24. Rossi then does not confirm Professor Bignami's observation, according to which Padre Pio had "an evident dermatographism all over his chest, and on his back, too".

[53] Ibid.

[54] *Rossi*, p. 25. Rossi continues and says: "But even supposing that at first, for a moment, the phenomenon did manifest itself in Padre Pio because of a morbid excitement: Would it be equally easy to maintain that this excitement has been and still is keeping the phenomenon alive, after over three years? I ask: How could a man live under the constant pressure of this morbid state, capable of continually reviving the painful signs on the exterior? Or at least, I wonder how he would be able to conduct himself always with tranquil serenity and perfect calm, and to perform his duties uninterruptedly, as Padre Pio does."

[55] This demonstrates that the willingness to unite himself to the Lord's suffering is not a fact originating outside Padre Pio.

[56] *Rossi*, p. 31.

[57] Ibid., pp. 31–32. On Padre Pio's marked inclination toward humor, see *Il Beato Padre Pio*, p. 319.

[58] Ibid., p. 38.

[59] Ibid., p. 39.

[60] Ibid., p. 40.

[61] Ibid., p. 41.

[62] Ibid., p. 17.

[63] The originality of Rossi's contribution to the knowledge of Padre Pio's mystical profile is quickly verified through a short account that, with less information, discusses this topic, in Gerardo Di Flumeri, *Il Beato Padre Pio*, pp. 430–33.

[64] *Rossi*, p. 41.

[65] Ibid.

[66] Ibid., p. 42.

[67] Ibid., p. 45.

[68] Ibid., pp. 45–46.

[69] On the relationship between Padre Pio and the Holy Office in the following years, see appendix V, years 1922–1968, pp. 292–94, below.

Notes to Chapter 2

[1] D. Domenico Palladino's further denunciations of Padre Pio are kept in the Archive of the Congregation for the Doctrine of the Faith. Cf. ACDF, S. O., Dev. Var., 1919, I, *Cappuccini*, Padre Pio da Pietrelcina, folder V, Padre Pio, document 132; 143.

[2] "A testimony, that of the archpriest, that we could describe as being on the razor's edge: cautious, but not too much, toward Padre Pio, severe in denouncing a part of his flock, which has abandoned the sheepfold", in Luciano Lotti, *Padre Pio piccolo chimico? La verità della fonte Rossi*, in "Studi su Padre Pio", VIII3 (2007), p. 540. This won't be Prencipe's only act in the Padre Pio affair. In fact, the Archive of the Holy Office contains many letters and reports sent by him to denounce what was going on in the convent in San Giovanni Rotondo. ACDF, S.O., Dev. Var., 1919, I, *Cappuccini*, Padre Pio da Pietrelcina, folder III, Padre Pio, document 74; folder IV; document 120 bis; folder V, document 134; document 140; 152–54.

[3] Regarding the change in Palladino's deposition, Lotti very acutely observes his change of direction. Luciano Lotti, p. 541. About his admission of guilt, toward the end of his life Domenico Palladino declared he did not believe what he had stated about Padre Pio, but had done so on account of the orders he had received from his bishop. Diocesan Tribunal of Manfredonia, *Transumptum processus in Curia Sipontina constructi super vita et virtutibus Servi Dei Pii a Pietrelcina*, (Manfredonia, 1989), vol. I, pp. 400–403.

[4] *Rossi*, p. 60.

[5] The occurrence of "doctrinal" conversions, even before moral ones, is from a theological point of view, a fact perfectly befitting the life of a true believer. Christianity, in fact, as Benedict XVI has often pointed out, is not an ethical decision, but an encounter with a divine person, an encounter that needs love to develop and mature. On this subject, besides his many speeches and homilies, see Benedict XVI, *Deus Caritas Est*, 1; see also his *Address to the participants in the Fourth National Ecclesial Convention* in Verona, October 19, 2006, which can be found on the official website of the Holy See, www.vatica.va.

[6] *Rossi*, p. 68.

[7] To have a better understanding of this philosophy—for which knowledge of God cannot be gained through a rational, speculative process, but rather through the religious sentiment, where the union between the divine and man is possible—a brief but effective analysis can be found

in Nicola Turchi, *"Teosofia"*, in *Enciclopedia Cattolica*, vol. XI (Vatican City: Ente per l'Enciclopedia Cattolica e per il Libro cattolico, 1953), pp. 1984–86.

[8] *Rossi*, p. 69.

[9] On this topic, the Capuchin superior declares: "On account of the name of, and the acquaintance with, Padre Pio, and after asking for his advice, the following persons have embraced the religious life, or are on the path toward it:

1. several young ladies who have become nuns: Padre Pio was able to provide for the first necessities of the vestition, thanks to donations received and reserved for this purpose;
2. Fr. Gaetano Morelli of the *Scuole Pie*, former rector of the *Collegio Nazareno* in Rome, entered the novitiate of our Capuchin Province of Sant'Angelo;
3. Prof. Arturo Palagi of Florence, professor of science and mathematics, now in this convent, is about to put on our religious habit;
4. a Russian painter who entered the Trinitarians in Livorno."

Finally he adds another important piece of information: Many who had been away from the Faith, having encountered Padre Pio "have resumed practicing the religion", *Rossi*, p. 69.

[10] Ibid., p. 72.

[11] Ibid., p. 76.

[12] Ibid., p. 89.

[13] Ibid., p. 97.

[14] Ibid., p. 96.

[15] This means the Lord's apparitions never stopped until the Apostolic Visitation.

[16] It is remarkable that Padre Pio received not only exhortations, but, in a way, "reproaches" regarding the spiritual life. It's clear that, in this case, "reproaches" is to be understood in a very broad way.

[17] On this subject, a detailed study of mine is about to be published that provides a historical outline of the theological debate on this aspect of the Capuchin's life, and also offers some considerations for future reflections.

[18] *Rossi*, p. 98. It is astonishing that Padre Pio reduces everything to ordinary soap! This episode is further proof of his "indifference" towards supernatural phenomena.

[19] Ibid., p. 98.

[20] Ibid.

[21] *Rossi*, p. 101.

[22] Ibid., pp. 101–2.

[23] Ibid., p. 102. Regarding miracles, too, Padre Pio's humility shines through. The Visitor asks for some confirmations with respect to alleged healings, and Padre Pio answers: "I don't know. I have prayed for the needs of the people who recommended themselves to me, poor people, needy people, etc. This is what I know."

[24] Ibid., p. 104.

[25] Ibid., p. 105.

[26] Ibid., p. 113.

[27] Ibid., p. 114.

[28] Ibid., p. 116. Actually, the Capuchin doesn't write, but receives, letters in French, showing that he can translate it easily into Italian. Padre Pio's only letter in French, of five lines, is addressed to Father Agostino of San Marco in Lamis, and contains a short greeting. A question, though, remains open: How could Padre Pio know French to the point of easily translating it? A few hypotheses could be advanced, but more clear is the explanation given in a similar situation. In 1912, before his pastor in Pietrelcina, Salvatore Pannullo, Padre Pio read and explained a letter in Greek by Father Agostino. Asked how he could do it, Padre Pio credited his guardian angel with it. *Epistolario*, p. 301; p. 302 n. 2.

[29] Ibid., p. 118.

[30] Appendix IV.

[31] The speaker is referring here to a conversation between Padre Pio and Fr. Raffaele D'Addario.

[32] Ottaviano Schmucki, "*Le stimmate di San Francesco e le stimmate di Padre Pio*", in *Atti del Convegno di studio sulle stimmate del Servo di Dio Padre Pio da Pietrelcina, San Giovanni Rotondo, 16–20 Settembre 1987* (San Giovanni Rotondo: Edizioni Padre Pio da Pietrelcina, 1988), pp. 154–55.

[33] This is a statement of Padre Pio reported by Fr. Raffaele D'Addario in 1967 and published in *Le stigmate*, p. 107.

[34] *Rossi*, pp. 96–97.

[35] *Le stimmate di San Francesco*, p. 157.

[36] *Le stigmate*, p. 107. The conversation is, from his point of view, further proof of Padre Pio's awareness of the identity of the "mysterious person".

[37] *Rossi*, p. 97.

[38] In the same conversation we learn that the stigmatization of Padre Pio happens in the context of a larger project of our Lord, who reveals to him his wish to unite "souls with his Passion".

[39] On this subject, the reading of John Paul II's *Salvifici doloris* allows us to gain an exceptionally close understanding of the Capuchin's spirituality.

[40] *Epistolario*, pp. 350–52.

[41] Cf. the testimony referred to in the *Positio* of Saint Gemma Galgani, in *Summ.*, p. 332.

Notes to Chapter 3

[1] A brief historical account of the immediate circumstances, and of who was present at these medical visits, is offered in Giuseppe Pagnossin, *Il calvario di Padre Pio* (Conselve, Padua: Tipografia Maffeo Suman, 1978), vol. I, p. 82. All the reports and the testimonies regarding Padre Pio's stigmata have been helpfully published in *Le stigmate*.

[2] *Rossi*, p. 106.

[3] Ibid. Festa, talking about the lesion on the left hand's palm, analogous, in his report, to the one on the right hand, declares that it was of "circular shape, [with] a diameter of almost an inch", in *Le stigmate*, p. 187.

[4] *Rossi*, p. 108.

[5] To be precise, Romanelli says "in an almost corresponding place", cf. *Le stigmate*, p. 148.

[6] Ibid., p. 188; *Misteri di scienza*, p. 160.

[7] In his report, Festa had instead observed perfectly identical dimensions on the left hand and the right. Cf. *Le stigmate*, pp. 187–88.

[8] *Rossi*, p. 108.

[9] It would have been helpful to have some more anatomical and morphological details about these "two buttons". It seems that a hypothetical parallel could be established here between Saint Francis' stigmata—a sort of fleshy excrescence—and those on Padre Pio's feet. Regarding these two "buttons", in his report Romanelli affirms that on the palms of the hands there is a "bright membrane, quite raised at the center, forming a very little button", in *Le stigmate*, p. 148. Therefore, he, too, saw two "buttons", albeit on the hands only.

[10] *Rossi*, p. 24.

[11] So far, this detail had not been clearly known from the doctors' reports in our possession.

[12] *Rossi*, p. 108.

[13] Ibid., p. 109.

[14] On this subject, we can agree with Gaetano Intrigillo: "The lesion on Padre Pio's side will always be the subject of discussion, with regard to both shape and exact position", in Gaetano Intrigillo and Maria Grazia Siliato, *Sindone e Stimmate*, in *Atti del Convegno di studio sulle stimmate del Servo di Dio Padre Pio da Pietrelcina, San Giovanni Rotondo, 16–20 Settembre 1987* (San Giovanni Rotondo: Edizioni Padre Pio da Pietrelcina, 1988), p. 102.

[15] *Le stigmate*, p. 149.

[16] Ibid., p. 150.

[17] Ibid., p. 176.

[18] Ibid., p. 83.

[19] Ibid., p. 189.

[20] Ibid., p. 207.

[21] Ibid., p. 295.

[22] Ibid., p. 130.

[23] We don't have information about the date of the examination of the stigmata on the chest conducted by Father Nazareno. More biographical information on Father Nazareno is found in *Le stigmate*, p. 66, n. 1.

[24] *Le stigmate*, p. 66.

[25] *Rossi*, p. 109.

[26] Ibid., p. 110.

[27] Cf. Luzzatto, p. 142.

[28] For example, see *Rossi*, pp. 61–62.

[29] Ibid., p. 23.

[30] Ibid., p. 110.

[31] Gaetano Intrigillo and Maria Grazia Siliato, p. 89. As we have seen from Monsignor Rossi's interrogation, this is not historically true, even though Intrigillo could not know.

[32] A picture of the shirt was reproduced in *Atti del Convegno di studio sulle stimmate del Servo di Dio Padre Pio da Pietrelcina, San Giovanni Rotondo, 16–20 Settembre 1987* (San Giovanni Rotondo: Edizioni Padre Pio da Pietrelcina, 1988), p. 85.

[33] Gaetano Intrigillo and Maria Grazia Siliato, p. 90.

[34] Stefano Campanella, *Il Papa e il frate* (San Giovanni Rotondo: Edizioni "Padre Pio da Pietrelcina", 2005), p. 54. We have no trace of other

statements by John Paul II recalling this circumstance that may offer further elements or possible confirmations.

[35] Cleonice Morcaldi, *La mia vita vicino a Padre Pio* (Rome: Edizioni Dehoniane, 1997), p. 48.

[36] Campanella, p. 34.

[37] *Rossi*, p. 24.

[38] Cf., for example, what Padre Pio says regarding the first manifestations of the invisible stigmata in *Epistolario*, p. 233.

PART TWO

Votum
on Padre Pio of Pietrelcina

by

His Most Reverend Excellency
Monsignor Raffaello C. Rossi
Bishop of Volterra

in

ACDF, S. O., Dev. Var., 1919, I, *Cappuccini*,
Padre Pio of Pietrelcina, Folder I,
Padre Pio, Document 21
[*Printed version of the report by Apostolic Visitor
† Msgr. Raffaello C. Rossi*]

SUPREME SACRED CONGREGATION OF THE HOLY OFFICE

(Month of January 1922)

Order of the Capuchins
ON PADRE PIO OF PIETRELCINA

Most Reverend Eminences,

[1] For some years, a humble Capuchin religious of the Province of Foggia, Padre Pio of Pietrelcina, of the convent of San Giovanni Rotondo, has been the object of such admiration, discussion, veneration, and curiosity that have well passed the short borders of northern Apulia to spread and appear not only in all of Italy, but also in foreign regions, even the far-away Americas. Y.E. [hereafter Your Eminences] already know the cause of all this. Reputation for an extraordinary virtue, rumors about graces and "miracles" that are said to have been obtained by Padre Pio, the "gift" of the stigmata with which he allegedly has been favored, a set of events and singular circumstances around his person—Padre Pio lives in the midst of populations prone to religious enthusiasms—all this is what has touched hearts and divided opinions.

[2] With great prudence, the diocesan ecclesiastical authority began by keeping itself apart from the popular movement: Then it watched, and gave private instructions to the town's clergy that they should not take any part in the almost

unanimous praise. At the moment of the Visit it appears to me that it stood aside not very favorably disposed, if not quite toward the person of Padre Pio, certainly toward what was said about him.

[3] In the meantime, the H. See [hereafter Holy See] was also watching, and—with the H.O. [hereafter Holy Office] gathering reports and depositions, presented by Father Gemelli, O.F.M., on his own behalf, and by the Bishop of Foggia on behalf of a third party[1]—started asking the local ordinary, the Archbishop of Manfredonia,[2] and the Capuchin General Curia, for the appropriate information. Along with the answer, the Holy Office also received from the Curia the reports of three doctors who had visited and examined Padre Pio.[3] The Holy Office, then, submitted everything to the examination of a Qualificator, so that he may report back. The Most Reverend Father Lemius, once appointed, studied the documentation and made his report: It followed exactly the conclusions of the Most Reverend Relator, who had primarily suggested the dispatch of a Visitor, a role with which Your Most Reverend Eminences willed to entrust me and which loomed difficult enough and was not devoid of challenges. But the Lord deigned to assist me, and therefore I am able to present Your Eminences with the results of the Visitation. Are they definitive? Unfortunately, no, but they can certainly provide, I think, sufficient assurance regarding what could be the object of appropriate and grave fears. The future will reveal what today cannot be read in the life of Padre Pio of Pietrelcina.

*

*   *

---

[1] S. O. *Lemius* Report, pp. 16, 20, and 26.
[2] Ibid., p. 28.
[3] Ibid., pp. 30–75.

[4] Of him here is the "story", in brief, as can be inferred from the information gathered and from the copious depositions whose full text Your Eminences will find in the compendium.

[5] Padre Pio, whose given name is Francesco Forgione, was born in Pietrelcina, the first station after Benevento, along the Benevento-Campobasso railway, thirty-four years ago. In 1902 or 1903 he entered the Order of Capuchins of the Province of Foggia, and for his novitiate and his studies he went from convent to convent; however, many times the state of his health forced him to go back to breathing his native air. He was said to be suffering from bronchial pneumonia; in reality, the medical exams never confirmed this positively. To me, after frequently interacting with him for eight days, he gave the impression that he was truly suffering from said illness: It is, though, just an impression, caused above all by a light cough noticed in the Religious, a cough that generally characterizes those suffering from pulmonary ailments. During one of his frequent stays with his family, Padre Pio was ordained as a priest, around 1910. After the outbreak of the war, he served as a soldier, although intermittently and briefly, actually staying as an in-patient at the hospital in Naples. Afterward, he was sent to Foggia, then to San Giovanni Rotondo, where he currently resides.[4]

[6] A set of circumstances, in which I think he had no part, brought him to San Giovanni Rotondo; perhaps he wasn't even aware of them. But it seems there was someone who was working to move him, that is, who took advantage of the "opportunity" of Padre Pio, with the intention—which we want to think was good—of serving the Faith.

I am reporting what I was told, during the inquiry and outside it.

---

[4] Compendium, depositions 6 and 18.

At that time, the superior of the Capuchins of San Giovanni Rotondo was a Father Paolino, a rather intrusive religious. During the vacancy of the office of archpriest, he had started hearing confessions in the town's churches, without asking for the appropriate faculties, as if he were in his own church, so much that the new archpriest—the current one—once in office, was forced to have recourse to the ordinary. Obviously, the superior was looking for "people": His church, far from town, was isolated; it needed to be enlivened. It seems he started talking about a holy monk living in Foggia (rumors about the extraordinary things happening around Padre Pio already existed); in turn, some devout people started making donations so that the holy monk would pray . . .* The preparation was long, the insinuation light, subtle, incessant. . . Then two, three brief visits of Padre Pio: He would come, counsel, and go back . . ., until, a small group of devout women having lobbied, it seems, to have Padre Pio definitely transferred to San Giovanni Rotondo, the wish was granted, and Padre Pio settled in the town where he is now, and where he enjoys, if not perfect health, at least better health than he had previously enjoyed in other convents of the province.[5]

[7] After some time, the event of the "stigmata" occurred, and what propaganda then! Not only by Father Paolino, but other religious as well: by a certain Father Raffaele—a religious who enlisted as an officer; by a certain Father Placido, another religious, as far as I can remember, who was far from spiritual; by a layman, a former priest. . . And after the propaganda, and because of it, came the crowds. Father

---

* Suspension points indicate pauses in thought by the author that were in the original text. Omitted text is indicated by bracketed ellipses.
[5] Ibid., dep. 1.

Paolino, I was told by the archpriest—from whom I gathered these facts and impressions—got more than he had
hoped for: He wanted the townspeople at the convent; he
saw people from all over the world flock there. We are, in
fact, at the peak of the "wonders" of which Padre Pio was
the center and cause, with I do not know what degree of
awareness on his part: This was the moment of the extraordinary "graces", which were multiplying by the day, of the
"miracles" that were said to occur under everyone's eyes
and that excited hearts to the point of delirium. "I [the
archpriest, a grave and serious priest, told me]—eyewitness
to the frenetic enthusiasm of the five, six thousand people
shouting 'miracle', crowding around him who had received
the grace and then parting to let him go through, so as to
form a double living wall around him—got an idea of what
must have happened when our Lord performed real miracles before the crowds who acclaimed him!"

[8] What was true of all that was said to be happening?
This enthusiasm which, again and again, for several months,
animated and agitated such a host of people, was it the result
of true wonders occurring under everyone's eyes, or was it
a case of collective autosuggestion? Time, the removal of
people who seemed to use their imagination and words too
freely, and the prudent reserve of the new religious who
replaced the former ones have settled many things back
within more proper boundaries. The declarations that Padre
Pio made, perhaps for the first time, to me, in the solemnity
of the inquiry and under the invocation of the Name of
God, provided the opportune clarifications, and would
change many minds, if known. Today it is easier to discern
human action from what could be divine action: but not at
that time. Padre Pio was a saint who performed miracles,
and this was not up for discussion. There were some who,
with supine ignorance, claimed him to be Jesus Christ

himself.[6] As a saint and miracle worker, notwithstanding his reluctance, he would go up to a window that looks on the church's square, so that he, in his surplice and stole, could bless the acclaiming crowd; he was made to give the same blessing from an opening above the high altar, from where a painting of our Lady would be taken down for the occasion. The bandages wet with the blood from the stigmata were taken around town, and the "pious"—devout women who would regularly go to the convent and have their confessions heard by Padre Pio—wore his picture around their necks (and some of them still do, although Padre Pio himself disapproves),[7] and lit candles before the image of this new saint! Meanwhile, he was made to celebrate the Holy Mass in church with the accompaniment of the organ, while the priests from out of town who happened to be present felt honored to be able to serve at the altar in a surplice[8]... One time, on May 5 of some year, there was even a panegyric of Padre Pio, recited by Father Benedetto *inter Missarum solemnia*...

[9] This was happening in San Giovanni Rotondo. But in the meantime the extraordinary news had spread, and kept spreading more widely, the work especially of the Neapolitan newspaper *Il Mattino*... It was a dark page in the first part of the story of this poor Padre Pio, whose name was used and abused, perhaps, to serve and cover up personal interests that were not always completely honest and transparent. The local correspondent for *Il Mattino* was a Freemason who frequented the convent: It seems that around there he had suspicious encounters with a young teacher—in

---

[6] Ibid., dep. 5.

[7] Ibid., depositions 5 and 20. This answers Fr. Lemius's observation: "Padre Pio has become a real center and object of a superstitious cult... *Why has he tolerated all this?*" (*Lemius* Report, p. 12).

[8] Ibid., dep. 11.

this maybe he was even helped and protected, since some religious certainly didn't shine for their exemplariness. . . It was necessary, then, to remove all doubts, and channel the interest the public had for the convent of San Giovanni Rotondo toward something very different from shady trysts. . . I came to know all this from the archpriest: But the religious also, without mentioning such details (of which they were perhaps unaware), confirmed to me that, if the friars had then showed more prudence and less credulity, and the journalist had provided less publicity, much of the noise would have been avoided, and many exaggerations would have been corrected.[9]

*

* *

[10] Sorting everything out and reporting and objectively considering old and new facts, this is what can be said of Padre Pio and the extraordinary things that are asserted about him.

[11] I'll start with a very brief *physical portrait*, and I think the one sketched by Professor Bignami[10] can be mostly repeated, so I will limit myself to the exterior appearance, with the changes dictated by my personal impressions: Padre Pio has a "pale complexion [but I wouldn't say *too* pale], sickly, suffering aspect [*not too much*, though]; droopy bearing [I'd rather say with Dr. Festa: slow and sometimes uncertain gait].[11] The demeanor of the person, which is modest and solemn [better, *composed*], the high and serene forehead; the look in his eyes, which is lively, sweet and sometimes wandering [but sometimes *vibrant*, too, the archpriest told me]; the expression on his face, which speaks of goodness

[9] Ibid., dep. 17.
[10] *Lemius*, p. 33. Cf. p. 34.
[11] Ibid., p. 49.

and sincerity: They all inspire sympathy." It is true. I couldn't obtain photographs to submit to the Holy Office. The cards that are circulating, at least those I saw, do not reproduce Padre Pio at all; I am almost tempted to believe that another Capuchin's portrait is passed off as Padre Pio's.

[12] From his physical portrait let us move onto another subject, which I would not know where to discuss later on, and which, after all, relates to the body: how Padre Pio eats and how much. Truth be told, Padre Pio has been presented as somebody who almost lives off air: There may be some exaggeration. He doesn't eat much, no; and especially when the "pilgrims" were most numerous, it was truly amazing how he could bear up in the confessional for so many hours without adequate nourishment. In fact, he doesn't take anything in the morning (although there are many people who don't eat anything for breakfast); his lunch certainly isn't lavish; he eats very little in the evening: some hot chocolate, sometimes not even that, thus reducing all the meals of the day to just one (and wasn't this the habit, for instance . . . of Monsignor Grasselli?); but everyone says he does eat. "As far as I know," declared Archpriest Prencipe, "he certainly does not eat much, but I was able to observe *de visu* [with my own eyes] that he does eat." [12] "[W]hen he used to eat lunch with us [now he takes it in the refectory with the boys at the minor seminary] I could see", these are Father Luigi's words, "that he didn't eat much, but, all in all, he did eat." [13] "He eats rather sparingly," testifies Father Romolo, who is headmaster of the minor seminary and as such takes his meals with Padre Pio, "and leaves food in every dish; he eats some of everything [. . .] but just a little bit. [. . .] [H]e eats more or less a third of

[12] Compendium, dep. 2.
[13] Ibid., dep. 11.

what I eat." [14] And Father Cherubino says Padre Pio's food
is sufficient, although he adds: "[N]evertheless, it's not always
proportional to his energy consumption, considering his
health and his work." [15] Clearly, then, his nutrition is not
abundant, but I don't think we are at the point of making
of Padre Pio a "phenomenon" in this regard, too. I rather
think that the illness that seemingly affects Padre Pio might
play a role in all this, and the Father Provincial seems to
hint the same thing in his deposition: "As for his nutrition,
it's strange—so much that I asked the doctors' advice, to
see whether we should intervene and request obedience.
*There are periods when he can't keep anything down: moments
when he takes to some food, which later he cannot tolerate.* Consulted, the doctors said not to force him, neither in quantity nor in quality." [16]

Moral and religious portrait of Padre Pio

[13] Padre Pio has always been a very good religious. They
all proclaim it in unison, both priests and Brothers. Still a
young student, he was so highly esteemed for his piety and
his spirit of observance that some superiors would even ask
for his advice—and they did so, truth be told, with so little
prudence as to provoke criticism and create discontent among
the religious, who then thought Padre Pio inspired some
measures that the superiors happened to take. [17] The Fathers
who behaved that way were Father Agostino of San Marco
in Lamis, now Provincial Councilor, and Father Benedetto,

---

[14] Ibid., dep. 13.
[15] Ibid., dep. 17.
[16] Ibid., dep. 16.
[17] Ibid., dep. 6.

also of San Marco in Lamis, currently working at the International College in Rome. Nevertheless, I'll repeat it, that doesn't mean that the *good* esteem Padre Pio enjoys is not *general.* Archpriest Prencipe, asked about the Padre's virtues— obedience, humility, etc.—testified that *it appears that he practices them.* He advanced some doubts about obedience: "I only know, from a religious of the convent, that the Father Provincial had forbidden private conversations in the guest quarters, but Padre Pio continued them".[18] However, Padre Pio, whom I interrogated on this point, explained that the Father Provincial granted him to stop those said conversations gradually, and he has actually tried to eliminate them little by little.[19] It is settled, then, that he didn't disobey the superior. Canon Palladino, while disapproving of some religious, and of certain women, called Padre Pio *a good son, a prayerful person and a good priest;*[20] Father Lorenzo, the superior, declared he thought him *most exemplary* as a young man,[21] and now *a simple man, devoid of duplicity, very kind, dedicated to piety—ordinary piety. In matters of obedience, he hears the superior's voice when it manifests itself clearly; with regard to chastity, [. . .] angelic; as for poverty,* about that there is *nothing in particular to say;*[22] about him, *observant.*[23]

Father Ignazio has *no doubt about* Padre Pio's *virtue;*[24] in fact, he says that if one wanted to sketch his moral-religious portrait, *one is at a loss.* He is a *good religious, humble; he does what the superiors want. And so, he is obedient.* He

[18] Ibid., dep. 2.
[19] Ibid., dep. 23.
[20] Ibid., dep. 5.
[21] Ibid., dep. 6.
[22] Ibid., dep. 7.
[23] Ibid., dep. 6.
[24] Ibid., dep. 9.

concludes: *Certainly, I am not as intimately acquainted with him as I am with other religious.*[25]

Father Luigi attests that, as a young religious, Padre Pio was by all accounts *very good. His classmates say that when he was a student, they would often find him in tears.* Now, in Padre Pio's life he doesn't *see anything extraordinary:* He leads *a simple life, common, ordinary.*[26] From Father Romolo we know that he was thought to be *a good young man and a good religious.* Now, according to him, *Padre Pio is like a child, quite a simple soul, because he says things as a young child would, although in serious matters he leaves you speechless.* He does not practice the virtues *to a heroid degree* but he *possesses a delicate conscience.* As far as obedience, Father Romolo asserts that *there were never,* as far as he knows, *clear and definite orders from the superiors* to Padre Pio regarding a specific issue. He has heard it said that *Padre Pio's obedience should be put to the test, but then no one does.* But he believes that if Padre Pio *received a definite, clear order, he would immediately bow his head.*[27]

Father Lodovico designates him as *a religious leading a holy life;*[28] Father Cherubino: a *good religious, who inspires trust and devotion in whoever talks to him.*[29]

Finally, the Father Provincial doesn't hesitate to say he was able to notice in Padre Pio, since his youth, *docility, obedience, and exact observance of his duties as a religious and as a student. Among his classmates, too, he exercised some influence, on account of his candid manners, kind, charming, and charitable. Even for the townsfolk, the sight of Padre Pio was edifying.* Nowadays, the Father Provincial appreciates and admires *his composure and his unfeigned piety, his obedience, his purity, his modesty.*

---

[25] Ibid., dep. 10.
[26] Ibid., dep. 11.
[27] Ibid., dep. 13.
[28] Ibid., dep. 15.
[29] Ibid., dep. 17.

Remarkable is his humility before the extraordinary manifestations of which he has been made a sign, while *one cannot suppose the existence in him of a duplicity that would be the opposite of his candor: He always lives true to his nature.*[30] On this last point, the same testimony was made, for instance, by Father Ignazio,[31] Father Luigi,[32] Father Romolo.[33] It is also unanimously thought that Padre Pio is very *simple,* so that *he rather needs direction and advice.*[34]

[14] A chorus of approval and praises, then, all the more credible because they are not exaggerations: Padre Pio's piety, at least judging from the outside, is thought to be common, ordinary, not much different from that of his Brothers. Credible, also, since the "good" Religious is not spared even small reproaches: it is noted that, in the choir, he doesn't distinguish himself by his special composure[35] (to me, frankly, it seems he does as many Capuchins more or less do: a consequence, then, of education and formation, not of lack of virtue); it is noted that he doesn't always keep silence in the hallways[36] (in this case, too, a habit that is ... common, as I myself was able to observe); that he is a little prone to judging his superiors—perhaps, it is added, he may have his reasons;[37] that on the Rosary hanging from the side he wears a little cross with Jesus Crucified, while the Constitution mandates a simple wooden cross;[38] that, especially when he is summoned to see visitors, he sometimes reacts with irritation, although he

[30] Ibid., dep. 16.
[31] Ibid., dep. 9.
[32] Ibid., dep. 11.
[33] Ibid., dep. 14.
[34] Ibid., dep. 17. Cf. depositions 13 and 16.
[35] Ibid., dep. 13.
[36] Ibid.
[37] Ibid., dep. 14.
[38] Ibid., dep. 13.

immediately represses it,[39] etc. More remarkable is the Father Provincial's observation: *I have also seen his human side*—a complaint Padre Pio expressed in a letter to the Father Provincial, when the Provincial himself prudently removed from the convent those religious who had provoked so much noise. But—and here lies the virtue—soon Padre Pio reconsidered, and, in a second letter, he asked to be forgiven for the complaint he had expressed:[40] a complaint he had advanced, after all, only on account of affection among Brothers.[41]

[15] I must admit Padre Pio made a rather favorable impression on me, although I had gone [to San Giovanni Rotondo] rather unfavorably prejudiced... A serious religious, distinguished, dignified, but also frank and casual in the convent. In church he assumes a measured gravity, as is only appropriate, after all. He doesn't have (*salva reverentia* [with all due respect] for others) the abandoned, careless manner of not a few of his Brothers (apart from the less-than-perfect way of staying in the choir): half-sitting down, half-genuflecting, with the arms on the pew and the head on the forearms—a consequence, I'll repeat, of the received education. The composure of his person is constant, grave, recollected, without exaggeration or affectation.

Some have mentioned the tight fit of his habit: It's not true; I'd say there is propriety. As for the use of a *fine* shirt: First of all, I would say that his special health concerns and the circumstance of the wound on his chest could require the use of unusual undergarments, but then, how about the other religious? In the convent I have noticed a great variety, of quality and of color, in the garments that stick out

[39] Ibid., dep. 6.
[40] Ibid., dep. 16.
[41] Ibid., dep. 24.

of the habit: At least two Fathers, also ill, wore a white shirt. After all, these are hard times: Everyone uses what he has, and so the young use what is left from their military service.

When talking, Padre Pio is generally polite and respectful, although, with what is known of him, one would never expect to hear from his mouth that *"per Bacco"* [by Jove] which sometimes escapes him. One would not expect him ever to use as an interjection, in the middle of an animated (but measured) conversation, the Holy Name of God, with habitual "my God, my Jesus" [or] to comment easily, I won't say on specific persons—I've never heard of this—but on townsfolk, or on local flaws, etc. Imperfections can therefore be observed in him, yes; but, after all... he is walking toward perfection; why declare he has already reached it? "Perfection cannot be acquired quickly", writes Saint Teresa.[42] "When the world sees anyone setting out on that road [of perfection] it expects him to be *perfect all at once.*" Somewhere else, speaking of ecstasy and of the kind of confessor who is "so scrupulous and inexperienced", she writes: "He thinks that people to whom God grants these favours *must be angels* and [. . .] *this is impossible while they are in the body.*"[43]

Let's continue. In conversation, Padre Pio is very pleasant; with his Brothers, he is serene, jovial,[44] even humorous, and this certainly is a sign of a good disposition.

If we also want to take a look at a *little* virtue, as Saint Francis de Sales would say, that is, at precision, I will say

[42] Saint Teresa of Avila, *The Life of Teresa of Jesus: The Autobiography of Teresa of Avila*, E. Allison Peers, ed., trans. (New York: Image Books, 1960), chapter 31, p. 268.

[43] Saint Teresa of Avila, *The Interior Castle*, E. Allison Peers, ed., trans. (New York: Image Books, 1972), Sixth Mansion, chapter 1, p. 119.

[44] Cf. Compendium, dep. 6.

that, while Padre Pio, as far as this aspect is concerned, is impeccable on his person, he doesn't seem to be as tidy in the way he takes care of his things... in his cell, the various drawers are somewhat disordered: sheets of paper, gloves, quinine, candies for the boys, images, everything rather muddled...

Few books: a commentary on the Holy Scriptures by Father Sales, Scaramelli, Sardou, something by Father Ventura, various booklets. By the bed, a terracotta image of the Nazarene; one of the B.V. [Blessed Virgin] on paper, with a hanging calendar attached to it.

[16] As far as the practice of the specific, "major" virtues, in the eight days of my stay and during a Visitation conducted in the utmost reserve and exterior secrecy, I could not possibly put Padre Pio through grave and long-lasting tests, but I was able all the same to observe his deeply felt and profound *humility*, so that—as it is univocally attested—he lives in the utmost simplicity and indifference, as if nothing had ever occurred around his person, and he wasn't still the object of so much attention and of an admiration that on the part of many is absolute veneration. Asked what he thought of the crowds that in the past would flood in, he told me that not even he knew the reason: "I remember", he added, "they would say: 'We're coming to confession'".[45] And on a different occasion: "I was terrified. I tried to listen to everyone as far as possible, and to work. Even in the Community we were invaded. We had to resort to the *Carabinieri*".[46]. He had also expressed to a Brother his amazement as to "why everyone was coming to observe me, my things".[47] I asked how it was that it never occurred

[45] Ibid., dep. 24.
[46] Ibid.
[47] Ibid., 14.

to him, to protect his own virtue, to ask to be transferred to a different convent. He answered: "I did desire solitude, because I have even been assaulted. I didn't ask anything because I've always followed the rule of deferring to my superiors, since they know everything".[48]

Informed that there had been too much talk—about his "stigmata" also—Padre Pio, on the last day of my stay, literally told me: "But, blessed be the Lord, why do they make so much noise about this! This explains why so many foreigners come here." And as I went on to mention to him the small group of women who habitually frequent the church and who talk more than necessary, he commented: "It is good that I am told and warned, but the real commotion was made by someone else", and here, opening himself up with great animation and liveliness, he went all over again through the newspapers' publicity and the release of the report by Dr. Romanelli of Barletta. "And yet," he went on, "only the three of us knew about it: the Father Provincial, the doctor, and myself. I didn't talk; the Father Provincial, I cannot believe it, since he once reproached a religious who talked too much... Who, then? The doctor? I take these things with resignation, but it pains me that all this could displease others, and maybe the Lord."

[17] As for *obedience*, I believe Padre Pio isn't lacking it. Besides his verbal assurances of always wanting to submit to the Church and to the legitimate authority,[49] he gave me an outstanding proof of obedience by putting in my hands, upon my first hint and without the slightest objection, all the letters he received from the former provincial, Father Benedetto. And my request, necessary on so many levels, had also an audacious side to it, since through it I asked

[48] Ibid., 20.
[49] Ibid., depositions 20, 23, and 24.

him to hand me a spiritual correspondence that could also reflect the secrets of his conscience. I actually felt the need to express the reservations which even a Visitor must sometimes express, but without difficulty he handed over everything for me to see and read. Moreover, once back in Volterra, when I expressed the desire to see the letters again, he promptly sent them with renewed feelings of submission, and since it occurred to him, while sending the letters, that he had by an oversight kept some that he hadn't found right away, he hurried to send me these, too, separately.

[18] Still, a "hasty" observer could see two clouds fall on Padre Pio's person with regard to Christian and religious *modesty*: one, because he was once seen talking with a young lady in the guest quarters;[50] another one, because of the liberties that the "pious women" somehow took with him, while he, ill, was being treated in the same guest quarters.[51]

But as far as the first case is concerned, Padre Pio was in the company of this young woman with the utmost discretion for reasons of ministry, and the malice was all on the part of two young men who peered into the room, and imagined they saw who knows what: One of them was the young lady's former fiancé!

As for the second instance, of women who would touch the ill Religious "to take hold of his holiness" (!), it was all the product of deluded minds and small brains, and the occasion had been imprudently created, alas, by the superior. But Padre Pio, who out of obedience and necessity had submitted to living outside the cloister, was never aware of what was going on and never had doubts, as is clear from the questioning that was prudently conducted on this matter.[52]

---

[50] Ibid., dep. 4.
[51] Ibid.
[52] Ibid., depositions 21 and 24.

It has also been observed that he addresses some women as *tu*. Let's not be surprised and let's not dwell on it too much: We are in southern Italy. He told me, "I hardly ever use *lei*: I use *tu* and *voi* indifferently." [53]

Now that all this has been reported and explained, we can rest assured that even with regard to this most important Christian, religious, and priestly virtue, Padre Pio is unassailable—as all witnesses, after all, attest. "His demeanor toward women *is proper, religious*", testified Father Lorenzo, the superior: "*With regard to chastity, I believe him to be angelic.*" [54] "*As far as chastity is concerned,*" declared Father Romolo, "*his tact is extraordinary: As to this, nobody doubts he is an angel.*" [55] The Father Provincial says he admires *his purity and modesty*; [56] Father Lodovico attests that, when relating to women, *he shows politeness, reserve, and at times has even been austere*; [57] Father Cherubino, finally, testifies that Padre Pio treats all women *with affability and sweetness, but is always most reserved.* [58]

[19] *Poverty.* Some religious might have been not quite sure about Padre Pio's practice of *religious poverty*. It's true that at first he managed some money, but it turns out he had been given such faculty by the then-provincial. [59] This handling of money not being regular, though, the current Father Provincial has disposed otherwise, [60] and now Padre Pio doesn't manage the donations received: He only expresses his desire that they be used regularly according to the

[53] Ibid., dep. 23.
[54] Ibid., dep. 7.
[55] Ibid., dep. 13.
[56] Ibid., dep. 16.
[57] Ibid., dep. 15.
[58] Ibid., dep. 17.
[59] Ibid., dep. 8.
[60] Ibid., dep. 16.

benefactors' aims and intentions. Actually, while he receives alms for the poor, he doesn't think at all about his own family, which is poor and provided for by the Father Provincial, unbeknownst to Padre Pio.

[20] As far as *prayer*, nothing extraordinary appears from the outside in Padre Pio, besides that *special recollection* that the superior noted;[61] but, by Padre Pio's own testimony, he seems favored sometimes with apparitions and intellectual visions, and, more or less, with a spirit of elevation,[62] which, if it doesn't quite reach the highest degrees of infused prayer, is nonetheless always to be acknowledged and admired in a soul. The Most Eminent Fathers will better understand this point by reading deposition 22.

[21] Finally, regarding the *celebration of the Holy Mass*, which was also the object of comments, I believe one must be measured and indulgent in providing judgment.

Padre Pio obviously celebrates with devotion—actually, with . . . too much devotion: five minutes for the *Memento* of the living; four or five for the *Memento* of the dead; two minutes for the consecration of the chalice—measured with watch in hand. But then he has his own little liturgical flaws. For example, I didn't see him bow his head at the name of the Holy Father in the Collect; he doesn't open and close his hands well at the *Oremus*; he doesn't incline toward the crucifix at the *Per D.[ominum] N.[ostrum] Iesum Christum*; when turning the pages of the missal with one hand, he also keeps the other hand up in the air; he doesn't bow perfectly toward the altar at the *Munda* and at the *Te Igitur*— maybe because of the pain in his ribs; he is not entirely precise in the ceremonies of Communion. . . All things to which a . . . *saint* should pay attention. But does this stem

---

[61] Ibid., dep. 6.
[62] Ibid., dep. 22.

from his coldness or carelessness? No. Again, I believe it all stems from his formation, from the instructions imperfectly received at the time of his priestly ordination. And the spirit of devotion thus remains intact and safe.

[22] All this I had to report conscientiously and note, based on the collected depositions and on my personal observations, to present, as accurately as possible, *Padre Pio's moral and religious portrait*, a portrait which can be summed up in a few words: *Padre Pio is a good religious, exemplary, accomplished in the practice of the virtues, given to piety and probably elevated to a higher degree of prayer than it seems from the outside; he shines especially because of his sincere humility and his remarkable simplicity, which did not fail even in the gravest moments, when these virtues were put to the test, a test truly grave and dangerous for him.*

Extraordinary facts *ad extra*

[23] So much has been said! And so little is true! Groundless claims,[63] words undeservedly attributed to Padre Pio. "They make me say what I don't think", he complained to me, "God's will be done!" And another time: "There has been recklessness on the part of some who wanted to use my name for things I would have never dreamed of either saying or revealing. It was crazy, and I have to thank the Lord that the greatest grace I know I received concerning this matter, was indeed the grace not to lose my mind and my health, so numerous were the lies that were told."[64]

[24] Archpriest Prencipe's depositions[65] report, in all the details, the "miracles" that caused so much sensation in San

---

[63] Ibid., dep. 11.
[64] Ibid., dep. 24.
[65] Ibid., dep. 1–3.

Giovanni Rotondo. I would ask the Most Reverend Eminences to read it now in full. Well, not even one "miracle" holds true, for example:

1. Rumors had it that a boy crippled by a humpback was at least partially made straight: In reality, this couldn't be verified.

2. People talked about the healing obtained by the Chancellor of the magistrate's court in San Giovanni Rotondo, who had dislocated his foot. In order to heal, he had to go to a spa.

3. People acclaimed the miracle of "Santariello", a poor idiot of Lilliputian height—hunchbacked, crippled, cross-eyed. I saw him: He is a pitiful wretch.[66]

4. A mute little girl was taken to Padre Pio. The crowd had the illusion the little girl had talked: a miracle! The scenes on . . . the Jordan's bank were renewed. The archpriest came forward out of the crowd, called the little girl's mother, and together with other relatives and doctors he locked himself inside the post office. "Little one, speak. . ." The little girl wouldn't. "But she did speak", the mother and the relatives all said, "Now the emotion keeps her from speaking." The next day the archpriest went back: The little girl didn't speak. . . After fifteen days, the mother went back to Padre Pio, so that he may *terminate* the grace. . .

5. Much noise was also made about the case—of a very different nature—of the bell of the parish church, a bell which was said to have cracked as a result of . . . Padre Pio's prayers, *in vindictam*

[66] Ibid., dep. 11.

against the archpriest, who had denied the Capuchin Fathers a permission ... I say *much noise*
because I myself heard talk about it in Rome. Well,
the Most Eminent Fathers will be able to see for
themselves in deposition 2. It's all laughable! And
the ignorant people shouted miracle! ...

[25] It happened sometimes that the implored grace was
not immediately... granted: But Padre Pio assured it would
happen on such and such a day, or another day, so the faithful would leave with this hope—and wait. That day would
come, but the grace would not happen; so they would go
back to Padre Pio, and Padre Pio again assigned a new dead-
line, and so on. I questioned Padre Pio about these allega-
tions, and he frankly answered that he had never given such
assurances; that you don't give the Lord deadlines; that it
was all coming from the mouths of the persons involved.
He would only tell them: "Trust in the Lord; I will com-
mend you to him" and similar encouragements,[67] when he
was not... more clear! The poor archdeacon of the cathedral of Trivento knows something about that. He was suffering from gout, and with difficulty he made the trip to
San Giovanni Rotondo. When he presented himself to Padre
Pio to beseech the grace to heal, adding: "This year I came
here instead of going to a spa", he was coldly answered:
"You made a mistake, you should have gone there!" I know
the archdeacon was very upset, and he left saying, "That's
deceiving people! ..."

[26] To think that so many idle words had cast such
an unfavorable light on this poor Capuchin! I'll take the
liberty then to call to the attention of the Most Eminent [Fathers] his genuine and honest depositions, since

---

[67] Ibid., depositions 20 and 24.

they reveal him to be not at all like an unscrupulous miracle worker or an enthusiastic instigator of mobs. He is a poor friar who, as far as I know, keeps his place and unwittingly has become the center of such attraction. These past years many things have been attributed to him which, had they even been true, he wouldn't have liked to see talked about: Whenever he was able, he never failed to raise his voice: *After all*—these are his own words—*of many of these things that were said to be true or made up, the last one to know, or the one who knew the least, was [Padre Pio himself].*[68]

[27] If no proven extraordinary facts happened in San Giovanni Rotondo, it would seem that they happened somewhere else, according to the reports sent to the convent in great numbers. At first, in the fervor of the enthusiasm, up to seven hundred letters would come in every day.[69] Now the number is much lower—sixty, seventy a day: Invariably they are letters asking for his intercession—as can be seen from the sample that I requested to be copied, and from authenticated copies that I deposited at the Holy Office—or letters of thanksgiving for spiritual or temporal graces that are said to have been granted on account of Padre Pio's prayers, some of which mention, for instance, true cases of sudden and unhoped-for healings. Suffice it to refer to the case of Maria Cozzi, a woman who was a patient in the main hospital in Florence, afflicted by an epithelial carcinoma of the tongue, and who was found perfectly healed the very moment she was supposed to undergo surgery (August 1919); also, the more recent case of a Canadian young man suffering from tuberculosis with hemoptysis, who was healed to the point that there was

---

[68] Ibid., dep. 24.
[69] Ibid., dep. 9.

not even a trace of the illness in him, after two "appari-tions" of Padre Pio.[70]

To be sure, these, shall we say, prodigious cases have been neither subjected to formal examinations, nor expounded with due documentation and in the proper legal form, but they nevertheless make us ponder, in general and since they confirm each other, whether the Lord truly is availing him-self of this pious Religious in order to once again manifest his goodness and his might.

[28] Since I am talking about the subject now, I will say that these letters generally used to be destroyed; now they are kept—it is a real archive: There must be at least twenty thousand—but Padre Pio only sees the few that are strictly personal or exceptional.[71] The superior and other religious go through the correspondence: They write back to whom-ever has sent postage for this purpose, to those who sent offerings (for Masses, for sacred functions, for the poor: few for the convent), to some to whom it would be impolite not to write back.[72] Usually, the answer is: *Padre Pio prays and sends his blessing,* or an image of our Lady with these two words written by Padre Pio on the back: *Heavenly blessings.*[73] He then entrusts to the Lord all the intentions for which the people who write implore prayers. It's not true that there are pre-made answers that are put into the envelope;[74] the only prepared things are the images I mentioned above,[75] which Padre Pio signs—reluctantly, sometimes[76]—generally during the evening recreation.

[70] Letter by Father Naldi of Florence, June 10, 1921.
[71] Compendium, dep. 9.
[72] Ibid., depositions 7 and 9.
[73] Ibid., dep. 9.
[74] Ibid., depositions 7 and 9.
[75] Ibid., dep. 9.
[76] Ibid., dep. 7.

[29] To complete this section about graces that were, or were not, granted, on account of Padre Pio's prayers (as it is asserted), it cannot be neglected to recall also other "graces", of a purely spiritual kind, which appear to have been obtained through the name, the example, and the words of Padre Pio: namely, the conversions of Jews and Protestants, the repentance of sinners, the intention, then carried out, on the part of some good people to lead a more perfect life. . . .[77] Are these unimpeachable attestations of Padre Pio's superior virtue? To be sure, evil itself can, in God's hands, be an instrument for good, and, for the elect, *omnia cooperantur in bonum* [Rom 8:28]: These changes of hearts could, in God's designs, be explained even without considering them to be the effect and proof of Padre Pio's holy life; but anyway, it is helpful to note that they did happen, and that those who received such graces openly trace their origin to Padre Pio.

[30] Another extraordinary fact is that of *bilocation*. One such case caused a stir in San Giovanni Rotondo, but it had all the appearance of a case of an overly excited imagination, of hysteria: It can be read, well narrated, in Archpriest Prencipe's deposition 3. The same archpriest learned of another case in Foggia,[78] and a third one—about a baker in Torre Maggiore—is alleged.[79] As usual, I challenged Padre Pio on each episode: With childishly candid answers, he admitted to the first and third, explaining how they had happened. He flatly denied the veracity of the second: In fact, it was ascertained that it had been a Father Pio *of Benevento*... To avoid useless repetitions, allow me to refer to depositions 20 and 24. In the meantime, though, it is

[77] Ibid., dep. 8.
[78] Ibid., dep. 3.
[79] Ibid., dep. 6.

indispensable to concede that, until proven otherwise, these facts hold true, and we have two sources for them: those who attest they have met Padre Pio and have talked to him, and Padre Pio who confirms, *protesting that he has never mentioned a word to anybody and has done so now* (during the inquiry) *for the first time.*[80] Therefore, there is no need to fear a possible collusion between the two parties.

[31] Conclusion. *Regarding the extraordinary events that occurred, as it is maintained, at the hands of Padre Pio, the popular imagination, fomented even by those who should have been more careful, has run as wild as it could. But of the most celebrated episodes, those that would have occurred exactly because of Padre Pio's personal intervention, not even one holds true. As for the cases which are told happened in places far from San Giovanni Rotondo, so far they haven't been presented with sufficient documentation. For the so-called "bilocation" episodes, on the other hand, it seems there may be the support of Padre Pio's sworn deposition, which, until proven otherwise, is to be considered sincere, since imposture and perjury would be in too stark a contrast with the life and the virtues of the Padre himself. Similarly until proven otherwise, it seems such a grave and continuing delusion cannot be assumed in Padre Pio, since he is so calm, serene, and uniform in all that concerns his life that it appears that nothing abnormal affects his spirit.*

Extraordinary facts concerning the person of Padre Pio

[32] It is said, even though those who say so can't provide any details—but Padre Pio confirms such statements in his depositions—that things not ordinary, even extraordinary, have happened to the person or around the person of Padre

---

[80] Ibid., dep. 20.

Pio since years past. In particular, there have been reports about some *noises* heard in the convent in Foggia, while the Community was in the refectory and the Padre in his cell, ill,[81] about apparitions of animals:[82] apparently, diabolical assaults and harassments.[83] Padre Pio says he has also had heavenly apparitions, which have now become rarer:[84] Others, too, relate this.[85]

But today, extraordinary facts of a higher order are the *"stigmata"*, the *scent*, and the *temperature at 118.4° F.*

THE STIGMATA

[33] The stigmata *are there*: We are before a real fact—it is impossible to deny it. *What they look like*, I have tried to describe amply in the appropriate report, drafted during the examination of the "stigmata" themselves.[86] I only hope for the benevolence of the Most Reverend Fathers, because the words of the report do not stand out for the appropriateness of the terminology, such as an expert doctor would have been able to use. And after all, I didn't conduct the examination according to medical criteria: I was simply an observer, even though a diligent one, to the utmost. As for Padre Pio, he *resigned himself* to endure the examination: His face betrayed his interior suffering—it didn't escape me. Then, that evening he told me: "How much I have felt the burden of obedience today! But the Lord made me feel it all at the beginning: Afterward, things went better!"

[81] Ibid., depositions 1, 11, and 13.
[82] Ibid., dep. 12.
[83] Ibid., depositions 13 and 18.
[84] Ibid., dep. 18.
[85] Ibid., depositions 6 and 11.
[86] Ibid., dep. 21.

[34] The "stigmata" *on the hands* are very visible, and caused, I think, by a bloody exudation: There is absolutely no opening or breaking up of the tissues, at least on his palms: It might be said there is on the back of the hands, even though I don't think there is, but then it must be agreed that the hypothetical opening doesn't penetrate through the hand cavity and doesn't come out on the palm. Without being a specialist, but only on account of an elementary process of observation, I would certainly agree with Dr. Festa's opinion, against that of Dr. Romanelli, who maintains the existence of a wound from palm to back. After all, if the tissues were broken up, Padre Pio wouldn't be able to use the joints of the hand and close it; instead, he can move it and close it *almost* completely.

On the inferior extremities the "stigmata" were about to disappear: What was possible to observe resembled two buttons with whiter and more delicate skin; but Padre Pio assures that the "stigmata" "at times [. . .] are more noticeable, at times less so; sometimes they look like they are about to disappear, but they don't, and then come back, flourishing again":[87] So it may be the case that those on the feet, too, could now be open again.

In his side, the sign is represented by a triangular spot, the color of red wine, and by other smaller ones—not anymore, then, by a sort of upside-down cross, such as the one seen in 1919 by Dr. Bignami and Dr. Festa.[88] This is the sign that gives out the most blood. I had neither the desire nor the opportunity to perform a more extensive examination, which, given my task and my ignorance in medical matters, would have come to nothing: I did notice, though, that no other dermographic phenomenon appears around

---

[87] Ibid., dep. 24.
[88] *Lemius*, pp. 35, 49.

this bloody spot, and Padre Pio assured me that nothing like that is on his person. This would therefore represent a change from what Prof. Bignami reported: "There is also an evident dermatographism all over his chest, and on his back, too."[89]

[35] When, and how, did these signs manifest themselves? I questioned Padre Pio; he lowered his eyes, then, with the hint of a smile, he told me: On September 20, 1918, while he was praying after the Holy Mass, suddenly he was overtaken by a powerful trembling; then he had a vision: Jesus Crucified appeared to him, he talked to him, he told him he would unite him with his Passion. When Padre Pio came to, he saw the blood dripping from his hands.[90]

Perhaps only Father Benedetto knows these details, at least from Padre Pio himself, who has been very reserved. And this testifies in his favor, as does the care that was taken since the beginning in concealing the extraordinary fact: It was some devout women who realized it in church. Nevertheless, it was only too natural that various hypotheses were aired to explain these "stigmata" (all the more because until now, it was not known precisely what Padre Pio has testified about their origin). At this point, therefore, it is necessary to summarize them and discuss them.

[36] I. Is it likely, in this case—as has been written[91]—a pathological self-stigmatization *ab intrinseco*? In other words, are these "stigmata" the manifestation of a morbid condition?

II. Is it likely, in this case, a self-stigmatization *ab extrinseco*? In other words, were these stigmata

[89] Ibid., p. 34.
[90] Compendium, depositions 18 and 20.
[91] *Lemius*, pp. 6 ff.

caused by either suggestion or the voluntary application of artificial means?

III. Is it likely that Padre Pio's "stigmata" might be of divine origin?

IV. Is it likely that they might be of diabolic origin?

[37] I would like to begin by absolutely ruling out this *last hypothesis*. Padre Pio's most righteous life, his virtue, his piety are arguments too powerful to believe that the devil, if he fights Padre Pio, as it seems he does, has over him a power that only the subject, for diabolical ends, can give him. It would be necessary to find in Padre Pio a *culpable* form of obsession, or quasi-obsession, to think of a diabolic stigmatization. But it is very clear that in Padre Pio's case there is no such obsession. Therefore, *the hypothesis is ruled out*.

[38] I will consider now the *first hypothesis*: *Are* Padre Pio's "stigmata" *manifestations of a morbid condition?* The Most Reverend Father Lemius, who asked himself the question, answered that, on one hand, Padre Pio's temperament seems to be predisposed toward this phenomenon—very scarce nutrition, dermatographism or autographism—but upon meeting him, he could not understand how someone suffering from a neuropathic disorder could endure the hard work of the ministry, and how it was that phenomena resulting from such a condition—such as inflammation, etc.— never appeared on him.[92] Well, now the Most Reverend Father should remove from his report the arguments in favor of this proposed thesis, or at least introduce some doubts, because it's true that Padre Pio eats little—let's even say very little—but it's also true that this *very little* is not as incredible as it was once believed, and anyway, he eats as much as is sufficient for him to live. As for dermatographism,

[92] Ibid., p. 7.

it needn't be discussed any further, since besides the local-
ized "stigmata", no dermatographic sign is found on Padre
Pio: It can be verified and it is what Padre Pio asserts.

And if dermatographism is identified with autographism, then
Padre Pio, questioned—and it was impossible not to question him—answered under the sanctity of the oath that he
never produced on his person signs that would have then
appeared visible depending on fixations and obsessions.[93]

After all, it is anything but proven that the stigmata can be
a morbid consequence of autosuggestion: On this topic, Father
Poulain can be opportunely consulted; in his work *The Graces
of Interior Prayer*, he is very skeptical about it, thinks it problematic that the imagination could have so much power, and
ends by writing: "If we say that the imagination is capable of
producing the stigmatic wounds, we are forced to state it as
a fact without any experimental proof."[94]

But even supposing that at first, for a moment, the phenomenon did manifest itself in Padre Pio because of a morbid excitement: Would it be equally easy to maintain that
this excitement has been and still is keeping the phenomenon alive, *after over three years*? I ask: How could a man live
under the constant pressure of this morbid state, capable of
continually reviving the painful signs on the exterior? Or at
least, I wonder how he would be able to conduct himself
always with tranquil serenity and perfect calm, and to perform his duties uninterruptedly, as Padre Pio does. *Therefore,
it seems to me that the hypothesis of pathological self-stigmatization
ab intrinseco cannot be endorsed, or, at least, I think current data*

[93] Compendium, dep. 23.

[94] Fr. Augustin François Poulain, S.J., *Delle Grazie d'Orazione. Trattato di
Teologia Mistica* (Turin: Marietti, 1912), chapter 31, sections 8–10. English
Edition: *The Graces of Interior Prayer: A Treatise on Mystical Theology* (London:
Kegan Paul, Trench, Trubner & Co. Ltd., 1910), chapter 31, sections 8–10,
p. 556.

*are not sufficient to support it and transform it into certainty. It
would be necessary to keep studying and, especially, waiting.*
[39] *As for the second hypothesis*—self-stigmatization *ab
extrinseco*—there are three possibilities:

1. Self-stigmatization through external suggestion;
2. same, through autosuggestion;
3. same, procured with chemical and physical means.

The probability of a self-stigmatization through external
suggestion (first case) is assumed by Father Gemelli, who
casts the suspicion that the former provincial, Father
Benedetto—who has been Padre Pio's educator, coun-
selor, and protector, and still is his spiritual director—
might have contributed to this suggestion, through his
tenacious and enduring influence.[95] Some of Father Benedetto's phrasings—if only Father Gemelli knew!—might support this suspicion: For instance, three months before the
"vision" and the "stigmata", he wrote to Padre Pio, "It is
not Justice, but the crucified Love that *crucifies you and wants
to unite you with his most bitter suffering*" [emphasis by Rossi].[96]
A month before, he wrote about a *vocation to co-redemption*
in Padre Pio, about a *painful union* of Padre Pio with O.L.
[hereafter our Lord], about *transverberation*, and about an
inexplicable *wound*: "*The fact of the wound* completes your
passion just as it completed that of the Loved One on the
Cross." [97] Might the mention of a *wound* have powerfully
influenced Padre Pio? And don't the words of the previous letter come back in our Lord's mouth, in Padre Pio's
"vision": *I unite you with my Passion?* . . . Padre Pio is not
new to making some of Father Benedetto's "beautiful"

---

[95] *Lemius*, p. 18.
[96] Compendium of the appendix, Letter of June 7, 1918.
[97] Ibid., Letter of August 27, 1918.

phrases *his own*:[98] Might he not have done it one more time? Is it not peculiar the correspondence between the September "stigmata" and the "wound" mentioned in August—between the "vocation" of Padre Pio *to be united* with our Lord's Passion and Father Benedetto's very same words (in June), which we would be tempted to call prophetic? Might it not be that, through suggestion, the wounds indicated by Father Benedetto formed on Padre Pio, and that, through suggestion, he thought he heard from our Lord those words that were nothing but Father Benedetto's resonating in his mind?

It could be, obviously. Given the continuing, intense influence (four words in a letter wouldn't be sufficient per se to produce such grave effects); given in how much esteem Padre Pio holds Father Benedetto (and it is a great deal); given the authority Father Benedetto has over Padre Pio, as a former superior and as spiritual director; then the hypothesis of suggestion *is not impossible*, according to some—but not to me. But could it even be likely? . . . I would like to offer separately the following considerations:

a. Father Benedetto's letters are, generally, *answers* to letters from Padre Pio—in particular, the letters of June 7 and

---

[98] Here is an example. On *May 8, 1919*, Padre Pio wrote to someone: "You, too, help with your prayers this Cyrenian who bears the cross of many, so that in him the apostle's words may come true: *to compensate for and perfect what is lacking in Christ's Passion.*" Well then: Isn't this thought one of Father Benedetto's, who, on *June 17, 1918* had written to Padre Pio: "Justice has nothing to vindicate in you, but in others, *and you, as a victim, owe on behalf of your brothers what is still lacking in Jesus Christ's Passion.*"

One more. On *January 26, 1921*, Padre Pio wrote to a sister: "You would like to know who is causing you joyfully to suffer so much, and to complain about what you ardently desire; to feel intoxicated in your suffering and to endure it with utmost distress! Don't you know that God alone can reconcile the opposites in a soul and make *in pace amaritudo tua amarissima?*" Well, didn't Father Benedetto write these *exact* words, *ad literam*, to Padre Pio, as it appears from his letter of January 6?

August 27, 1918, as is clear from the context. If, then, Father Benedetto wrote of wounds, of transverberation, of crucifixion, he wrote as the *second*, not as the *first*; he wrote because Padre Pio had already written to him on the same topics. It should be said then that . . . Padre Pio influenced Father Benedetto, not vice versa! . . .[99]

b. But let's suppose the opposite: Let's assume for a moment that Father Benedetto succeeded in producing in Padre Pio a psychological phenomenon such as the one in discussion. Then a difficulty already mentioned (in a different context) arises again: a suggestion that *after three years, for three straight years* produces a continuous bleeding? A suggestion that is the irresponsible work of a religious who lives almost two hundred fifty miles away, who rarely goes to San Giovanni Rotondo, who writes, yes, but only about once a month, and writes letters that these days, rather than being about the stigmatic disciple and his spiritual direction, are about the hunger for. . . the mystical apostolate of the director himself? . . . Frankly, I don't think this is the case.

Concluding, I would be of this opinion:

a. that Padre Pio might have not received very good spiritual direction by Father Benedetto, who I think—even though I do not know him, and only judging from reading his correspondence with Padre Pio—does not possess the qualities needed to direct souls on a mystical path: first of all, because he has a *wrong* conception of mystics; secondly, because he

---

[99] If we could consult Padre Pio's correspondence with Father Benedetto, I think it would help enormously in gaining intimate knowledge of Padre Pio in the process of the extraordinary events happening to him, and in understanding Father Benedetto's part in it. But it is spiritual correspondence, and so far it would have been bold to request it . . . If the Holy Office will think it opportune, the documents will be the object of a supplemental study. In that case, it would be a very good thing also to request the chronicle that Father Benedetto is allegedly writing.

insists *on wanting to be* a "mystical" director, when it *is the Lord who makes* the mystics what they are; and finally, because, also according to the testimonies of others, he is *too credulous and enthusiastic* before allegedly extraordinary events;

b. that Father Benedetto, with his oral and written teachings, may have had a heavy influence on the special ascetic and mystical education of Padre Pio; but

c. *that his action could not have been so powerful as to influence Padre Pio deeply and even produce in him the "stigmata", which would be too disproportionate an effect compared to the cause, I don't think it happened. Nevertheless, caution may suggest a prudent, restrictive measure concerning the relationship between the two religious, which, without being specific to the case of Padre Pio, might be part of the more general measure I will propose—separately, in the appendix—with respect to Father Benedetto.*

We will now examine the second alternative within the hypothesis of self-stigmatization *ab extrinseco*: self-stigmatization *through autosuggestion.* The Most Reverend Father Lemius writes "that the autosuggestion related to extreme acts is one of the possible, but by no means necessary, manifestations of hysteria; and that after all, hysteria itself is only probable in Padre Pio's case, not certain".[100] I think I can complete this assessment, rewording it. Padre Pio is not hysterical at all; he is absolutely normal, from what can be seen, from what is known: So testified the superior, Father Lorenzo,[101] and Father Ignazio.[102] Even Padre Pio himself—a dubious judge in his own trial, yes, but not so much as to deny him good faith in his own matters—has said that "by the grace of God" he has never suffered from nervous disorders, hysteria, and the like.[103]

---

[100] *Lemius*, p. 8.
[101] Compendium, dep. 7.
[102] Ibid., dep. 10.
[103] Ibid., dep. 23.

In agreement with the Most Reverend Father Lemius, therefore, *it is appropriate to rule out a stigmatization self-inflicted through autosuggestion.*

The third alternative remains: self-stigmatization *produced through physical and chemical means.*

A serious, legitimate suspicion arose on account of a deposition that could not be discounted,[104] and Father Lemius collected it in his report: It couldn't have been otherwise.[105] One day Padre Pio, through a young woman whom he had urged to keep great secrecy, asked a pharmacist in Foggia, a relative of the aforementioned young lady, for a bottle of pure carbolic acid; another day, for four grams of veratridine, a caustic substance, a very powerful poison that is stocked in very small quantities in few pharmacies. What did this mystery hide? Were the stigmata a sham, a vulgar fraud? Did Padre Pio, at the cost of suffering pain, cause them, did he cultivate them, did he make them grow artificially, so as to increase the fame of his "holiness" ... ? The "mystery" is revealed: I don't think there is reason to doubt the sincerity of Padre Pio, who was required to take oaths that should have struck a chord in his priestly soul and *under whose sanctity he attested he had not artificially caused or completed the stigmata.*[106] The secrecy, if it was even requested, would have been requested not on account of the Brothers,[107] "especially considering", says Padre Pio, "that in the past [during the war] I was almost alone with the Father Guardian.[108] If anything, the only purpose was to prevent the people who had to carry it [the

104 *Lemius*, pp. 20–28.
105 Ibid., p. 9.
106 Compendium, depositions 23 and 24.
107 Ibid., depositions 19 and 22.
108 Ibid., dep. 19.

carbolic acid][109] from knowing that it was a medicament requested without a doctor's prescription."[110] It should be observed how the drug obtained in Foggia by the young woman had then to be transported to San Giovanni Rotondo by "the chauffeur driving the bus route between Foggia and San Giovanni".[111] Padre Pio requested *carbolic acid* to disinfect syringes needed for shots[112] and *veratridine* for ... a prank to be played during recreation!! Padre Pio had experienced the effects of this powder mixed, in an imperceptible dose, in the tobacco offered to him by a Brother.[113] Without knowing anything about poisons, without even considering what veratridine was (and that is why he asked for *four* grams), he requested it to repeat the joke and laugh at the expense of some Brothers! ...[114] That's all. Instead of malice, what is revealed here is Padre Pio's simplicity, and his playful spirit.

But there was another way in which Padre Pio could, *praeter intentionem*, preserve the "stigmata": that is, by using, as it seems, other medicaments, for example, iodine.

Besides the fact that he used it, according to Father Lemius' report, to *disinfect* the sores—and it certainly "sounds odd that stigmata that may be miraculous need disinfection"[115]— the application of iodine, given that it was *old iodine*, easily could have contributed, because of the development of hydroiodic acid, "to intensify preexisting skin alterations" and to produce more "in normal tissues".[116] This could

---

[109] The request for the veratridine was made in writing, and the original document does not mention secrecy.

[110] Compendium, dep. 19, cf. dep. 22.

[111] *Lemius*, p. 27.

[112] Compendium, depositions 19 and 22.

[113] Ibid., dep. 9.

[114] Ibid., dep. 19.

[115] *Lemius*, p. 12.

[116] Ibid., p. 37.

explain at least the *preservation* of the stigmata. Taking into due account, during the Apostolic Visitation, the correct observations mentioned above, this is what results today from the sworn depositions:

1st. Padre Pio used iodine not to disinfect the wounds, *but to stop their bleeding.*[117] "I didn't even know whether it would work. I saw others use this medication, when they happened to cut themselves, to stop the bleeding",[118] declared Padre Pio. Therefore, the singularity and oddness of disinfecting potentially miraculous stigmata do not have reason to be.

2nd. He made use not only of iodine, but also of petroleum jelly or starch glycerolate—but always for obvious reasons: "They had me use a little petroleum jelly when the sores would lose their scabs."[119]

3rd. The use of iodine was discontinued, precisely to avoid (though independently from superior reasons) the effects the iodine could produce on skin tissues: "[A] doctor told me to stop, since it could irritate even more".[120]

4th. Finally, it has been about two years[121] since Padre Pio has used anything, that is, *he does not apply any medicament on the "stigmata"*, even though—it should be noted— *the "stigmata" still persist.* Therefore, their permanence is independent of the application of these medicines: *We can then conclude that they were not caused or preserved with physical and chemical means, which, after all, would have been in absolute contrast with Padre Pio's proven virtue, and, if true, would have found no explanation other than a morbid condition, which cannot really be observed in Padre Pio.*

[117] Compendium, depositions 6 and 18.
[118] Ibid., dep. 22.
[119] Ibid., dep. 18.
[120] Ibid.
[121] Compendium, depositions 18 and 23.

[40] It remains to be seen whether the Capuchin's "stigmata" are *of divine origin* (*third* hypothesis): not an easy analysis, and a very difficult judgment.

Father Poulain writes: "It has been shown [. . .] that the saints' stigmata presented very great differences from those of [. . .] hypnotized persons." [122] Following this author, I will now set out these differences, and, with the appropriate applications to this particular case, I will try to infer separately the possible consequences.

"1st. *With the first* [that is, saints' stigmata] *there are true wounds; the flow of blood is often very abundant. There is nothing similar with the others. There has merely been a swelling or a more or less coloured exudation. It is a coarse imitation only.*" Now, in Padre Pio's case we do have something that is neither a simple swelling, nor a mere colored sweat: Blood—*real blood*, as doctors have confirmed [123]—sometimes flows out, and remedies have been used to try to stop it, but to no avail. Because of this, at least once Padre Pio could not celebrate Holy Mass. [124] We have then here the first of the two characteristics of miraculous stigmata; but can we say that we also have the second one, that is, *true wounds*? Admittedly, today the feet do not show sores, but signs of a former decomposition of skin tissue—decomposition, though, that could have very well been a sore in the past, as seems to be the case according to the reports of Dr. Romanelli and Dr. Festa, [125] but not confirmed by that of Professor Bignami. [126] There is no wound in the ribs, and never was, according to Bignami and Festa, [127] whereas Dr. Romanelli found one, and described

[122] Delle Grazie d'Orazione, pp. 555–56.
[123] *Lemius*, pp. 39, 40; 48–50.
[124] Compendium, dep. 15.
[125] *Lemius*, pp. 39 and 48.
[126] Ibid., p. 35.
[127] Ibid., pp. 35 and 49.

it as a "lacerated wound, linear, with definite, slightly wrinkled edges, involving soft tissues".[128] Today a diffused, triangular-shaped redness can be observed on the ribs, a kind of superficial inflammation, a "superficial skin abrasion"[129] from which flows enough blood to dampen clothing and bandages. Finally, it would seem that on his hands, where the stigmata are most visible, there is only an abundant sweat that causes dark, bloody scabs; as I said, there might be wounds on the back of his hands, but we cannot be sure. Dr. Bignami and Dr. Festa[130] did find *lesions* on his hands, while Dr. Romanelli[131] found *holes*, originating on one side and terminating on the opposite—holes, though, not really seen, but only deemed to exist through palpation.

We return then to the question: Can it be asserted that, in Padre Pio's case, we do have the *real sores* characteristic of miraculous stigmata? There is no easy answer. Today it should be possible to answer properly; yesterday the situation seemed different, although not even the doctors could agree on the details. In conclusion, it seems to me one can say

1. that Padre Pio's "stigmata" do present the supernatural character *of the outpouring of blood*;
2. that it is prudent to suspend one's judgment as far as the character *of the real sores* is concerned, even though there seem to be enough reasons to lean toward the presence of a supernatural gift— the signs on Padre Pio, for instance, are not limited to the mere swelling mentioned by Father Poulain; actually, there is no swelling at all.

---

[128] Ibid., p. 35.
[129] Ibid.
[130] Ibid., p. 35 and 37.
[131] Ibid., p. 39.

But let's even suppose that Padre Pio doesn't have, and never had, *real sores* on himself—would this be reason enough to rule out the existence of a supernatural phenomenon and of a divine gift? Would God really establish limits to his action? Can we really circumscribe mystic occurrences within certain and immutable conditions, within absolute terms, thus turning mysticism into a science? Or have we not had cases of invisible stigmata, for instance, of real stigmata with absolute absence of external wounds? ...

Another essential characteristic of true stigmata according to Father Poulain[132] is that they are "*located* in the same places as they were on Christ's body". Now, *there is no doubt that this happens in Padre Pio's case*, and it is such a peculiar fact, and so out of the ordinary, that Professor Bignami felt bound to write: "What is impossible to explain with the knowledge we have of neural necrosis is the perfectly symmetrical location of the lesions described." [133]

I will now continue with the list of differences between true and false stigmata, according to Father Poulain.

"2nd. *The first* [the true ones] *often persist for several years, or reproduce themselves periodically every week. The others are transient.*"

In this respect, there is no doubt: Padre Pio's "stigmata" have lasted *for over three years now*, and in this regard, then, they could be said to be of divine origin.

"3rd. *It is not possible to cure the first by means of remedies.*"

This is indeed Padre Pio's case. Iodine and starch glycerolate, used to stop the bleeding, did not prove effective to this end, nor could they close the wounds. And not just this, but I am told that once, one of Padre Pio's hands had to be treated by doctors, then bandaged, then treated again

[132] *Lemius*, n. 11.
[133] Ibid., p. 37.

periodically, so that, according to the experts themselves, it should have returned to normal within eight days. But it was actually after these eight days that the treated and bandaged hand was bleeding so much that it prevented Padre Pio from celebrating Holy Mass![134] *Here, then, would be found another distinctive characteristic of true stigmata in those of Padre Pio.*

"4th. *The first are often very painful* [and actually, in a different passage Father Poulain writes that it is an essential characteristic of true stigmata *to cause atrocious pain*]. *This fact has not been noted with the others.*" In fact, Padre Pio has testified that his "stigmata" give him "[p]ain always, especially on some days when they bleed. The pain is more or less intense: Sometimes"—and these are Padre Pio's own words—"I cannot bear it."[135] Not only that, but Padre Pio has added: "I felt pain in those same areas [that is, where there are now the visible signs], of the kind that I felt later on. These pains started around 1911–1912, during my first years of priesthood."[136] These pains were "intermittent, because there were breaks. They generally happened from Thursday evening through Saturday morning, and occasionally on Tuesdays, too."[137] Therefore, *the pain* considered a sign of supernatural stigmata *is present in Padre Pio's case*, and has been there for a long time, so it may be presumed that his "stigmata" could have been *invisible* for a certain period of time.[138]

"5th. *The first have always been accompanied by ecstasies.*" On this point, in truth, it is difficult to provide much clarification. Padre Pio certainly is a prayerful friar, but it is

[134] Compendium, dep. 15.
[135] Ibid., dep. 19.
[136] Ibid., dep. 20.
[137] Ibid., dep. 22.
[138] Cf. dep. 12.

not yet clear which degree of mystic elevation he has reached. Padre Gemelli writes that "he doesn't show any of the characteristics of a mystic"; [139] a Brother claims instead that "he has the appearance of a profound mystic." [140] It is a fact, though, that according to sworn depositions by Padre Pio himself, his "stigmata" were granted by our Lord *during a thanksgiving prayer following Holy Mass*, in a "vision"....[141] Was it ecstasy? If not an illusion, it certainly was at least something more than ordinary absorption in prayer...

"6th. *Contrary to what is observed in all natural wounds of a certain duration, those of the saints exhibit no fetid odour [...] (sometimes they even emit a perfume), no suppuration, no morbid deterioration of the tissues. And the remarkable thing is that any non-stigmatic wounds from which they may suffer follow the normal course.*"

Well then, here is another circumstance in favor of Padre Pio and his "stigmata", whose miraculousness would then have further sanction. *No suppuration* in the Capuchin's wounds—it's very obvious and even the doctors observed it:[142] A very vivid and pleasant *fragrance* emanates instead from the "stigmata" or, better still, from his whole person, of which I will talk separately. Are we then really before Saint Francis of Assisi's marvel, renewed somehow in one of his sons? I do not know. I said it is very difficult to pronounce judgment on the divine origin of Padre Pio's stigmata, and it would be imprudent, at least now, to decide, without hesitation, favorably—or unfavorably. Suffice it to

---

[139] *Lemius*, p. 17.
[140] Compendium, dep. 15.
[141] Ibid., dep. 18.
[142] *Lemius*, p. 40.

highlight the circumstances which, in case, could provide some light and criteria for a future judgment.

[41] *To summarize, what I believe can be certainly affirmed today is that the stigmata at issue are not a work of the devil, nor a gross deceit, a fraud, the trick of a devious and malicious person.* And this, if I am not mistaken, could be enough today to reassure the ecclesiastical Supreme Authority on the "case" of Padre Pio of Pietrelcina. *I would like to add that his "stigmata" do not seem to me a morbid product of external suggestion, either, although prudence may recommend some measures of observation and precaution. For the reasons I explained above, neither would I believe them to be a product of autosuggestion. But those who have more expertise than I can voice a more authoritative judgment on the matter, and, anyway, time will make known what today is so hard to demonstrate.*[143]

THE SCENT

[42] This very intense and pleasant fragrance, similar to the scent of the violet—as it was well described by the Bishop of Melfi—is attested by everyone, and may the Most Eminent Fathers let me attest it, too. I have smelled it, just as I have seen the "stigmata". And I can again assure the Most Eminent Fathers that I went to San Giovanni Rotondo with the resolute intention of conducting an absolutely *objective* inquiry, but also with a real *personal unfavorable*

---

[143] Rumors had it that on Padre Pio's forehead the signs of the *crown of thorns* were also starting to be visible. I saw nothing: Father Superior Lorenzo didn't notice anything (Deposition 7); questioned, Padre Pio answered laughing: "Oh, for the love of God! What do you want me to answer! Sometimes I've found some small blisters on my forehead or my head, but I never gave them any thought, and I certainly never dreamed of telling anyone!" (Deposition 24.)

prejudice regarding what was said about Padre Pio. Today I am not a ... convert, an admirer of the Padre: certainly not; I feel complete indifference and I would say almost coldness, so much did I want to maintain a serene objectivity in writing my report. But, to clear my conscience, I have to say that, faced with some of the facts, I could not retain my *personal* unfavorable prejudice, even though I did not manifest anything on the outside. And one of these facts is the *fragrance*, which, I'll repeat, I have sensed, just like everyone else:[144] The only one who does not notice it is Padre Pio.[145] Where does it come from? This is an even more perplexing question than that other: Where do the "stigmata" come from? Because with the "stigmata", one could, if he wanted, bring up, support, and defend suggestion and autosuggestion, but, as far as I know, such morbid conditions cannot produce smells. Therefore, again, we are either before the devil's work (and this is to be ruled out, for the reasons already stated), or we are before divine action—and on this I cannot pronounce myself; otherwise, we are certainly before a trick, a fraud, or, at the very least, before an innocent use of perfumes on the part of Padre Pio. But the idea of deceit doesn't hold true when compared with the Religious' virtuous life,[146] just as it would be hard to explain, for the very same reason, such secular vanity in him: At any rate, either fraud or simplicity, the fact is, in his cell Padre Pio has nothing but... soap—and I have thoroughly examined his cell with the utmost care. But since it is clear that it would be possible to keep something ... smuggled out of the cell, what really

[144] Compendium, depositions 6, 11, 13, 15, 16, 17. Archpriest Prencipe also testified to me he has smelled it.

[145] Ibid., dep. 19.

[146] Ibid., Cf. dep. 13.

counts is Padre Pio's sworn statement in which he attests
to never using, and never having used, perfumes.[147]

And after all, if he really, for whatever reason, used this
fragrance on himself, the scent should be sensed more or
less at all times. But that is not the case: They say it is
sensed at times, *in waves*, inside the cell and outside, when
he walks by, in his spot in the choir, even from a distance:
One such case occurred to Archpriest Prencipe, who noticed
it in the parish church when giving Communion to one of
the people who was closest to Padre Pio; it happened to
Father Lorenzo, the superior, while the others with him
didn't sense it.[148] It is to be noted that Father Lorenzo is a
very serious priest, prudent, and at the beginning "skeptical" about what was said of Padre Pio. Moreover, the bandages with the blood that flowed out of Padre Pio's wounds,
his *zucchetto*, his gloves,[149] his hair that was cut two years
ago keep this scent... Where does it come from? I have
observed and reported a fact. The Most Eminent Fathers
will judge.

THE TEMPERATURE AT 118.4°F

[43] Here's another odd fact which, if validated, "would
be most astonishing, like something miraculous",[150] since
it is well known that the human body doesn't seem capable
of reaching such high temperature. But in Padre Pio's case
it has happened more than once, and for a few years now,[151]
and Father Lorenzo, the superior, who was extremely dubious

---

[147] Ibid., depositions 23 and 24.
[148] Ibid., dep. 6.
[149] Ibid., depositions 11 and 15.
[150] *Lemius*, p. 11.
[151] Compendium, dep. 20.

about it—as he was about the rest—had to convince himself of the reality of it when the proof occurred in front of his very eyes and in his very hands.[152] It is not to be believed, though, that this is Padre Pio's permanent state: quite the contrary, and this explains how Monsignor Menghini, for instance, didn't notice it. The fact occurs in special *spiritual* circumstances; the illness that brings about this temperature, or of which this temperature is a sign, is—so declared Padre Pio—"a moral, rather than a physical illness". Padre Pio feels in himself "internal feelings, the consideration, or some representation, of the Lord. Like in a furnace, still always conscious." [153] And in fact, a Brother attests that even under the strain of this fever, Padre Pio is not knocked down, but gets up, moves about, and can do everything.[154] It can't be denied this is most unusual and exceptional! In the eight days of my stay in the convent, I didn't have occasion to observe this abnormal phenomenon in the Religious; the superior's deposition, which is added to that of Padre Pio, is powerful. I don't think, therefore, that the fact can be doubted. Its explanation, though, remains obscure, so various hypotheses are presented. Again, I cannot help but rule out any diabolical intervention, any human fraud. Whether this phenomenon, besides being exceptional, is also miraculous, the Lord will reveal when he thinks the time is right.

*

*   *

[44] At the end of this long report, and before concluding with any proposals, I will somehow return almost to where I began (sections 7 and 8): *What is going on around Padre Pio today, in the convent and in the town?*

---

152 Ibid., dep. 6.
153 Ibid., dep. 19.
154 Ibid., dep. 9.

[45] Things have now a different look compared to that in the past: more serious, calmer. The popular enthusiasm has waned:[155] Of those who regularly frequent the convent and the church, few are from San Giovanni Rotondo—mostly, the "pious women", good women, no doubt, but who should probably keep their visits less frequent, and stop the ridiculous flaunting of that portrait of Padre Pio they wear around their necks.

Padre Pio says of them: They do not obey; what spirit of submission to their spiritual director! . . .

But if Padre Pio were to leave the convent, I believe that, given the fanaticism of the locals, we should fear a renewed, fierce opposition on the part of the people of San Giovanni Rotondo: And I won't say anything of the "pious women", who, at the mere rumor of a measure they thought taken against Padre Pio, threatened a religious with spreading so many stories, both true and *false*, so as to cause his transfer and the superior's, too!

[46] More frequent than the locals' visits are those of people from out of town, some of whom are grave, serious, coming even from abroad. There are two or three women and young ladies who months ago took up "residence" in San Giovanni Rotondo,[156] and who invariably every morning and every evening walk up to the convent church to hear the Holy Mass and the vespers celebrated by Padre Pio. Among them, Mrs. Morselli of Rome, who, widowed, went there with her daughter—still a child—to find peace and comfort.

[47] In the convent, all is well. The religious who in the past had provoked so much noise were all transferred by the current Father Provincial,[157] a wise and prudent man,

---

[155] Ibid., cf. dep. 4.
[156] Ibid., depositions 7 and 20.
[157] Ibid., dep. 16.

who used to be in the Capuchin General Curia in Rome. The religious who make up the Community of San Giovanni Rotondo are serious, reserved, prudent: No measure regarding them is necessary. Special rules have been set up concerning the receiving of laymen in the guest quarters, in the convent, and in the refectory; photographers and journalists are forbidden to approach Padre Pio; it is forbidden to give away and circulate bandages or other objects belonging to Padre Pio. In any case, the Father Superior is storing away the blood-stained bandages.[158]

[48] Something resembling publicity—although much less than in the past—does go on in the church. Padre Pio celebrates the Holy Mass every morning at ten—*de officio diei* Mass—and distributes Holy Communion to the faithful who wait for that hour to communicate from his hands. After the Holy Mass he withdraws to the sacristy for the thanksgiving prayer, which he says, as far as I have seen, standing up, leaning on the vesting counter with his head in his hands. In the meantime, the visitors wait silently in the sacristy itself. Next, the kissing of his hands and a few short conversations happen. The Mass is not by invitation, as it has been said—everyone is free to enter the church—but those who desire to see Padre Pio are encouraged to take advantage of that service, during which everyone can easily see Padre Pio.[159] In the evening, it is once again Padre Pio who celebrates the sacred service that needs to be held (after which, more hand-kissing), but since he is always the celebrant, it has happened that, when nobody else is available, the Father Superior himself had to serve as deacon...[160] It wouldn't be a bad thing if all this remaining outward show

[158] Ibid., dep. 6.
[159] Ibid., depositions 6 and 12.
[160] Ibid., dep. 14.

could be eliminated, and many wish for this to happen;[161] so far it has been kept up to proceed prudently and gradually,[162] and to let those who want to see Padre Pio see him in public, without disturbing him privately. As for the Holy Mass, it was left at 10 A.M. to avoid displeasing those who desire it to be celebrated by Padre Pio, and who probably wouldn't be able to go up to the convent church— which is rather far from town—at an earlier hour. It seems there may also be some personal "physical" difficulties, as he calls them, on the part of Padre Pio, although he would, in the end, sacrifice on account of obedience.[163] In short, it seems it's not that easy to change the hour of this Mass.

*

*   *

[49] *Appendix*. I couldn't find a better place to deal with this topic, so I'll make it the subject of a brief appendix, almost *extra formam*.

In Rome, in the Saint Bridget Monastery in Via delle Isole, there is a Sister Giovanna, who used to be a spiritual daughter of Padre Pio. Last February, the Mother Superior, lamenting the spiritual meddling of Father Benedetto of San Marco in Lamis, extraordinary confessor, complained of the following:

1st. Padre Pio apparently wrote a letter to the aforementioned Sister Giovanna, insisting that she choose Father Benedetto as spiritual director: Sister Giovanna did not want to—one director, I imagine the ordinary confessor, being sufficient for her.

2nd. This Sister Giovanna reportedly said that "Padre Pio visited her in spirit and she was transported with him to an

---

[161] Ibid., dep. 13.
[162] Ibid., dep. 12.
[163] Ibid., depositions 13 and 24.

indescribable spiritual height, and that our Lord told her the following: 'I have incarnated you in my Divinity to make an oracle of you, immediately, without any distinction of beings'; he went on: 'You will be the voice of the Most High.' " Strange "visions", then, and dangers for her virtue and perfection.

[50] On this subject we have a letter by Padre Pio dated January 26, 1921, which is attached in the compendium, document 26. In it is the idea that Sister Giovanna should make use of Father Benedetto's spiritual ministry, as well as the mention of something extraordinary that happened to Sister Giovanna, which might be the strange "vision", or rather, the dream, of the deluded religious.

[51] Because these documents were among others concerning Father Benedetto, I failed to question Padre Pio in person about their content. I compensated by sending him a copy of the letter and a form with questions for him to answer. Faithfully and promptly, Padre Pio answered (compendium, document 27). Of the "dream", *he doesn't know or remember anything,* nor does he keep Sister Giovanna's letters, so he is unable to answer thoroughly. It should not be ruled out, however, that he might have been too credulous: After all, it's clear from his answers that he thinks of Sister Giovanna almost as a privileged soul... As for the advice Padre Pio gave her—"I urge you to confer every once in a while with the Most Reverend Father Benedetto about your spiritual life" (this is the advice lamented by the Mother Superior)—it was indeed given by Padre Pio, *but its ultimate source is... Father Benedetto,* who, unable personally to place poor Sister Giovanna under his *mystical* guidance, had written to Padre Pio not even a month earlier, on December 31, 1920: "I also meant to let you know that Sister Giovanna, for reasons I do not know, did not come to confession: Perhaps she thinks she can do without it? If you write

to her, urge her, without revealing in any way that I informed
you, to seek as much enlightenment as possible, and show to her
how the saints were not content with only one helping hand in the
ways of the spirit, but sought one hundred—with the exception of
some enlightened, and of sure competence, spiritual directors".

[52] If Father Benedetto's mystical cravings will be reined
in, it will be all the better for Padre Pio, and more souls
will find peace.

Conclusion

[53] Most Reverend Fathers, I have finished. It is time to
draw some practical conclusions, and it can be done by saying in short: that, as far as I can see and save errors or better judgment, Padre Pio is a good religious; that, of the
"graces" beseeched, as it is said, through his prayers, many
do not hold true—many are only asserted, but lack a legal
proof; that whatever is extraordinary in what happens to
the person of Padre Pio cannot be explained, but it certainly does not happen either by diabolical intervention, or
through deception, or with fraud; that the popular enthusiasm has greatly waned; and that the religious Community
in which Padre Pio lives is a good Community and one
that can be trusted.

It is now necessary to continue to be prudent and to wait; a
transfer of Padre Pio being unthinkable, his superiors must be urged
to observe and keep watch—tacitly, not in an obvious way; the
countenance of the "pious women" must be corrected, and their
visits to the church and the convent should be less frequent: In all
this, Padre Pio should be more assertive; Padre Pio should be char-
itably counseled to be more cautious in his believing in the spiri-
tual elevation of certain souls. Any form of external publicity that
is too evident must be reduced as much as possible. The Holy

Office must be kept current on all new facts concerning Padre Pio, whether in progress or after the fact. As for his relationship with Father Benedetto, it will be a sufficient measure if, as I will propose in due course, Father Benedetto is given prudent general advice regarding the direction of souls, mentioning in particular the grave prudence that must be used with respect to Padre Pio, either when interacting with him, or when writing to him. It would be a very good thing if we could acquire, to consult it, the Chronicle of Padre Pio, *which Father Benedetto is said to be composing, or at least to acquire whatever he is gathering to write someday on the life of Padre Pio.*[164]

Embracing the purple of Your Most Reverend Eminences, I am Your Eminences' very humble and obedient servant.

Volterra, October 4, 1921

† Br. Raffaello C., Bishop of Volterra*
Apostolic Visitor

N.B. *After the compendia concerning the report on Padre Pio, there is a brief appendix with the respective compendium on Father Benedetto.*

---

[164] Ibid., dep. 16.
* Bishop Rossi signed his name with the title for a religious brother because, though he was a priest and bishop, he was a Carmelite.

COMPENDIUM

In this compendium are reported in full the depositions received by the Apostolic Visitor, organized by the name of each witness, and not following the chronological order of the sessions. Nevertheless, since the interrogations are naturally interrelated, to explain the relations and to understand the reason for some of the questions asked of the witnesses, a chronology of the sessions has been put at the end of the compendium, with the appropriate references to it.

NUMBER I

First Deposition of Can. Dr. Giuseppe Prencipe, Curate Archpriest of San Giovanni Rotondo

June 14, 1921—9 P.M.

Before me, the undersigned Apostolic Visitor, charged by the Supreme S. C. of the H. Office [hereafter Holy Office] with conducting an inquiry about Padre Pio of Pietrelcina, Capuchin, has appeared, summoned, in San Giovanni Rotondo, Archd[iocese] of Manfredonia, in the parish residence, the *Most Illustrious and Reverend Mr. Dr. Giuseppe Prencipe*, curate archpriest, son of the late Pasquale, of San Giovanni Rotondo, age forty-nine, who, after taking the oath *de veritate dicenda* [to tell the truth] on the H. [hereafter Holy] Gospels, testifies what follows.

Padre Pio was preceded by the fame, spread by his then-Brothers, of wondrous facts, especially about a noise of chains heard in the convent in Foggia, about the devil, appearing in the form of a woman, etc. Given this fame, crowds flooded to come see him: It should be noted that he hadn't come to live in the convent in San Giovanni yet, but he came two or three times. Later on, I believe, the Father Guardian [the title Capuchins give their superior], pressed by a group of devout women, found a way for Padre Pio to be transferred to this community. Padre Pio was not a confessor: He spent his days counseling devout women; he didn't preach. Then the "stigmata" occurred, and with them the tales of many extraordinary phenomena which happened, by way of his influence, to these devout women who frequented the convent, phenomena reported in *Il Mattino* of Naples by the correspondent in San Giovanni, Adelchi Fabbrocini, an elementary schoolteacher and a Freemason. I must confess that I didn't have the luck to experience any of these events in San Giovanni.

I should add that I called some of these pious women to know what extraordinary things had happened to them, but I couldn't learn anything, since they said silence had been imposed on them.

As for the healings, the rumor did spread of countless healings, but I couldn't verify *de visu* [with my own eyes] the veracity of any, at least of those that were called "miracles", and always within San Giovanni Rotondo. And of some of these healings, made known by the Brothers, their insubstantiality has been revealed, especially the one concerning a crippled man who walks like before. I will note that the Brothers had almost an impelling urge to exaggerate.

I'll mention a relevant instance. Two *mute* women were taken to Padre Pio: It was said that their healing would occur; but it didn't, even after Padre Pio's prayers. They came back two, three times: nothing. While Padre Pio, questioned, answered: "I didn't say it would happen, I said to pray", the others insisted it had to happen.

In fact, I intend to declare that I didn't observe anything irregular in Padre Pio, that is, concerning his life, at least as far as I know, since I don't frequent the convent every day.

Given the late hour, the present session is concluded. All of the above having been duly read and accepted, the Most Ill. Rev. Dr. Giuseppe Prencipe was dismissed, upon the oath *de silentio servando* [to maintain silence] taken on the Holy Gospels. In confirmation of everything that precedes, it is signed.

Giuseppe, Arc. Prencipe*

Acta sunt haec per me, Visitatorem Apostolicum

L.✠S.**   Br. Raphael C., Episc. Volaterr. *Visit. Apost.****

NUMBER II

Second Deposition of Can. Dr. Giuseppe Prencipe

June 15, 1921—8:30 A.M.

Before me, the undersigned Apostolic Visitor, again has appeared the *Most Ill. and Rev. Mr. Dr. Giuseppe Prencipe*, whom, taking again the oath *de veritate dicenda* on the Holy Gospels, I interrogated as follows.

---

* The signature of the witness as it was written on the deposition.
** L.✠S. likely signifies *locus sigilli*, the place for Bishop Rossi's seal.— TRANS.
*** The signature of Bishop Rossi as written on the depositions. He signed with the title of a religious Brother, as he was a Carmelite.

Q. Whether he needs to revise anything of what he has testified last night.

A. No.

Q. Whether he has anything to add.

A. Still regarding the "miracles". On June 12, 1919, the big bell of the parish church cracked while it was pealing festively. The relationship between me and the convent was most cordial. Around June 25, a priest of the parish advised a friend to have his child baptized by Padre Pio at the convent, which is almost a mile away. Given the crowds that went to the convent, I observed that this authorization would open the doors to many more authorizations that could be requested, and so to irregularities in the parish. Having spoken with Padre Pio and the then-Father Guardian, I also noticed they were somewhat reluctant to take on this ministry, agreeing with me on the future annoyances that would be caused to me and to them. I then asked the aforementioned priest to cautiously dissuade his friend from his desire. In less than fifteen minutes after this conversation, malicious rumors spread that the pastor, offended, had refused [to grant the authorization] in order to aggravate Padre Pio. After a few days the order of the events was reversed, and, while the cracking of the bell had happened about ten days before, it was said that Padre Pio, to retaliate against my refusal, had obtained that the bell would break. The Father Guardian, seeing that things were getting ridiculous, especially in the eyes of sensible people, was compelled to come and celebrate [Mass] in the parish church, and, at the moment of the Gospel, to speak opportune words to the people, so as to stop the rumor.

Q. What seemed to him to be Padre Pio's attitude with respect to these "wondrous" facts tied to his name.

A. With me, silence.

Q. What he knows of the alleged stigmata.

A. First from the group of pious women who frequented the convent, and later from the then–Father Guardian, I learned that Padre Pio had been honored with the
stigmata. Having found the courage to ask Padre Pio
about the way he had received these stigmata, about
other relevant circumstances, etc.—since people were
spreading different versions, and I, flooded with letters
from everywhere, wanted to be able to answer precisely
and avoid contradictions—Padre Pio answered: "I cannot
talk."

Q. Whether it is true that Padre Pio eats very little.

A. As far as I know, he certainly doesn't eat much, but I
was able to observe *de visu* that he does eat. He is of sickly
constitution; ill, he had been transferred from the convent
to the guest quarters, these so-called devout women taking turns caring for him, an irregularity the Father Provincial took care to stop. During his illness he couldn't
easily keep food in his stomach: to show the degree of
fetishism reached by the Brothers, I know that they would
show what Padre Pio had not been able to keep in his
stomach. Those so-called devout women never fail to provide Padre Pio with what was necessary.

Q. Concerning Padre Pio's spiritual and moral character,
his practice of the virtues, obedience, humility, etc.

A. Yes, all of this appears. I only know, from a religious of
the convent, that the Father Provincial had forbidden private
conversations in the guest quarters, but Padre Pio continued
them.

All of the above having been duly read and accepted, the
Most Illustrious Reverend Dr. Giuseppe Prencipe was

dismissed, upon the oath *de silentio servando* taken on the Holy Gospels. In confirmation of everything, it was signed.

Giuseppe, Arc. Prencipe

Acta sunt haec per me, Visitatorem Apostolicum

L.✠S.   Br. Raphael C., Episc. Volaterr. *Visit. Apost.*

NUMBER III

Third Deposition of Can. Dr. Giuseppe Prencipe

June 18, 1921—4:30 P.M.

Before me, undersigned Apost. Visit. [hereafter Apostolic Visitor], appeared, summoned, in his parish residence, the *Most Illustrious and Reverend Dr. Giuseppe Prencipe*, curate archpriest of San Giovanni Rotondo, Archdiocese of Manfredonia, who, having taken the oath *de veritate dicenda* on the Holy Gospels, so answered and testified.

Q. If he needs to revise anything of what he has previously testified.
A. No.

Q. About the present "miracles" that have occurred through the intercession of Padre Pio of Pietrelcina.
A. Once the rumor spread that Padre Pio performed "miracles", I was taken by an intense desire to see something personally, so I would often go to the convent to observe *de visu* some sort of extraordinary event, a miraculous healing, since there were many cripples—from the town and

foreigners—who would go there. But I never had the luck to see any extraordinary phenomena. To tell the truth, perhaps I was not worthy. More than once I pressed Padre Pio himself to do something extraordinary in San Giovanni, even just the miracle of a bilocation for the conversion of the incredulous—especially for the conversion of a medical doctor, a friend of mine, who had told me these precise words: "If I saw Padre Pio come into my room, at night or during the day, or if I saw Santariello (a monstrous cripple) really standing straight on his legs and healed in his eyes (he's cross-eyed) and in his mind (he's a half-wit), I would be the first to believe in the supernatural." Padre Pio laughed at my words, and only once did it seem to me that he believed in the miracles attributed to him, when he said these words: "The San Severo one isn't enough?" He meant to allude to a young lady who recovered her sight: a miracle I was never able to verify, despite the volume of information I acquired.

The miracles that generated the biggest commotion here in San Giovanni Rotondo are the one of the mute women, about which I have already testified; the one of the hunchback; the one of the court clerk; and the one of crippled Santariello.

1. I'll say what I have heard; although the incident of the hunchback happened here, I wasn't present. But I went on purpose to Foggia to see the hunchbacked child's father and listen to the story of the grace obtained. I don't know the names of the persons involved. The little hunchback was in fourth grade: I went to my friend the deputy principal of the elementary school, to identify the child in school, but he was absent that day, and his teacher of three years told the deputy and me: "The poor little hunchback has crawled since he was a small boy; on the Feast of Our Lady of Sorrows, which is venerated in Foggia, he received a first grace; and he was able to stand up straight and walk

on his own legs. He had four or five little humps along his spine. After going to Padre Pio, two or three disappeared; the others stayed." She didn't say anything else.

2. "Miracle" of the chancellor of the magistrate's court in San Giovanni Rotondo. On the occasion of the armistice, during an evening party among friends, our clerk had a little too much to drink and going down the steps, he slipped and sprained his ankle. This sprain kept him immobile in bed for about two months. Afterward he began to get up, but he had to stay at home for another month, I believe, leaning on crutches. Then he got better, stopped using the crutches, and with a cane he started going out and climbing the courthouse steps. He was therefore on his way to recovery, so much so that he resumed his walks with his friends. At this point, from Lucera came the royal prosecutor (the name was Milone, I think), who wanted to visit Padre Pio, with what purpose I do not know. By chance, that day Professor Tangaro of Foggia, and I think the chancellor of the magistrate's court in Lucera and the editor of *Il Mattino*, Mr. Trevisani, were also there. The prosecutor and the local deputy magistrate also invited our chancellor to go with them to the convent. The chancellor declined, explaining that the sprain he suffered didn't allow him to walk such long distance. The next day after lunch the invitation was repeated a second time. This time he accepted, and very slowly he walked to the convent. The following narration was given to me by the chancellor himself the next day: "I was wandering around the two hallways on the first floor of the convent, which were packed with people waiting their turn to go to Padre Pio for confession—he was hearing confessions in a corner of those hallways. Suddenly, I heard this one word: 'Cane!', but I didn't know who said it, to whom it was directed, and to what purpose. I had gone to the convent with no intention of receiving a

grace. At this word, two friends of mine who were beside me shook my arms and said: "Chancellor, don't you hear that?' Padre Pio said I should throw the walking cane away, because a grace had been granted. At these words I felt as if a flame was going up from my feet to my hair: I started sweating, the people turned their eyes on me, a voice came out of that crowd: 'Grace, grace!', and my friends insisted, 'Throw the cane away, throw it away', because there was this conviction that, if one didn't obey there, the grace would not come. 'Walk,' said my friends, 'you're healed!' I started moving, and I felt no more pain in my foot. The loud shouting made the prosecutor and the others come down; they came to me, they took my arm, they made me walk; I didn't feel any pain. I came back to town without my walking stick. I called for the doctor, who concluded the dislocated bone had not returned to its place." This is what he said. Just the following day, I, and everyone else in town, could clearly see that the alleged healing had not happened. The chancellor was forced to resume the use of a walking cane, until his summer vacation, when he went to a spa.

3. The miracle of "Santariello". A young man in his forties, cross-eyed, a half-wit, pale, hunchbacked, with deformed legs, one round foot turned backwards. Santariello himself, as well as other eyewitnesses, told me this about the alleged miracle. Padre Pio was sitting down in the square in front of the convent church, before a large crowd. The young cripple, I do not know whether by his own will, or advised by a Capuchin Father, presented himself to Padre Pio to ask him something. "What would you like me to do for you?" Padre Pio apparently said. And the cripple—and I believe this petition had also been suggested to him by the friar—answered: "Give me the grace of healing." "Well," said Padre Pio, "throw away these crutches." The young

man says one fell, but the other stayed in his hand, so Father Placido, Capuchin, quickly took it away from him, saying: "Walk, you're healed." The poor man started walking as best as he could, floundering, leaning right and left against the people who surrounded him filling the air with deafening cries of "miracle".

That evening he came back to town, and everyone was very disappointed to see that a miracle had been alleged where there wasn't even the shadow of one.

At this point the witness relates an episode of bilocation:

I heard the story from the sick woman's own mouth, Mrs. Bambinella D'Enrico, wife of Mr. Luigi Massa, automotive entrepreneur. She had been sick for eight days. The fever had not gone beyond 102.2°F. The doctors had diagnosed only a mild bronchitis, and reassured the husband that it was not serious. One of the doctors, suspecting constipation, prescribed a dose of calomel, which upset her whole body. "The idea grew in me", said the woman, "that the doctor had poisoned me, and this nightmare of an idea lasted around two hours. Then the idea of dying, that I was to die, took over, and it loomed large in my mind for over two, three hours. So I called my husband and my children, and I expressed my last wishes. Then my mind clearly went from the idea of death to embracing the hope to heal, and I don't know for how long I clung to it, and I thought the healing could come from Padre Pio. If the grace didn't happen, it would be not because of me, but because of my husband. So I called him: 'If I die, I'll die because of you, because you don't believe.' My husband protested, but I refused to believe otherwise and I was even more frantic. Around 2 A.M. my husband went to call for the doctor to visit me. In leaving, my husband took the lamp from the room where we were, and moved it to the next room. At that moment I saw Padre Pio in the room, against the wall (N.B.: on which the lamp projected shadows and light). Once my husband came back to the room, I said: 'I saw Padre Pio', but my husband, despite all his searching, couldn't find anything. After about one hour, the same experiment of the lamp taken out of the room was repeated, and again Padre Pio was there, and again the search produced no result. Again, I railed against my husband, accusing him that, if I died, I would die on his account, because he had no faith." The husband finished the story: "Frankly, I had my doubts about Padre Pio's holiness and the pos-siblility of a miracle; but since my wife insisted, I became very agitated, and I said, 'I would believe in Padre Pio if you were healed this very moment.' At these words my wife sprang out of bed, and stood up in front of me. I had her lie back down in bed. At the same time, a nursing infant started crying; his mother wanted him, then she held him and nursed him—and she hadn't had any milk in eight days. But immediately afterward, the milk disappeared again. Toward the middle of the night, the woman fell in a deep sleep, and the next morning she was feeble, yes, but healed."

I will say that this woman's family is mentally disturbed: A brother attempted suicide; another brother is half-crippled and markedly cross-eyed.

Another example:

One day I was in Foggia, when a lieutenant from my same town came toward me and said: "Yesterday I was called by the lieutenant general commanding the division, who told me: 'This morning Padre Pio of San Giovanni Rotondo came to me to talk about some soldiers causing trouble'; it was a group of soldiers stationed, I don't know, either in a convent or close to a convent. I answered it couldn't be, since Padre Pio was in San Giovanni. 'I assure you', said the general, 'that Padre Pio came to me.' "

I didn't know what to say to the lieutenant, since the day before I had talked to Padre Pio in San Giovanni Rotondo. I went back there and headed for the convent, to ask Padre Pio about the episode, but while I was with the Father Guardian, talking about it, another Capuchin Father intervened and said, "Now there can't be any more doubts about yesterday's bilocation: Padre Pio himself said it to some devout women who had interrogated him, and to whom he answered, 'Yes, I took a trip.' Where? 'It doesn't matter.' "

When that Father left, the Father Guardian begged me not to report what the Father himself had said. For that day I decided not to ask Padre Pio for an explanation. But later I learned that it all had been a misunderstanding with the lieutenant general: a Padre Pio of San Giovanni Rotondo did go to see him, but it was a different Father residing in Benevento, and who had personally gone to Foggia.

Q. But faced with all these stories, what was Padre Pio's attitude?
A. True or false as these stories may be, I never heard that he rectified them.

Concluding, I will say that it would be my wish that some of my doubts turned out to be completely groundless, and that Padre Pio really were the man chosen by God, sent to my town to sanctify and shock the world with more wonders.

All these things having been read and accepted, the Most Illustrious Reverend Dr. Giuseppe Prencipe was dismissed, upon the oath *de secreto servando* on the Holy Gospels. In confirmation of everything, it was signed.

Giuseppe, Arc. Prencipe

Acta sunt haec per me, Visitatorem Apostolicum

L.✠S.   Br. Raphael C., Episc. Volaterr. *Visit. Apost.*

NUMBER IV

First Deposition of Can. Domenico Palladino, *Bursar of the Parish of San Giovanni Rotondo*

June 18, 1921—7 P.M.

Before me, the undersigned Apostolic Visitor, has appeared, summoned, in the parish residence of San Giovanni Rotondo, the *Most Reverend Mr. D. Domenico Palladino*, bursar of the parish, who, having taken the oath *de veritate dicenda* on the Holy Gospels, so testified and answered.

Q. About his personal identification.
A. My name is Domenico Palladino, son of the late Giuseppe, age thirty, bursar of this church.

Q. About Padre Pio of Pietrelcina, Capuchin.
A. I didn't know him, since a month after my priestly ordination I went into the army; but in 1918, when I came back for one day of convalescent leave, two young men, Michele Perna and Pasquale Ricci, came in the church after the Mass to see the archpriest. Not finding him, they told me, they went to the Capuchin convent to snoop, and while

they were standing by the fountain, they saw, through a small window of the guest quarters, Padre Pio conversing with a young elementary schoolteacher; they peeked through the window several times trying to avoid being seen. But the two [Padre Pio and the young woman] realized they were there, and the young woman tried to hide. Afterward, Padre Pio, seeing that, went out to the sacristy, and the young woman followed him. They sat close to each other, by a brazier, and talked. The two young men turned and went into the church: They meant to confront Padre Pio, because the episode had made a great impression on them. In the sacristy there was a terrible altercation between Padre Pio and the two young men, who insulted the Padre and threatened to write to the archbishop. They reproached Padre Pio for being alone with a young woman; he answered he was carrying out his ministry, but they said he should carry it out from the confessional.

The incident became known, and that evening the guardian and another monk, together with Can. D. Giuseppe Massa, came down [to the town from the monastery] to try to placate the two young men. They succeeded, and the incident was concealed. Several days afterward, the rumor spread that Padre Pio was performing miracles, so many people were flocking to the convent; but the privileged were the so-called "pious women", who hardly moved away from the convent and who rebuked other women who had not shown up before.

Hearing all that was being said about Padre Pio's "miracles", one day I and other priests went to the convent to see something. We received a cold welcome, compared with the past, and instead of coming and greeting us, the Fathers kept talking to the women. We approached the guardian, and a colleague asked him how many graces had been granted that day. The guardian answered: sixteen. So the colleague replied he thought there were twenty-four. "No," said the guardian, "the real ones are those I say", and among those was the grace to Santariello, who was present. We turned our eyes toward the church, and we saw our Santariello trying a step or two, and then falling down. Since we were surprised by this, the guardian said: "What do you expect? We, the healthy ones, need the cane: Imagine what he has been like recently!"

We left him and went to the garden, where Padre Pio was. After kissing his hand, we started talking about public and private health, and especially we happened to discuss the strike of the elementary teachers. Padre Pio made a tirade, and said that if he were the government, he would send them all to Apulia. A fellow priest told me that between sentences Padre Pio may have said, as if to himself: "*In dubio libertas*", but I didn't notice. After Padre Pio imparted a solemn blessing (we were priests) I went back a little baffled; we went into a few taverns to see the miracles claimed by the Father Guardian, but we couldn't see any.

I've never been back to the convent since.

Two women of good conscience bound by secrecy—obviously not the secrecy of the confessional—told me that, together with the other so-called "pious women", they would go to the convent every day—sometimes twice a day—lingering for a long time in the guest quarters, whenever Padre Pio was there, ill. The so-called "pious women" would touch Padre Pio's arms, feet, and side while he was asleep, with the sole purpose of receiving his holiness: They [the "pious women"] prompted them to do the same, but the two women, blushing, could hardly touch him, and they did so almost against their will. From that day on, they never went back to the convent. These "pious women" still frequent the convent: They own it. They would wear a portrait of Padre Pio around their neck. Padre Pio saw that: He could have prevented it.

All these things having been read and approved, the Reverend D. Domenico Palladino was dismissed, upon the oath *de secreto servando* on the Holy Gospels. In confirmation of everything, it was signed.

Domenico Can. Palladino

Acta sunt haec per me, Visitatorem Apostolicum

L.✠S.   Br. Raphael C., Episc. Volaterr. *Visit. Apost.*

NUMBER V

Second Deposition of **Can. Domenico Palladino**

June 19, 1921—5 P.M.

Before me, the undersigned Apostolic Visitor, has appeared, summoned again, the *Most Reverend Mr. Canon Domenico Palladino*, who, having taken the oath *de veritate dicenda* on the Holy Gospels, so testified and stated.

Q. If he needs to revise anything in the previous deposition. A. No. One evening, before going back home, I was visiting some gravely ill persons, as is my custom, being the treasurer of this collegiate church; when I entered the house of a sick woman I found one of those "pious women" who are always around Padre Pio, applying on the infirm a bandage wet with Padre Pio's blood while reciting a formula: "Saint Padre Pio, etc." (I will note that the ignorant common people would say that Padre Pio was Jesus Christ himself.) This episode happened to me another time or two, but as soon as these women saw me, they would hide. I believe Padre Pio is a good son, but I am greatly disgusted by the assiduity of these women who would spend so much time at the convent, all day long, even at lunch, even late into the evening, and who would spread to the four winds the news of Padre Pio's "miracles".

I was told, although I didn't hear it myself, that one of the monks who was here before may have said: "Our bad luck is to have Archpriest Prencipe."

I'll repeat, regarding Padre Pio, I think he's a prayerful person and a good priest, but the monks around him and these women have made me and others lose some of our esteem for him, so much that, while before I would hear Padre Pio's name mentioned with respect, now I hear it even cursed. Moreover, all that religious fervor that had aroused has waned, so that, while at the time of the "miracles" many who hadn't approached the sacraments went to confession, etc., now many don't even comply with the [Sunday] precept.

All these things having been read and accepted, the Reverend D. Domenico Palladino was dismissed, upon the oath *de secreto servando* taken on the Holy Gospels. In confirmation of everything, it was signed.

Domenico Can. Palladino

Acta sunt haec per me, Visitatorem Apostolicum

L.✠S.   Br. Raphael C., Episc. Volaterr. *Visit. Apost.*

NUMBER VI

First Deposition of Father Lorenzo of San Marco in Lamis *Superior of the Capuchins of San Giovanni Rotondo*

June 16, 1921—9 A.M.

Before me, the undersigned Apostolic Visitor, in the convent of the Minor Capuchins of San Giovanni Rotondo, today at 9 A.M. has appeared the *Most Reverend Father Lorenzo of San Marco in Lamis,* guardian of the convent, who, having duly taken the oath *de veritate dicenda* on the Holy Gospels, so testified and answered.

Q. About his name and personal details.
A. My name is Father Lorenzo of San Marco in Lamis, born Nicola Giavarella, son of the late Leonardo, age forty, superior of this convent since November 1919.

Q. He may relate what he knows about Padre Pio of Pietrelcina.
A. I think I got to know him around 1906 or 1907, when I was guardian at Montefusco and he came to that convent as a philosophy student. He didn't stay long at Montefusco because, on account of his health, he was transferred to other convents. For the time he was at Montefusco I can attest he was always exemplary, so much that the lector himself went to consult him in many disciplinary matters. Nothing extraordinary happened during that time.

From other convents—Campobasso, Venafro, and Morcone—he went back home, always because of his poor health. He was also ordained as a priest while he was staying at home (but there he would wear the religious habit). They said he was sick with bronchial pneumonia, but actually, when they examined his lung they didn't find anything.

I know that during the time he was home, the lector—who is now First Provincial Definitor and whose name is Father Agostino of San Marco in Lamis—as well as the then-provincial, Father Benedetto of San Marco in Lamis, went to consult him on issues concerning the province. So much that sometimes the religious would grumble about it: Sometimes a circular was sent out, and knowing that the superiors had gone to see Padre Pio, some would say: "They went to consult the saint in Mecca."

Q. If he knows the reason why the superiors would behave in such a way with a young friar, since the province certainly must not be lacking in religious whose age and prudence would likely make them good counselors.
A. Because Father Agostino, who had been his confessor, as well as Fr. Benedetto, who later became his spiritual director, found him to be most exemplary, not a grumbler.

Q. He may resume his narration.
A. During the first or second year of the war he was sent from home to Foggia, where he stayed for a few months; then he was sent here as spiritual director of the boys of the minor seminary, and he is still here. I will note that he was also drafted in the army and stayed for about two months, almost always at the hospital in Naples; then he was (at first temporarily, then permanently) declared unfit for military service.

While he was in Foggia, the then-superior, Father Nazareno of Arpaise, used to say that extraordinary noises were heard several times coming from Padre Pio's room; actually, one time the whole Community, gathered in the refectory, heard. They went upstairs and found him composed, and to the superior asking the reason of the noise, he answered: Don't be alarmed, it's nothing important. We suspected it was the devil.

Then he came here. Before I came, there was much talk about him: that he ran fevers of over 118°F; that he had received the stigmata; that he could read into people's hearts. To tell the truth, I didn't put much trust in these tales, so much that, being a military chaplain and having obtained a leave to go back to my hometown, I refused to come. Another time, though, I came, because the Capuchins in Bologna and Milano were asking for news, and I had always limited myself to saying that I had known Padre Pio for fifteen years and had always found him to be good, but that it seemed to me too much now to make him into a miracle-working saint.

It was also said, as I have already stated, that he had such high fevers, but even as superior I was sceptical. Once when Padre Pio had a fever, I wanted to use a thermometer: Padre Pio advised me not to, for it would break. I yielded, but a second time I absolutely wanted to try and the thermometer went up to 109.6°F—that is, up to the last mark—but it didn't break. A third time a thermometer that would read up to 113°F was used, and the mercury went up to 113°F; but it did not break. There were Dr. D. Franc. [likely, Francesco—TN] Antonio Gina, and Dr. Angelo M. Merla, the house doctor, a socialist. Another time I myself wanted to measure the temperature with a thermometer brought by Dr. Festa of Rome, one that would read up to 302°F, and it went up to 118.4°F. So I, too, believed in what was said.

Another peculiar thing: the scent that is perceived, acutely at times, and that comes from his person. I was and still am hesitant, and I cannot find an explanation. What makes me suspect that it's something uncommon is that it is some-times sensed, sometimes not; and it comes as if in waves: I sit next to Padre Pio in the choir, so I sense it well. The Father Provincial once told me he, too, was sceptical, but then he smelled it from the confessional in the back of the church, while Padre Pio was in the convent, on a very crowded day. And that fragrance had penetrated the tobacco box, the tobacco, and the cloak.

There are some who say they have smelled this scent of Padre Pio even from afar: It happened to me once, on the road back to the convent, but the others with me didn't sense it.

Q. What he knows and thinks about the stigmata.
A. I have only seen the ones on his hands, but not those on his side and feet.

Actually, I don't really know the origin of these stigmata. I was a military chaplain (it is said they occurred on September 20, 1918). The then-guardian, Father Paolino of Casacalenga, told me that not even he knew the true origin: Padre Pio initially wore a handkerchief, or he would pull his sleeve down, and the first to notice them were the devout women in church. Several times I asked the former provincial, Father Benedetto, to try to find out something, but he always answered me: "It is all written." Different versions circulate: that he received them in the choir, during the thanksgiving after Mass; that he received them while hearing the confession of one of the boys; it is not known which one is true.

Regarding the nature of these stigmata, according to Dr. Festa they are like seals, almost as if produced by fire, on the derma; according to Dr. Romanelli of Barletta, they are real holes from one side to the other. But Dr. Festa notes that if that were true, the fingers could not be moved normally, as Padre Pio is able to do. Once, before Padre Pio went downstairs to celebrate, I myself saw much blood flowing out of one hand.

As for the bandages soaked with blood, at first some of them circulated outside the 'convent: When I came here, I wanted them destroyed, but the Father Provincial told me it was not a good thing to do, so now I personally keep them.

Q. If he knows whether Padre Pio has ever applied medicaments to the stigmata.
A. I am not aware that he does, but I do know that at first—and I do not know if he still does—he used iodine to stop the bleeding.

Q. Whether he knows if, among the young boys of the minor seminary there were, and are, some who need injections.
A. There was a boy who for a month had malarial fever, but I don't know if they gave him injections.

Q. If necessary, who in the convent administers injections?
A. Now there are only Father Lodovico and Father Cherubino.

Q. If Padre Pio knows how to administer injections.
A. No.

Q. Whether, as far as he knows, Padre Pio has ever or still is directly receiving medicaments through people outside of the convent.
A. Not that I know.

Q. Whether pure carbolic acid is kept in the convent. Whether anyone makes use of veratridine.
A. We don't keep it. Only last year, in the summer, Professor Ribola, a teacher of the boys, would order it to dilute it and disinfect smallpox as early as possible.

I don't even know what veratridine is.

Q. Whether in the convent there is a Father Ignazio, whether he uses tobacco, and whether he uses veratridine, as far as the witness knows.
A. There is a Father Ignazio; he does keep tobacco in a box, but he never uses it, neither to smell it, nor to smoke it. I don't know whether he uses veratridine.

Q. Whether he knows of episodes of bilocation attributed to Padre Pio.
A. Tales are told, but I don't know how truthful they might be, because I am a little sceptical about this. It is said that he allegedly appeared to the automobile entrepreneur's wife, who was ill, one night at ten, and told her she would be healed if her husband, a blasphemous man, converted. The following day the husband came and had confession, and the woman apparently healed.

Likewise, in Bologna he allegedly appeared to a woman who had scalded her hand, and was in danger of gangrene on account of her diabetes: Padre Pio allegedly promised healing within nine or ten days, and so it was, apparently.

Somewhere else—in Torre Maggiore, in the Province of Foggia—a workman at a furnace couldn't turn it on, and he uttered blasphemies, against this new saint, too, Padre Pio. Padre Pio allegedly appeared, and it seems that within six hours the furnace turned on.

Q. About extraordinary things that happened, about sudden healings, etc.
A. They talk of a hunchback, of the chancellor of the magistrate's court who had sprained his foot, of a cripple who used to walk with two canes and now with one only—but it was before I came here.

Q. It is known that pictures of Padre Pio are being circulated, worn around the neck, candles are lit up before them, etc.
A. I know that these pictures apparently are reproductions of a picture taken in Foggia, but all means have been used to prevent this abuse.

Q. Is it true Padre Pio eats very little?
A. Yes, it's true.

Q. Is it true that he spends up to sixteen hours in the confessional?
A. In the past, yes, so much that he celebrates [Mass] even at 12:30 P.M. or 1 P.M.

Q. And how can so much work be explained, with so little nutrition?
A. Actually, I cannot explain it. In the morning, he doesn't take anything; at lunch generally some vegetables with oil; and until recently, in the evening a cup of hot chocolate, but not anymore. Not wine, but beer; no coffee.

Q. Does Padre Pio take anything during the day, between meals?
A. No.

Q. But there are devout women who provide him with food.
A. Yes; they would bring beets, peas, etc., according to the season. But not anymore.

Q. Why does Padre Pio celebrate [Mass] so late?
A. So he can attend to confession beforehand. The Mass he celebrates is the conventual: Before, this Mass was celebrated early, but now it has been arranged at that hour

out of consideration for the faithful who come here and so take the opportunity to see Padre Pio.

Q. He may talk about the spiritual, ascetic, mystical nature of Padre Pio.

A. His is a jovial, simple nature. Every once in a while he has an irritated reaction, especially when someone is looking for him, which he immediately acknowledges. He is observant: He comes to the choir, to the meditation, etc., except for the morning, because he needs time for cleaning. He is a good religious, with a special recollection when praying. There are no episodes of asceticism or better details. Only one time, he was talking—and if need be, he can be witty—and I noticed he seemed for about a minute to talk to himself.

Q. About Padre Pio's attitude regarding the things happening around him, the people's clamor, the touting of miracles, etc.

A. Padre Pio has kept an indifferent attitude.

All these things having been read and accepted, Father Lorenzo, superior, was dismissed, after taking the oath *de silentio servando* on the Holy Gospels. In confirmation of everything, it was signed.

Fr. Lorenzo of S. Marco in Lamis
Capuchin Superior

Acta sunt haec per me, Visitatorem Apostolicum

L.✠S.&   Br. Raphael C., Episc. Volaterr. *Visit. Apost.*

NUMBER VII

Second Deposition of **Father Lorenzo of San Marco**
in Lamis *Capuchin Superior*

June 17, 1921—10 A.M.

Before me, the undersigned Apostolic Visitor, in the convent
of the Minor Capuchins of San Giovanni Rotondo, has again
appeared, summoned, the superior, *Father Lorenzo of San
Marco in Lamis*, who, having taken the oath *de veritate dicenda*
on the Holy Gospels, so testified and stated.

Q. If he needs to revise anything of what he previously
testified yesterday.
A. No.

Q. Whether it's true that a *Chronicle of Padre Pio* is being
written.
A. I know that the former provincial, Father Benedetto, is
collecting documents. If there is something singular, it is
told to him or to the provincial.

Q. Whether in the convent they have copies of memoirs,
reports, etc.
A. No. The convent only keeps, by order of the provincial,
a book where the thoughts of distinguished persons coming
to see Padre Pio are written down.

The witness here shows me the book.

Q. Whether they have pre-made notes to reply to whomever
writes to Padre Pio.
A. No. A reply is written each time. Only holy cards are
prepared beforehand.

Q. But doesn't Padre Pio say anything about this halo that surrounds him? About this having to write, to prepare holy cards?

A. Sometimes he is reluctant, but we need to please so many who are asking—bishops, provincials—and who actually would like to have something that Padre Pio has used, but we don't give anything.

Q. Does Father Benedetto write often to Padre Pio?
A. Every once in a while, more or less every month. The letters are given to Padre Pio sealed.

Q. About Padre Pio's demeanor toward women.
A. Nothing in particular to say: His demeanor is proper, religious. I think he doesn't use either *tu* or *lei*, but *voi* with everyone.

Q. Is it true that Padre Pio is starting to show the signs of the crown of thorns?
A. Some have told me so, but I haven't noticed anything.

Q. Whether he knows a Domenicuccio.
A. No.

Q. Whether he knows some Fiorentini sisters, and who they are.
A. Yes, actually, one is a director of the tertiary order. Excellent women, as far as I know. Almost elderly.

Q. Is it true there are people from out of town who have been staying in San Giovanni Rotondo for a long time to be able to frequent the convent? And who are they?
A. Yes. A woman from Turin has been here for five or six months now; a woman from Stigno (in the Province of

Trento)—the family went to Florence—has been here since before Easter. They come to Mass, then go away, and come back for vespers.

Q. As far as the witness knows, does Padre Pio suffer from hysteria, or some form of neuropathic disorder?
A. No.

Q. He may offer a more detailed religious and moral portrait of Padre Pio.
A. Padre Pio is a simple man, devoid of duplicity, very kind, dedicated to piety—ordinary piety. In matters of obedience, he hears the superior's voice when it manifests itself clearly; with regard to chastity, I believe him to be angelic; as for poverty, I have nothing in particular to say. He regularly observes the other religious virtues.

As for prayer, he dedicates some time to it in the morning, then he goes to hear first the men's confessions, then the women's; he celebrates Mass with devotion—he can be rather long at the *Memento.* I have noticed a few flaws in his Mass, especially in the words of the Consecration, and I informed him: I think he may have some scruples; I heard some words being repeated. This flaw is also observed in the formula of the sacramental absolution. After the Mass, the thanksgiving prayer—for twenty to thirty minutes—then he has lunch. Then he rests like everyone else; afterwards, he attends the Office; then he stays in the choir for fifteen to thirty minutes; then, if need be, he goes to hear confessions. In the evening he attends the communal prayer and Rosary, and then he stays for a while in the choir to pray, since he doesn't come to dinner. He goes back to the choir at 10 P.M. with the other religious.

As far as I know, he doesn't get up at night to pray.

All these things having been read and approved, Father Lorenzo was dismissed, upon the oath *de secreto servando* on the Holy Gospels. In confirmation of everything, it was signed.

Fr. Lorenzo of S. Marco in Lamis
Capuchin Superior

Acta sunt haec per me, Visitatorem Apostolicum

L.✠S.   Br. Raphael C., Episc. Volaterr. *Visit. Apost.*

NUMBER VIII

**Third Deposition of Father Lorenzo of San Marco
in Lamis Capuchin Superior**

June 20, 1921—11 A.M.

Before me, the undersigned Apostolic Visitor, has again appeared, summoned, the *Most Reverend Father Lorenzo of San Marco in Lamis*, superior of the convent of the Minor Capuchins of San Giovanni Rotondo who, having taken the oath *de veritate dicenda* on the Holy Gospels, so testified and answered.

Q. If he needs to revise anything in the previous depositions.
A. No.

Q. About Padre Pio's spirit of obedience, especially considering his exceptional circumstances.
A. I have never told him anything in the form of an order; when I have stated some things in terms of a wish (for example, to change the time of the Mass), sometimes he gave me reasons, in view of which I left things as they were.

Padre Pio of Pietrelcina (May 25, 1887–September 23, 1968). The picture dates back to 1918, the year of the visible stigmatization (which occured in the convent's church of Santa Maria delle Grazie, on September 20th.)

In the upper left corner, the first picture of Padre Pio, Capuchin, taken in 1911. The others date back to 1919, after the stigmatization had already occured.

On the next page we see the saint portrayed in the funda-mental moments of his life: the Holy Mass and the celebration of the sacrament of penance.

© Voce di Padre Pio Archive

© Voce di Padre Pio Archive

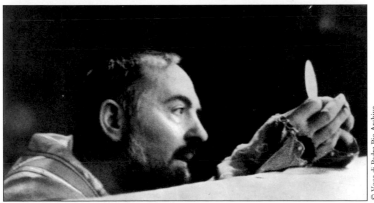

Padre Pio's stigmata clearly visible during the Eucharistic celebration

*Msgr. Raffaello C. Rossi,
Apostolic Visitor to San
Giovanni Rotondo in 1921,
and the author of the* Votum,
*the previously unpublished
document reproduced in this
volume.*
*Below: Monsignor Rossi during
a ceremonial signing. With him
is Monsignor Montini, later
Pope Paul VI.*

Above: Msgro. Pierino Galeone, among the most important witnesses at the beatification process, while talking with Padre Pio.

On the opposite page (top): a portrait of Father Benedetto of San Marco in Lamis, who was provincial and Padre Pio's spiritual director during the years of his novitiate and his stigmatization.

On the opposite page (bottom): Padre Pio with Father Agostino, his second spiritual director.

The first page of the Votum, *fully reproduced in this volume, and the signatures of Padre Pio and Msgr. Raffaello Carlo Rossi at the end of one of the depositions made during the inquiry.*

Q. About Padre Pio's spirit of poverty and his practice of it. *A.* There is nothing noteworthy to say. Regarding the donations that are sent to him with the explicit purpose of helping the poor, he used to manage them himself, with the verbal assent of the provincial of that time; now he gives the money to the bursar, and then, with a written permission signed by the Father Provincial, he proceeds to distribute it, either according to his own judgment or through a devout person chosen for this purpose. In fact, speaking of poverty, Padre Pio has a special predilection for the poor.

Then the witness says:

I must remark how the name of Padre Pio has brought here some non-baptized and Protestants who received here the sacraments and entered the Church. They are the following:

1. A Jew from Florence, whose eyes were so ill he had to wear black bandages: Having already been sufficiently instructed [in the Faith], he received baptism and had his First Communion here. After he left, his sight improved, so much that, having quitted the black bandages, he now wears glasses like many others. He had come here to obtain a grace; Padre Pio told him: "Become a Christian first, and the rest will follow."

2. A non-baptized Protestant Dutchman, who came here moved by the desire to be baptized by Padre Pio: Not being sufficiently instructed, he went back to Rome, was instructed by Father Benedetto, and came back again: He received baptism, and, since the Bishop of Melfi was here, he also received his confirmation and First Communion.

3. A Protestant born to German parents: He stayed the time necessary for the instruction, then was baptized *sub conditione* [conditionally] and received Communion after he abjured.

4. A young Protestant woman from Holland: She, too, was here several days for her instruction, then received baptism *sub conditione*; she abjured, received Communion and went to Foggia for her confirmation. Now she lives in Capri, but she has come back three or four times to see Padre Pio and do her devotions with him.

5. A young woman from Estonia, daughter of Protestant pastors: She stayed here for a few days. Since she was already sufficiently instructed, she received baptism *sub conditione* and Communion, after she abjured.

Moreover, these persons also came here:

1. A man from Milan, a follower of theosophy: He recognized his errors; he stayed here for about a month, receiving Communion every day.

2. A young British woman, also a follower of theosophical doctrines: She mended her ways. She remained here almost two months, and still comes back every five or six months.

On account of the name of, and the acquaintance with, Padre Pio, and after asking for his advice, the following persons have embraced the religious life, or are on the path toward it:

1. several young ladies who have become nuns, whom Padre Pio was able to provide for the first necessities of the vestition, thanks to donations received and reserved for this purpose;

2. Father Gaetano Morelli of the Scuole Pie, former rector of the Collegio Nazareno in Rome, who entered the novitiate of our Capuchin Province of Sant'Angelo;

3. Arturo Palagi of Florence, a professor of science and mathematics, now in this convent, is about to put on our religious habit;

4. a Russian painter who entered the Trinitarians in Livorno.

Finally, many people, especially men, who had lived away from the sacraments, resumed practicing the religion after coming here.

All this having been read and approved, the Reverend Father Lorenzo was dismissed, upon the oath *de secreto servando* taken on the Holy Gospels. In confirmation of everything, it is signed.

Fr. Lorenzo of S. Marco in Lamis
Capuchin Superior

Acta sunt haec per me, Visitatorem Apostolicum

L.✠S.   Br. Raphael C., Episc. Volaterr. *Visit. Apost.*

NUMBER IX

First Deposition of **Father Ignazio of Jelsi** *Capuchin*

June 16, 1921—10 A.M.

Before the undersigned Apostolic Visitor, has appeared, summoned, in a cell of the convent of San Giovanni Rotondo, Archdiocese of Manfredonia, the *Reverend Father Ignazio of*

Jelsi (Province of Benevento), Capuchin, who, having taken the oath *de veritate dicenda* on the Holy Gospels, so testified and answered.

Q. About his name, age, etc.

A. My name is Father Ignazio of Jelsi, born Salvatore Testa, son of the late Pietr'Angelo, age thirty-nine, Capuchin priest, from Jelsi. I have been in this convent since October 12, 1919.

Q. About Padre Pio of Pietrelcina.

A. As a personal opinion, I can say I have no doubt about the virtue of the Padre, to whom I am very close, since for any material thing he may need he turns to me, in my position as bursar, and since I act as secretary for the correspondence. Generally he doesn't read the correspondence, except for a few letters that I give to him: The lack of time prevents him.

On average, about seventy letters arrive each day—now mainly from Spain, Brazil, Argentina, etc. Essentially, the letters describe miseries, maladies, spiritual afflictions and ask for the help of Padre Pio's prayers. Not so much from abroad, but from Italy donations also arrive for the offering of Masses, for the poor—actually, for these there is a specific administration, since Padre Pio absolutely refuses that the Community receives what the benefactors have destined otherwise.

Thank-you notes also arrive almost every day. A reply is generally sent to those who write with certified mail, or send donations, or include a stamp; then, of course, a reply is sent also to those to whom it is opportune to respond, for example, to communities: In fact, many are those who write, nuns especially.

The replies are vague: *Padre Pio prays and sends his blessing*. We don't venture anything else. Padre Pio, on the other hand, can reply in a decisive way, and I can recall some special cases when Padre Pio did so.

Q. Whether he is aware of extraordinary events that have occurred, as it is said, through the prayers and the work of Padre Pio.
A. Yes, on account of these letters that are written; but nothing happened before my eyes. Some things are rumored, but they refer to a time when I was not in this Community.

Q. Whether the letters are kept.
A. Since I have been here, yes, by order of the provincial. Before, when even six or seven hundred letters would arrive every day, they were burned.

Q. What does Padre Pio say of all this commotion made about him?
A. He never talks about it. He stays indifferent, as if nothing were going on.

Q. What do the boys of the minor seminary say of their spiritual director?
A. They are happy.

Q. About Padre Pio's health.
A. You can never count on it. Now he is well, now he suffers. A precise opinion cannot be given, since the origin of the illness is unknown: It's not known whether it might be rheumatism, or a cold, etc. A 118.4°F fever was observed, but he is not knocked down: He gets up, moves about, and can do everything.

Q. About the stigmata.
A. I have only seen those on his hands; I've never dared ask him to see the others, to avoid humiliating him and

depriving him of my trust. Those on his hands, one time that they were bleeding, seemed to me like a blood scab on the palm and like coagulated blood. My opinion is that there may be a hole filled with blood. Regarding the sore in his side, as far as I know it soaks so many bandages.

Q. Whether the witness smokes or sniffs tobacco.
A. No, nothing.

Q. But you have a tobacco box.
A. In my room, but I don't use it.

Q. Have you ever put anything special in this tobacco?
A. No.

Q. Whether, specifically, he has ever put veratridine in it.
A. No, I have the veratridine. In another convent we had a pharmacy for the Community, which was very numerous: There was no pharmacy in town. A pharmacist gave me one gram of it, and I still have some. One evening, joking with the Brothers, I made them try the effects it produces when it is drawn close to the nose. Padre Pio, too, took some, and he had to go back to his cell because he couldn't stop sneezing.

Q. About the chronicle it is said is being written about Padre Pio.
A. We don't write here, only some visitors leave their names with some thoughts. They say Padre Pio's spiritual director keeps records of everything. The director is Father Benedetto of San Marco in Lamis, currently in Rome. Of course he is in contact with Padre Pio through an ongoing correspondence. He writes, in a sealed envelope, and sends the letter inside another one, addressed to the superior.

Here Father Ignazio hands over some of the great many letters from people who ask for something or give thanks.

Q. How can the friars reply to all these letters?
A. As much as we can, day by day. For foreign languages, a missionary Father who happens to be here helps, or some local professors.

Q. Whether they have pre-made notes, holy images signed by Padre Pio, etc.
A. Notes, no. Images with a blessing, the signature, sometimes with a longer thought, yes—so we can send many of them and please many people.

All this having been read and approved, Father Ignazio was dismissed, upon the oath *de silentio servando* taken on the Holy Gospels. In confirmation of everything, it was signed.

Fr. Ignazio of Jelsi
Capuchin Priest

Acta sunt haec per me, Visitatorem Apostolicum

L.✠S.　　　Br. Raphael C., Episc. Volaterr. *Visit. Apost.*

NUMBER X

Second Deposition of **Father Ignazio of Jelsi** *Capuchin*

June 17, 1921—11:30 A.M.

Before me, the undersigned Apostolic Visitor, has appeared, summoned again, in the convent of San Giovanni Rotondo, the *Most Reverend Father Ignazio of Jelsi,* who, having taken the oath *de veritate dicenda* on the Holy Gospels, so testified and stated.

Q. Whether he needs to revise anything in the answers given during the previous interrogation.
A. No.

Q. Does Padre Pio ever use, or has he ever used, medicaments on his sores?
A. Given his virtue, no.

Q. From what illness does Padre Pio suffer?
A. They even granted him a military pension, on account of his tuberculosis, and now they suspended it, since it was found that the illness was pre-existing. The local doctors, on the other hand, say there is nothing. And, according to Padre Pio, the bacteriological analysis done in Naples gave a negative result.

Q. Does Padre Pio suffer from nervous disorders of any kind, is he hysterical?
A. I've always seen him normal; I am not aware of such disturbances in him.

Q. About a religious and moral portrait of Padre Pio.
A. One is at a loss. He is a good religious, humble; he does what the superiors want. Certainly, I am not as intimately acquainted with him as I am with other religious. He is humble, I'll repeat, so much that if not for that, with all that has been going on around him ... And so, he is obedient.

All this having been read and accepted, Father Ignazio was dismissed, upon the oath *de secreto servando* taken on the Holy Gospels. In confirmation of everything, it was signed.

Fr. Ignazio of Jelsi
Capuchin Priest

Acta sunt haec per me, Visitatorem Apostolicum

L.✠S.   Br. Raphael C., Episc. Volaterr. *Visit. Apost.*

NUMBER XI

First Deposition of **Father Luigi of Serra Capriola**
Capuchin

June 17, 1921—8 A.M.

Before me, the undersigned Apostolic Visitor, in the convent of the Minor Capuchins of San Giovanni Rotondo, has appeared the *Most Reverend Father Luigi of Serra Capriola,* who, having taken the oath *de veritate dicenda* on the Holy Gospels, so testifies and states:

Q. About his personal details.
A. My name is Father Luigi of Serra Capriola, Capuchin priest, son of the late Francesco, born Nicola Consalvo, age forty-five, living in this convent since September 1919. I had already been here for a year and a half, about five years ago, at the beginning of the war.

Q. About Padre Pio of Pietrelcina.
A. I have been teaching since 1919. He was one of my students for a very short time; I saw him a few times in

passing, in some convent where he studied. I remember that several rather prodigious things were said about him: that he had ecstasies in Venafro; that once he had written a letter in Greek, without knowing this language (one day, indirectly, having the occasion of speaking about it, he may have hinted that he had *forgotten* it, so he must have known a little of it); that in Foggia many noises were heard, even by the Brothers, while he was in his cell. These are all things I heard.

In Foggia he was ill and wasn't performing any ministry; he started a more active life—services, etc.—here. To be sure, it was common knowledge that Padre Pio had always been a very good religious, and his classmates say that when he was a student, they would often find him in tears. To the "prodigious" events most religious gave little credence, except for the three or four who related them (for example, Father Benedetto). Father Benedetto is the spiritual director: He writes to him, and we believe that some letters he published in his little book, *Ai desolati di spirito*, [To the spiritually despondent], are letters he wrote to Padre Pio. It is also said that Father Benedetto is keeping notes to write a biography of Padre Pio. I came here around Easter of 1915, and shortly afterward Padre Pio came, more on account of the desire of Father Paolino, the guardian, than for a change of climate, and here, feeling better, he remained. At that time he didn't have the faculty to hear confessions: The archbishop gave it to him once the fame of prodigious events started spreading. Since he came here with this kind of fame, some devout women would come to receive spiritual counsel (he didn't hear confessions yet). What I saw is that at that time he would fall ill every once in a while, and sweat in an extraordinary manner, so much that they had to change his undergarments. Father Paolino said that then the thermometer would read over 104°F. I attributed it to a natural predisposition, while Father Paolino presented it to me as a supernatural phenomenon. Nothing extraordinary happened at that time. It is said that several thermometers also broke; so I was told.

Then I was drafted in the army, and in the meantime—actually, beforehand—Padre Pio was also drafted.

Once I came back from my military service to live in other convents, I learned from the papers the news that was spreading regarding Padre Pio (the episode of the hunchback, his life, his nutrition, his apparitions, etc.). Then I came to San Giovanni Rotondo, when the influx of people, which had seen its climax during June, July, and August 1919, was still going on. But I didn't see anything extraordinary, any healings, etc., and as far as I know, nothing happened, at least here. In the past there had been talk about the chancellor of the magistrate's court in San Giovanni Rotondo who had been granted the healing of his foot—he had fallen down the stairs—but it seems that he himself cast doubts on the episode. There was also talk about a cripple from San Giovanni Rotondo, who allegedly started walking without his cane: Father Paolino broke the news to me while I was in Venafro; when I came here I saw again this cripple, whom I had known before, and who used to walk with two canes but now only uses one. He is as much of a cripple as he was before: Only instead of leaning on two canes, he now leans on one. I noted a sort of frenzy in everyone, a great exaggeration, but when I came here I didn't exactly find everything as it was rumored.

I also found that Padre Pio celebrated [Mass] after hearing confessions for a very long time, around 11:30 A.M.; this Mass was considered a solemn one: The people waited in great numbers, and the priests from out of town who happened to be there considered it an honor to serve at the altar. Padre Pio celebrated Mass in a surplice, etc. Little by little we have abolished this. The Mass was always accompanied by the organ—I think it was almost always chanted—and they even had to change the school hours. But music was played even if the Mass was read. Now, only the Sunday Mass is chanted. All in all, there was great pomp.

As for Padre Pio, he said neither yes nor no: He let others do as they wished. Simplicity, always indifferent before any honor, etc. We have never seen him abandon his simplicity.

As for the stigmata, I have only had occasion to see those on his hands—at the altar, while serving as a deacon: I've never dared ask to examine them. I was present when a military doctor saw them: He came to visit him and see if Padre Pio, as someone suffering from tuberculosis, was entitled to a pension. I was also present when other visitors saw them. As for the rest, I know it from what the doctors who visited him have said.

As for the smell, I can attest I, too, have experienced it, both in his room and often while walking down the hallway, close to him, and in the room where I am, where he slept for a few nights, when they were redoing the floor in his, and where he left a bandage wet with blood. I have sensed the scent on his cap and gloves, too. I couldn't explain the nature of this smell.

Q. On the origin of the stigmata.
A. It is not known with precision. They say they occurred on Friday, September 20, 1918, in the choir, before a crucifix that is now in the library. The first to notice them were some devout women who frequented the church, and then Father Paolino.

Q. What he thinks of said stigmata.
A. I could not attest that they are a supernatural occurrence, since I understand there may be stigmata of a different nature, and that there have been many stigmatized. I believe they

are one of the signs of sainthood, but not the only one, nor the decisive one, and that it must be accompanied by others, and include the whole life of the stigmatized.

Q. So then in this regard, what do you think about Padre Pio? Are the other signs present?
A. As for his life, I do not have anything to remark; I do not see anything extraordinary, no apparent signs of an extraordinary life. It's a simple life, common, ordinary. In the evenings he stays longer in the choir or in church, while we're having dinner; he is attentive, more than the others.

Q. On Padre Pio's practice of the religious virtues.
A. I couldn't indicate anything extraordinary or heroic; all is commonplace, like the rest of his life. I think he's always been treated with a sort of regard. I cannot say that there have been acts that seemed to be not virtuous.

Here the witness notes that Padre Pio, while speaking to others, seems to say something peculiar—it may be ejaculations—some say he speaks to his guardian angel. . .

Q. About what is said regarding Padre Pio's scant nutrition.
A. Before, when he used to eat lunch with us, I could see that he didn't eat much, but, all in all, he did eat; now he eats with the students of the minor seminary, so I do not know. Back then, he would eat angel hair pasta, vegetables with oil, potatoes with oil, dairy products, a few bites of sponge cake made for him by the devout women, and especially fruit. In the evening, the same, but much less. Now in the evening he doesn't even go with the students: He doesn't come down; he eats something, always different—sardines, then he started taking a cup of hot chocolate, and fruit when available. He drinks beer. And many evenings he doesn't eat anything at all.

Q. On his use of medicaments.

A. Pills, quinine, etc., and it seems that on his hands he also used iodine.

Here the witness says Padre Pio fell seriously ill on the Feast of the Immaculate [Conception] in 1919, and on May 5, 1920: We thought he was going to die; the rumor had spread that he would die at thirty-three, the age he was about to turn then. He healed and got better. They said he must fall ill on solemn feasts: The devout women said he suffered for some sinner.

All these things having been read and approved, Father Luigi was dismissed, upon the oath *de secreto servando* taken on the Holy Gospels. In confirmation of everything, it was signed.

Fr. Luigi of Serra Capriola
Capuchin

Acta sunt haec per me, Visitatorem Apostolicum

L.✠S.   Br. Raphael C., Episc. Volaterr. *Visit. Apost.*

NUMBER XII

Second Deposition of Father Luigi of Serra Capriola *Capuchin*

June 19, 1921—8 A.M.

Before me, the undersigned Apostolic Visitor, in the convent of the Minor Capuchins of San Giovanni Rotondo, has appeared of his own will the *Most Reverend Father Luigi of*

Serra Capriola, who, having taken the oath *de veritate dicenda* on the Holy Gospels, so testified:

I have heard that the archpriest of Pietrelcina allegedly stated that Padre Pio has already had stigmata, internally, for five years; the archpriest allegedly related further details.

I remember two men who came here to give thanks for a grace they had been granted.

I recall I've heard from Padre Pio himself that he had talked with an old man who had appeared to him in the guest quarters: He had been dead for many years and the guardian Father Paolino apparently tracked down his personal details at the City Hall. I also heard that one evening, while he was alone in the choir praying, he heard a noise like a load of small pebbles falling from the window.

Also, I've heard that while he was in Sant'Elia a Pianise, still a student, he saw a big black dog jumping from a window of a room where it is said noises had been heard: He himself related this.

We know from letters of other instances of healings that were allegedly granted.

I cannot, though, square these apparently prodigious occurrences with some things that are at least in themselves faults—at least objectively; subjectively, I think they may not be.

I've heard that while he was ill in the guest quarters, he was tended to by some women, and that these women once showed their displeasure at the presence of another, older, woman.

It is also a known fact that he received his penitent women in the guest quarters for their spiritual direction, one at a time—something we did not like, especially since a circular on this subject had come from Rome. We must certainly suppose that he did not mean to disobey; rather, the circular itself must have been benignly interpreted. Now there have been some changes in this area, and some of these women—who call themselves the "Spiritual Daughters"—got upset, because they thought we had no trust in them. The imperfection of these irregularities is certainly caused by the local fanaticism: Padre Pio is very simple. Until some time ago, these women stayed until late to talk, to kiss his hand, etc. So, if these irregularities could be eliminated, it would be a good thing.

I believe Padre Pio has been poorly directed.

The Mass he now celebrates at 10 A.M. is the conventual, in the sense that it's the *de officio diei* Mass: the Community is not present at all, since everyone is busy with his various duties, so it was decided that Padre Pio should celebrate it, to avoid the impression of a sudden change from the past custom. I think these devout women would be sad if another change had to be made: Padre Pio has pointed out how he cannot hear confessions before a certain amount of time has passed after the Mass.

Before, Padre Pio used to give away the donations sent to him, distributing them, they say, through a devout woman known as the "secretary": They sent him alms that he might use them as he thought best. It is supposed and thought for sure that he had the permission of the previous superiors. This way of doing things happened in the past: The current superior found out once (it was a matter of a significant sum of money), and apparently he was displeased; since then it has never happened again, as far as I know.

All of this having been read and approved, the Reverend Father Luigi was dismissed upon the oath *de secreto servando* taken on the Holy Gospels. In confirmation of everything, it was signed.

Fr. Luigi of Serra Capriola
Capuchin

Acta sunt haec per me, Visitatorem Apostolicum

L.✠S.   Br. Raphael C., Episc. Volaterr. *Visit. Apost.*

NUMBER XIII

First Deposition of Father Romolo of San Marco in Lamis *Capuchin*

June 18, 1921—7:30 A.M.

Before me, the undersigned Apostolic Visitor, in the convent of the Minor Capuchins of San Giovanni Rotondo, has appeared, summoned, the *Reverend Father Romolo of San Marco in Lamis*, Capuchin, who, having taken the oath *de veritate dicenda* on the Holy Gospels, so testified and answered.

Q. About his personal details.
A. My name is Father Romolo of San Marco in Lamis, born Michele Pennisi, son of Paolo, age thirty-five; I have been living in San Giovanni Rotondo for thirteen months. I am the director of the boys of the minor seminary.

Q. About Padre Pio of Pietrelcina.
A. It's since I have been here that I know him well. I saw him once in Foggia, for a few minutes; having learned he had the stigmata, I went to see him for eight days. I have

heard his friends and everyone say (before he received the stigmata) that he has always been a good young man and a good religious. Father Benedetto of Santa Maria [*sic*] in Lamis also related this episode: He was the confessor of a woman who would regularly receive Holy Communion. One day Padre Pio wrote to him to warn him that that woman was hiding a sin, and that the Lord was tired of it. Father Benedetto tried to find out about it; but the woman said she had nothing else to confess. She was so insistent that Father Benedetto said to himself: "Oh, look what Padre Pio makes me do!" But eventually he declared: "You committed such and such sin." And the woman repented. Since my memory is not so good, I wouldn't want to be wrong: Father Benedetto had in his care several good souls, but I think the one who told him about the hidden sin was really Padre Pio.

When I was in the army, I heard about the stigmata received by Padre Pio. So I thought: Father Benedetto was indeed right when two years ago he said it was God who acted through Padre Pio!

I even went to see him; I opened my heart to him, and I asked him many things: whether my grandmother who had died suddenly was saved—and he answered me: Her account is settled; whether I would be reunited with her in Heaven—he told me yes. But before he spoke, he would turn away, saying the words in a low voice, as if he were talking to another person.

Also, as I was with him on the evening of Good Friday, I asked him about a deaf-mute woman for whom, as rumors had it, Padre Pio's prayers would obtain a grace on the next day; I asked him whether she would receive the grace, and actually, I asked that he obtain it for her on the following day. Padre Pio answered: "She will be granted the grace, but the Lord doesn't want to be bound to a specific time."

Many times he has told me: "*Statutum est mori senex*" [It is decided that I die in old age]—but I do not know if he meant to joke.

Seeing these things, I would wonder: Either this man is an impostor, or otherwise how can he know the future? And since I could not consider him a fraud, I thought he was an extraordinary soul.

I know of another episode that seems to hint at the work of the devil against Padre Pio. One time, Father Agostino, now First Definitor, wrote a letter to Padre Pio, who was in Pietrelcina. The letter arrived so stained with ink that nothing could be read. Then the archpriest put the crucifix on the letter, and the stain disappeared enough to reveal the writing. Father Agostino wanted the letter back, and I myself have seen it stained with ink, so much that it was barely possible to decipher it.

In Foggia I have heard it said that loud noises were heard; one time, a bishop was also present; the religious noticed them, and since such noises would recur, they told Padre Pio: "Either you tell us what it is, or we'll go away." I was told Padre Pio answered that they should rest assured, since nothing would happen anymore. And I think that henceforth they apparently didn't happen again.

I know from Father Agostino that Padre Pio had frequent conversations with his guardian angel, with Saint Francis; that he had many fights with demons, etc.; and that he was even beaten up, but I do not know from whom Father Agostino learned about this last circumstance.

Q. Whether he has seen the stigmata, and what he thinks about them.
A. I saw them on the hands, but a sort of reverential awe kept me from asking to see the others. But even those on his hands, I never examined them, or touched them. Padre

Pio does so much good through the confessional, etc. How could the Lord allow for so long all this good, if the stigmata were not from him?

Q. Whether he has sensed the smell, and what he thinks of it.
A. I've noticed it many times, I think—I've defined it as some sort of lily scent. Many have smelled it, and if I'm not mistaken, I think I have, too. Actually, I can say I smelled it several times.

Q. Do you think Padre Pio makes use of fragrances?
A. Knowing his soul, I don't think so. I know (because he has said so) that in the morning he doesn't even have the time to comb his beard.

Q. Since Padre Pio eats in the refectory with Y.P. [hereafter Your Paternity] and with the students of the minor seminary, what do you think of his eating habits?
A. He eats rather sparingly, and leaves food in every dish; he eats some of everything, every food, whatever he is given, but just a little bit. Before, he couldn't eat anything but green vegetables, and couldn't keep them down; he also eats macaroni, almost no meat, but pork liver yes, beans, fish: You might say he eats everything, except meat, but he eats more or less a third of what I eat. Little bread; he drinks some beer, around half a liter, sometimes a little more. I know that throughout the day he drinks another half a liter. In the evening, Father Ignazio takes care of him: He gives him a cup of hot chocolate, rather thick. Sometimes an apple or two.

Q. On Padre Pio's nature, on his moral portrait.
A. I think in his behavior Padre Pio is like a child, quite a simple soul, because he says things as a young child would,

although in serious matters he leaves you speechless. I have to say, I sincerely don't see that he generally practices the virtues to a heroic degree, from what I have seen; an exception occurred once when he had a very painful headache: "I have something like a circle pressing", he said. I said: "Let's take turns." He replied: "I only have this one, what would be left for me then?" He wanted to keep it, and not give it to me.

I also know that his feet are always cold, and if they give him a foot warmer full of hot water, he doesn't feel any warmth, even though others can't even touch it: At least this is what he says.

Nevertheless, even though I don't see heroic virtues, I do notice that he possesses a delicate conscience.

There is that decree prohibiting talks with penitent women outside the confessional. The superiors noticed that despite this decree, which was publicly read even in his presence, Padre Pio kept talking with them in the guest quarters and in the sacristy. Since I heard many complaints from the Fathers, but nobody dared say anything to Padre Pio—because they said he knows; it was read in front of everybody—I went to Padre Pio, and I conveyed to him the existing prohibition. He hinted at his obedience to the superiors, and to the fact that he didn't do anything without advice. "Also," he said, "mine is an extraordinary case, and it would provoke a scandal to remove it suddenly." In short, I noticed almost displeasure: I don't know if there was a bit of attachment; I don't know whether he had other motives. It seemed to me, but I could be wrong, that he was hurt. After I said it, the guest quarters weren't used for talks anymore. When I mentioned to him that the issue could have reached Rome, he answered that he would have been happy (I'm not sure these were his precise words), and he himself would have apologized before the superiors. In short, from the entire context

I gathered he was acting legitimately, with a sure conscience, even though he then stopped.

As for the 10 A.M. Mass, the superior meant to move it
up on account of the Community. But Padre Pio made
known that for an hour after the Mass he cannot hear confessions anymore, for a reason he cannot tell anyone, and of
which he says: "I'm ashamed of it myself." I have to say,
though, that, as far as I know, there were never clear, definite commands from the superiors to him, regarding these
issues of the Mass and of the parlor. I've heard some say
Padre Pio's obedience should be put to the test, but then
no one does. But I believe that if he received a definite,
clear order, he would immediately bow his head.

Having reported to the superior Padre Pio's problem with
moving up the Mass, I told the superior to leave it at ten, and
he agreed. That evening I went to Padre Pio's room, and since
he looked nervous, I told him: "Don't worry, the superior
told me that you can say Mass whenever you want." He
answered me: "How could my conscience not worry, when I
know the superior wants Mass at 10 A.M., and I cannot say
it?" I say all this to highlight Padre Pio's delicate soul.

Q. About Padre Pio's practice of poverty.
A. To be sure, I don't see any heroism. But he's a child, a
petit enfant.

It seems that he couldn't be bothered with some things.
For instance, he talks in the dormitories, he has a cross
with a crucifix on his rosary, whereas the constitutions say
that the cross must be wooden. Maybe he was given it, he
is too simple, and so he wore it.

As for poverty, the Guardian complained that Padre Pio
should have given him a certain sum of money, quite a big
one, and Padre Pio had given it to somebody else in charge
of it instead—actually, I think it was a woman, who receives

all the money destined for the poor. But I think in this matter he must be obeying the superiors, otherwise he wouldn't do it.

Q. About Padre Pio's manners with women.
A. He is informal, like a child. He addresses them as *tu*; he says whatever he feels. But as far as chastity is concerned, he is extremely delicate. As for this, nobody doubts he is an angel. It's for this reason that the Father Provincial lets him have conversations in the guest quarters.

In my opinion, I think Padre Pio is a *petit enfant* who would need clear and definite orders in all the areas of his behavior, even though I have noticed a very sharp intelligence in his advice.

Q. About Padre Pio's spirit.
A. I think he must pray very much when he is in bed, because he has told me that in bed he cannot pray but mentally. When we are having dinner, he stays in the choir to pray. Nothing on the outside indicating recollection: I don't see that typical devout posture, but he always leans against the chair, kneeling on the cushions; when the Most Holy Sacrament is exposed, he sits on a straw-padded chair, covered with a pillow. He does all this maybe because of the stigmata, or on account of his delicate health.

Q. On Padre Pio's regular attendance of the functions in the choir.
A. I think he may be dispensed from them, because I seem to remember the superior once saying to me: "Instead of staying in the guest quarters, he could come to the choir." But as usual, nobody told him anything. It's as I said before: I don't think there ever was a precise order, only advice, wishes, etc.

Q. Why does Padre Pio have his meals in the refectory of the minor seminary, instead of with the Community?

A. Perhaps because he is the spiritual director of the school; perhaps because he doesn't want to be an object of curiosity on the part of the strangers who come to the refectory.

Q. What about his spiritual direction of the students?

A. Actually he is spiritual director: He should be teaching the catechism, but now I am doing it because I am less busy. This year that I have been here, he must have done just four or five lectures: He told me he doesn't have time. He hears the boys' confessions. In my opinion, his spiritual direction is good, although the confessions only last a few minutes each. After all, the direction rests more on me than on the spiritual director: Seeing that he can't [do more], I make up for it.

In conclusion, all things considered, Padre Pio is a good religious, with a God-fearing conscience, who would need clear and definite orders regarding his behavior: He has his own spiritual director, and I think he must follow him blindly, so much does he esteem him; and from what is said, I suspect he is also following the director in some of his external behaviors—for instance, the management of money, which is prohibited to us. But he must have been obedient.

All these things, with the additions and the notes, having been read and approved, Father Romolo was dismissed, upon the oath *de secreto servando* taken on the Holy Gospels. In confirmation of everything, it was signed.

                              Fr. Romolo of S. Marco in Lamis
[The printed document doesn't show the Bishop's signature here]

NUMBER XIV

Second Deposition of **Father Romolo of San Marco in Lamis** *Capuchin*

June 20, 1921—7: 30 A.M.

Before me, the undersigned Apostolic Visitor, in the convent of the Minor Capuchins of San Giovanni Rotondo, has appeared of his own will the *Most Reverend Father Romolo of San Marco in Lamis*, who, having taken the oath *de veritate dicenda* on the Holy Gospels, so testified and stated.

Q. Whether he needs to revise anything in the previous deposition.

A. No. I have to add the following:

— Padre Pio told me that when he was a boy, he would get up every morning to go and serve the early-morning Holy Mass, and he said this to me because I asked him why he would never get enough sleep.

Also, to show his practice of the virtue of chastity, I know from him that when he was very young, while in bed, he would hide his hands under the covers as soon as he would see his mother coming into his room.

— I have heard that during an ecstasy (Father Agostino and Father Evangelista must have witnessed it), witnesses heard Padre Pio allegedly say: "How could you, O Lord, be glorified in me, who am a good-for-nothing? I, who am not even a preacher?" And then he would apologize to the Lord for addressing him now as *tu*, now as *voi*.

— Padre Pio repeats very often the words of the sacramental absolution, especially the words *absolvo* and *tuis* (referred to *peccatis*). I also see that during the Holy Mass, the Consecration lasts for a very long time. I know from the guardian that when Padre Pio gets to that point, he suffers a kind of hell.

— During a conversation he was telling me that if the same things he counsels others about happen to him, he can't make up his mind, and needs advice.

— One day a boy at the minor seminary overheard Padre Pio, who was by an open window, pronounce the formula of the sacramental absolution, and the same thing happened another time in the sacristy: Father Ignazio told me about a woman who apparently heard him. I mention this because it might be related to some episodes of bilocation that are talked about, especially the absolution he imparted to a sick man far away, who told his family he had had his confession heard by Padre Pio.

— A young Capuchin student (one who is hyperscrupulous) told me that Padre Pio assured him he would never fall from God's grace again.

— Two or three times he mentioned to me, with his usual smile, some internal pains, as if he had a fire inside, and some pain in his bones—and these pains notwithstanding, he would do what he had to and perform his duties.

— I noticed in Padre Pio—at least two or three times—a bit of rush to judge the superiors (perhaps he might have had his reasons).

All these things having been read and approved, Father Romolo was dismissed, upon the oath *de secreto servando* taken on the Holy Gospels. In confirmation of everything, it was signed.

Fr. Romolo of S. Marco in Lamis

Acta sunt haec per me, Visitatorem Apostolicum

L.✠S.   Br. Raphael C., Episc. Volaterr. *Visit. Apost.*

After the deposition, the witness wishes to add, and adds, under the same oath *de veritate*:

The solemn holy services are always presided over by Padre Pio, so much that at least once—maybe out of necessity— the Father Guardian himself served him as a deacon.

But in the middle of all the commotion the whole world is making about him, I see that Padre Pio keeps his simplicity, as if nothing were going on. Actually, one day he wondered why everyone was coming—as he said—"to observe me, my things".

Again, the addition having been read and approved, Father Romolo was finally dismissed with the secret S. O. [oath observed] *de more* [according to custom] taken on the Holy Gospel, and it was signed.

Fr. Romolo of San Marco in Lamis

Acta sunt haec per me, Visitatorem Apostolicum

L.✠S.   Fr. Raphael C., Episc. Volaterr. *Visit. Apost.*

NUMBER XV

Deposition of **Father Lodovico of San Giovanni Rotondo** *Capuchin*

June 18, 1921—11 A.M.

Before me, the undersigned Apostolic Visitor, has appeared, summoned, in this convent of the Minor Capuchins of San Giovanni Rotondo, the *Most Reverend Father Lodovico of San*

Giovanni Rotondo, who, having taken the oath *de veritate dicenda* on the Holy Gospels, so stated, testified and answered.

Q. About his personal details.
A. My name is Father Lodovico of San Giovanni Rotondo, born Giovanni Miglionico, son of Matteo, age thirty-four. I have been living in this convent for eleven months.

Q. About Padre Pio of Pietrelcina.
A. He's a religious leading a holy life, and we are amazed that, as sick as he is, he can bear such exhaustion in the confessional, even though he eats so very little.

As for extraordinary events, I must testify that I have never seen anything with my own eyes. *Ex auditu*, yes, I have heard of them, one hears so many stories... There are two things on which I base my claim of Padre Pio's holiness: the stigmata and the scent he gives off, because this is not a natural phenomenon: he doesn't wash with scented soap bars, and does not make use of fragrances.

Q. About the stigmata specifically.
A. I see them constantly when I go to Mass. I know two doctors were sent for, and they said the stigmata cannot be explained naturally: They are an extraordinary phenomenon. I've only seen the stigmata on the hands, but I have seen the shirts stained with blood on the side. Professor Festa and another doctor dressed both hands in bandages and put a seal, and Padre Pio kept them this way for eight days. The doctors medicated them, then sealed them again: They said that if it were a natural phenomenon, within eight days it would have healed. Instead, after eight days so much blood came out that Padre Pio couldn't even celebrate Mass. I have heard these things from the Fathers who were here, because I wasn't present.

Q. Talk about the scent.
A. This scent is so intense that it's impossible to be in his room. Padre Pio doesn't notice it; if he did, he says, he wouldn't be able to sleep.

Q. Whether it is constant or intermittent.
A. In his room, it is constant; his things—some of them, such as his handkerchief and his *zucchetto*—always carry it. His person gives it off in waves. In 1919 I stopped by this convent; the Bishop of Melfi was here. When the Bishop was ready to leave, Padre Pio accompanied him outside the convent, on the square: His handkerchief fell, a Father who picked it up gave it to me, and I took it away to my convent in Umbria. The handkerchief was for twenty days in my suitcase; after such a long time, it still had the scent in all its intensity.

In the small drawer of the nightstand in my cell there was a bandage from Padre Pio's side. This small drawer has been in my cell for a year now, and every time I open it I notice Padre Pio's scent.

Q. About a moral and religious portrait of Padre Pio.
A. He devotes himself greatly to prayer—he protracts it, and one tires of waiting for him, especially if he's meditating. Even when he speaks, it seems that besides the person to whom he is speaking, there might be another one whom he might be addressing—it's commonly said that he speaks with his guardian angel.

Regarding his exterior devotion, he's very devout, and one only needs to look at him: He has the appearance of a profound mystic.

As for religious virtues, he is very submissive when the superior says something; he is humble: If he meets others, he gives up his place. As for poverty, he observes the prescriptions of the rule. Indeed, if someone wants to give

him a stipend for Mass intentions, he doesn't even touch
the money, but refers to whoever is in charge of it.

Q. About Padre Pio's conversation and manners.
A. He is kind and affable with everyone, always smiling—
sometimes he makes jokes, too.

Q. And how about his manners with women.
A. He shows politeness, reserve, and at times has even been
austere.

All in all, in my opinion he is a good religious who distinguishes himself from all the others.

All these things having been read and approved, Father
Lodovico of San Giovanni Rotondo was dismissed, upon
the oath *de secreto servando* on the Holy Gospels. In confirmation of everything, it was signed.

Fr. Lodovico of S. Giovanni Rotondo
Capuchin

Acta sunt haec per me, Visitatorem Apostolicum

L.✠S.   Br. Raphael C., Episc. Volaterr. *Visit. Apost.*

NUMBER XVI

Deposition of the **Reverend Father Pietro of Ischitella**
Provincial of the Capuchins of the Province of Foggia

June 19, 1921—10 A.M.

Before me, the undersigned Apostolic Visitor, has appeared,
summoned, in the convent of the Minor Capuchins of San

Giovanni Rotondo, the *Most Reverend Father Pietro of Ishi-tella, provincial*, who, having taken the oath *de veritate dicenda* on the Holy Gospels, so testified and answered.

Q. About his personal details.
A. My name is Father Pietro of Ischitella, born Domenico Paradiso, son of the late Francesco, age forty-one, provincial of the Province of the Minor Capuchins of Sant'Angelo since July 5, 1919.

Q. About Padre Pio of Pietrelcina.
A. I got to know Padre Pio when he was my literature student for six months, after the novitiate, and at that time I was able to notice his docility, obedience, and exact observance of his duties as a religious and as a student. Among his classmates, too, he exercised some influence, on account of his candid manners: kind, charming, and charitable. Even for the townsfolk the sight of Padre Pio was edifying (we were in Sant'Elia a Pianisi). I remember that whenever there was a procession, people were attracted by the collected bearing of this young man, who distinguished himself from his companions by his modesty, his eyes, etc. Then I lost sight of him, because I went out of the province: All I had during that time were reports. So one time when I stopped in Foggia, the Fathers there told me about physical temptations Padre Pio had suffered from the devil. I also had other reports from Father Agostino, who had him as a student after me.

Once elected provincial, I saw Padre Pio again on the occasion of the visit conducted by Professor Bignami of Rome. Then I came back often, at least once a month; and since the religious who made up the Community were perhaps too enthusiastic, I gradually changed the Community itself, instructing that there should be no interviews, everything should go on regularly, and the utmost discretion should be observed in all matters. Likewise, I gave the appropriate instructions to modify and limit the frequency of the conversations with penitents in the guest quarters, which are now closed, except in extraordinary cases.

As for the person of Padre Pio, first of all in his external behavior I have appreciated and admired his composure and his unfeigned piety. That goodness, that piety that is not demure—to me they seem truly natural. And this is the opinion of whoever approaches him, and of the religious family. He tries to conceal his suffering with special industry and ingenuity. I also admire his obedience, especially in a few instances when obedience undoubtedly cost him some sacrifices: as in the case of the doctors' visit, for which he bowed to the precept of obedience, or when the Fathers who loved him were removed—he was saddened by the measures that had been taken, and wrote to me about it. This is how I saw that he prefers precise orders from his superiors.

I have also admired his purity, his modesty, etc. But I have also seen his human side: This impression I got on the occasion of the removal of the Fathers—afterward, he asked me to forgive him for the letter he had sent. Candor is a virtue only so far: He let himself be carried away too much by the Fathers who comprised the Community—this is why I believe that in his exterior behavior he needs to be guided.

Great and remarkable is his humility before the extraordinary manifestations of which he has been made, and still is, a sign.

One cannot suppose the existence in him of a duplicity that would be the opposite of his candor: He always lives true to his nature.

As for his nutrition, it's strange—so much that I asked the doctors' advice, to see whether we should intervene and request obedience. There are periods when he cannot keep anything down: moments when he takes to some food, which later he cannot tolerate. Consulted, the doctors said not to force him, neither in quantity nor in quality. He doesn't request that what he likes best be bought. He drinks beer brewed by a lay Brother.

The scent. I've noticed it, without thinking it was coming from him: Then I was told, so I set out to find out about it, thinking that Padre Pio, in his simplicity, might have used fragrances that perhaps had been given to him. I didn't smell it in his room, but in the vegetable garden, yes.

I involved the Father Vicar so that he may find out, since he was always close by. He asked Padre Pio himself, who answered: "But I don't smell anything."

Regarding Padre Pio in general, I've sought the opinion of serious people, like the Bishop of Melfi, and the Archbishop of Simla: Their opinion was favorable.

Q. About the stigmata, what he thinks about their origin.
A. All things considered, after the medical examinations, and given their permanence, etc., I don't know to which natural cause they might be attributed.

Q. About Padre Pio's demeanor toward women.
A. On the women's part, there are some fanatics, yes, who (I don't know for which purpose, maybe because they don't have anything better to do) like to come across as Padre Pio's penitents. As for the Padre, I did hear that apparently he treats some with more familiarity, although I cannot attribute it to an intentional lack of decorum, but to his simplicity. Likewise, I was informed about a young lady, a little too scrupulous, who didn't want to receive Communion; reportedly, Padre Pio, while talking to her, gave her something like a little pat on her shoulder: The woman went away saying Padre Pio had caressed her; Padre Pio was warned.

Q. Regarding Padre Pio's practice of poverty.

A. When I was made provincial, Padre Pio told me he had some money he had received for the poor. I made him understand it was inappropriate for him to keep that money, and now he gives it to the bursar or to a spiritual daughter of his, who takes care of distributing it—when she herself doesn't receive the money directly from the benefactors. It's not good for the religious to occupy themselves with managing money, lest they give the impression they have an interest. The young woman who takes care of this is serious, discreet, prudent, and I have a very good opinion of her.

After all, I noticed not only the absence of irregularities in all this, but also that Padre Pio didn't even use the money he received to provide for the necessities of his own family. I provide for them, without Padre Pio knowing anything at all.

Q. Whether it is true he is writing a chronicle.

A. Not quite a chronicle: I had asked that a record be kept of notable facts, but the Fathers, because of their primary occupations, couldn't keep it up. I have ordered his correspondence be kept, especially the letters containing claims of graces, etc. Father Benedetto, yes, he is collecting all that is necessary to write the life of Padre Pio.

All of this read and verified, the Most Reverend Father Pietro, provincial, was dismissed, upon the oath *de secreto servando* taken on the Holy Gospels. In confirmation of everything, it was signed.

Br. Pietro of Ischitella*
Capuchin Min. Prov.

---

* Father Pietro signed with the religious title for a Brother, even though he was a priest and the provincial.

Acta sunt haec per me, Visitatorem Apostolicum

L.✠S.   Br. Raphael C., Episc. Volaterr. *Visit. Apost.*

NUMBER XVII

Deposition of Father Cherubino of San Marco in Lamis *Capuchin*

June 20, 1921—8:30 A.M.

Before me, the undersigned Apostolic Visitor, has appeared, summoned, in the convent of the Minor Capuchins of San Giovanni Rotondo, the *Most Reverend Father Cherubino of San Marco in Lamis*, who, having taken the oath *de veritate dicenda* on the Holy Gospels, so testified and answered.

Q. About his personal details.
A. My name is Father Cherubino of San Marco in Lamis, born Ciro Martino, son of the late Pasquale, age thirty-four, in this convent for about a year.

Q. About Padre Pio of Pietrelcina.
A. I am of the opinion that, considering all the facts, something extraordinary does appear [to be taking place].

The facts are, first of all, the stigmata, which for two and a half years, despite the treatments prescribed by the doctors at various points—like iodine and bandages applied on his side—have not healed, as I have learned from eyewitnesses. What's more, these sores, instead of producing pus, produce blood, as if deep internal tissues were damaged. Besides, if they were natural sores, they would be nauseating; instead, at times a sweet smell is sensed close to his person.

Second—Padre Pio's life is one of enduring suffering. He gets little sleep—one time, from something he said, I learned that he couldn't sleep a wink. Nevertheless, he works tirelessly, especially hearing confessions and listening to the people who turn to him for advice and consolation. As for food, although it is sufficient, nevertheless, it's not always proportional to his energy consumption, considering his health and his work.

Q. About Padre Pio's personality, and a moral and religious portrait of him.
A. Padre Pio, as far as his health allows it, endeavors to practice what the others practice. Regarding the religious vows, I don't have anything negative to say. As for prayer, he fulfills his duties, and since the active life takes up much of his time, he stays longer in the choir and in the church, even at different hours from the ones assigned to the Community.

Padre Pio is a good religious, who inspires trust and devotion in whoever talks to him. Also, he is very simple, and for this reason he rather needs direction and advice from those around him. And if in the past some minor inconveniences happened—concerning the townsfolk or the friars, but not Padre Pio—it was due to insufficient vigilance on the part of those around him, vigilance which, given the circumstances, could not be exercised.

Q. About Padre Pio's demeanor toward women.
A. He treats all with kindness and sweetness, but is much reserved. And those who frequent him carry on an exemplary—and extremely devout—life.

Q. About the extraordinary events.
A. I haven't witnessed any of them, but the correspondence we receive even from faraway regions clearly shows that

many people who had recommended themselves to Padre Pio's prayers write to give thanks for the graces they have received.

It seems the mission God entrusted to Padre Pio is to convert souls, and if some supernatural sign manifests itself through him it is precisely to attract souls to God. Therefore, if in the past there were inconveniences because of the extraordinary influx of people, it happened because of some partiality sparked more than anything by a few newspaper pieces written by people not knowledgeable, but worldly.

These things having been read and approved, Father Cherubino was dismissed, upon the oath *de secreto servando* taken on the Holy Gospels. In confirmation of everything, it was signed.

Fr. Cherubino of S. Marco
Capuchin

[In this instance, too, the printed document doesn't carry the Apostolic Visitor's signature]

NUMBER XVIII

First Deposition of Padre Pio of Pietrelcina *Capuchin*

June 15, 1921—5 P.M.

Before me, the undersigned Apostolic Visitor, has appeared, summoned, in the convent of the Minor Capuchins, the *Reverend Padre Pio of Pietrelcina*, who, having taken the oath of telling the truth on the Holy Gospels, testified and answered as follows.

Q. About his name and personal details.

A. My name is Padre Pio of Pietrelcina, born Francesco Forgione, son of Orazio, age thirty-four. I have been in this convent since September 1916.

Q. He may recount his life.

A. I entered the novitiate in Morcone, in the Province of Benevento, in January 1902 or 1903.

The following year I made my simple profession, and in due time, regularly, the solemn profession. From the novitiate I went to Sant'Elia a Pianisi, in the Province of Campobasso, to complete my literature studies; except for a few months in San Marco alla [la] Catola, I did all of my philosophical studies in the same convent in Sant'Elia, for around three years. I did my theological studies in Serra Capriola, in the Province of Foggia, and in Montefusco, for four years. I was ordained as a priest in 1910, during the course of my theological studies, having completed the second year, or more likely the third, I think. In the meantime, I was home on account of my poor health—malarial fever and, later on, bronchial pneumonia. I was in Foggia for a few months in 1916, then I came to San Giovanni Rotondo, where I still am. As for military service, I was in active duty only for a few days, also on account of my poor health: I was often sent on convalescent leave, until I was dismissed permanently the March preceding the armistice—I had been drafted in 1915. I spent those few days in the military in Naples, a patient at the hospital, while I spent the convalescent leaves in this convent of San Giovanni Rotondo.

Q. About when he was conferred the faculty to hear confessions and preach.

A. As for preaching, I have never preached; from around the time of my priestly ordination (1911), I was able to hear a few confessions in my hometown; here, [in San Giovanni Rotondo] I was conferred the faculty by the ordinary about three years ago; in Foggia I never heard confessions, since on account of my poor health I hadn't even requested the faculty to do so.

Q. What does he have to say about apparently extraordinary circumstances that have occurred to his person, e.g., in Foggia.
A. Since around 1912, I had heard noises that in Foggia started being heard also by others, who would come to see me—I was ill—to inquire what was going on. Also, I had malicious external visions, now under human shape, now under beastly shapes, etc. I haven't heard noises or had visions in years.

Q. Whether other episodes, beside the above-mentioned, of an apparently mystical nature have occurred to him.
A. Yes, apparitions of O.L. [hereafter our Lord], of our Lady, of Saint Francis, while I was awake.

Q. About when episodes of such nature started.
A. Since around 1911–1912.

Q. Whether, once the visions of an apparently diabolical nature ceased, the so-called apparitions continued and continue to this day.
A. Yes, even though they are rarer.

Q. Whether such apparitions were silent, or conveyed warnings, exhortations, etc.
A. Yes, I would receive exhortations regarding myself, as well as others, and even reproaches, always about the spiritual life.

Q. That he please give a detailed account of the so-called "stigmata".

A. On September 20, 1918, after celebrating the Mass, I stayed in the choir for the due thanksgiving prayer, when suddenly I was overtaken by a powerful trembling, then calm followed, and I saw our Lord in the posture of someone who is on a cross (but it didn't strike me whether he had the Cross), lamenting the ingratitude of men, especially those consecrated to him and by him most favored. This revealed his suffering and his desire to unite souls with his Passion. He invited me to partake of his sorrows and to meditate on them: At the same time he urged me to work for my brothers' salvation. I felt then full of compassion for the Lord's sorrows, and I asked him what I could do. I heard this voice: "I unite you with my Passion." Once the vision disappeared, I came to, I returned to my senses, and I saw these signs here, which were dripping blood. I didn't have anything before.

Q. Whether and how others noticed, and when.
A. Nobody asked anything directly, except for the director, Father Benedetto of San Marco in Lamis. He was not here—perhaps he heard of it; he wrote to me and later came here.

Q. What he has done to these "sores", since they have appeared.
A. I've tried to keep gloves on. Initially, I would use some iodine every once in a while, but a doctor told me to stop, since it could irritate them even more. They had me use a little petroleum jelly when the sores would lose their scabs; I used it several times, but I haven't in a long time. It may be over two years that I have used nothing at all.

The session is briefly suspended. Having duly approved and accepted the above statements, Padre Pio was dismissed with the oath *de silentio servando*, which he took on the Holy Gospels. In confirmation of everything preceding, it was signed.

P. Pio of Pietrelcina
Capuchin

Acta sunt haec per me, Visitatorem Apostolicum
L.✠S.   Br. Raphael C., Episc. Volaterr. *Visit. Apost.*

NUMBER XIX

Second Deposition of Padre Pio of Pietrelcina Capuchin

June 15, 1921—7 P.M.

About one hour later, the session is resumed, as above, and Padre Pio again takes the oath *de veritate dicenda* on the Holy Gospels.

Q. Whether he needs to revise anything in the answers of the previous interrogation.
A. No.

At this point the Visitor examines the cell, and doesn't find any kind of medicaments of relevance.

Q. Talk about the "scent" that is said to come from his "stigmata".
A. I don't know how to answer this question. I, too, have heard about this from people who came to kiss my hand.

But as for me, I don't know; I can't make it out. In my cell I have nothing but soap.

Q. What are the effects he suffers from these "stigmata".
A. Pain, always, especially on those days when they bleed. The pain is more or less intense: Sometimes I cannot bear it.

Q. What does he have to say about the temperature rising sometimes up to 118.4°F.
A. It's true—it happens when I am ill.

Q. What kind of illness does he mean.
A. I believe it is a moral, rather than a physical, illness.

Q. What effects does he experience, what does he feel.
A. Internal feelings, the consideration, or some representation, of the Lord. Like in a furnace, still always conscious.

Q. Whether he has ever used on himself carbolic acid, either diluted or pure.
A. No, except when the doctor used it to sterilize when he would give me an injection.

Q. Whether he has ever requested pure carbolic acid from people outside the convent.
A. I recall requesting some for the use of the Community— actually, of the minor seminary of which I was [spiritual] director, in case it wasn't available in the convent.

Q. Whether the request was made in such a way as to remain unknown to the Brothers themselves.
A. No, especially considering that in the past I was almost alone with the Father Guardian. If anything, the only purpose was to prevent the people who had to carry it from knowing

that it was a medicament requested without a doctor's prescription.

Q. Whether in the past he requested veratridine, and to what purpose.

A. Yes, I remember it quite well. I requested it, without even knowing its effects, because Father Ignazio, the convent secretary, once gave me a small quantity of such powder to mix it in tobacco—so I wanted it mainly to use it during recreation, so I could offer the Brothers some tobacco, which, with a small dose of this powder, prompts immediate sneezing.

Having duly approved and accepted the above statements, Padre Pio was dismissed with the oath *de silentio servando*, which he took on the Holy Gospels. In confirmation of everything preceding, it was signed.

P. Pio of Pietrelcina
Capuchin

Acta sunt haec per me, Visitatorem Apostolicum

L.✠S.   Br. Raphael C., Episc. Volaterr. *Visit. Apost.*

NUMBER XX

Third Deposition of **Padre Pio of Pietrelcina** *Capuchin*

June 16, 1921—4:30 P.M.

Before me, the undersigned Apostolic Visitor, has appeared, summoned, the *Reverend Padre Pio of Pietrelcina*, who, having taken *de more* the oath *de veritate dicenda* on the Holy Gospels, so testified and answered.

Q. Whether he needs to revise anything in his previous depositions.
A. No.

Q. Regarding his nutrition—whether outside the meals with the community he ever eats anything.
A. Ordinarily, no; unless I'm ill. I drink, sometimes.

Q. When did this raising of the temperature up to 118.4°F start?
A. It's been several years.

Q. What did the doctors have to say? What did they say while you were enlisted?
A. They were amazed, that's all. When I was enlisted I also had very high temperatures, but I always tried to hide it: One time, luckily, the nurse attributed it to a faulty thermometer.

Q. Regarding the "stigmata"—whether he really can't recall anything that might have been already there, before the manifestation of the sores.
A. I felt pain in those same areas, of the kind that I felt later on. This pain started around 1911–1912, during my first years of priesthood.

Q. And when these sores appeared, what did they look like?
A. They were red, dripping a little blood.

Q. Going back in your memory again, do you recall ever treating these sores, having applied anything, etc., besides what you have already testified?
A. No, besides what I have said.

Examined here the *petroleum jelly*; it turns out to be starch glycerolate.

Q. And what do you think is the origin of these so-called stigmata?
A. I don't know, I told the authority, the [spiritual] director.

Q. And what did the director tell you?
A. I think he didn't give his opinion. He told me: "Humble yourself ever more before the Lord."

Q. Who is your director?
A. The Most Reverend Father Benedetto of San Marco in Lamis.

Q. Since he is usually absent, how does he direct you?
A. Through letters, as far as it is possible, and when he comes here.

Q. How frequently does he write or come here?
A. A month doesn't go by without him writing to me, sometimes more, sometimes less. It has been several months since he has been here, because he is now in Rome.

Q. About the ability to read into people's hearts that is attributed to him.
A. A very few times I happened to feel inside me with clarity someone's fault, or sin, or virtue—of people of whom I had some knowledge, at least generally.

Q. Whether you remember having rebuked Dr. Romanelli of Barletta for some profanity he had pronounced, of which he had no memory.
A. I know I have rebuked him, but I don't recall precisely the reason.

Q. People also talk about episodes of bilocation. What does he have to say.

A. I don't know how it is or the nature of this phenomenon—and I certainly don't give it much thought—but it did happen to me to be in the presence of this or that person, to be in this or that place; I do not know whether my mind was transported there, or what I saw was some sort of representation of the place or the person; I do not know whether I was there with my body or without it.

Q. Whether he has noticed the beginning of this state, and the return to the normal state.

A. Usually it has happened while I was praying—at first my attention was turned to prayer, then to this representation, and then I would find myself exactly as I was before.

Q. That he please tell about specific episodes.

A. One night I found myself at the bedside of a sick woman: Mrs. Maria of San Giovanni Rotondo; I was in the convent; I think I was praying. It must have been over a year ago.

I spoke words of comfort; she begged me to pray for her healing. This is the substance. I didn't really know her personally. She had been recommended to me.

Another episode: A man [Padre Pio doesn't mention his name out of discretion] presented himself to me, or I presented myself to him, in Torre Maggiore—I was in the convent—and I rebuked him and reproached him for his vices, urging him to convert, and then later on this man came here, too.

I think there were other cases, but these are those I still remember.

Q. Whether he revealed to others these alleged episodes of bilocation.

A. No, not at all, in any way. This is the first time I talk about this, and I do it with you, in these terms. I don't think I even told my spiritual director, because I never gave it much thought. These people talked to me about it, but I was discreet; I neither denied it, nor confirmed it.

Q. There is talk of healings that were thought to be miraculous, obtained through your prayers. What do you have to say?

A. I don't know. I have prayed for the needs of the people who recommended themselves to me, poor people, needy people, etc. This is what I know.

Q. About the healing in Lucera—the hunchback who allegedly went back home healed.

A. I know I have prayed for those who recommend themselves to me, but I don't recall this specific case, since so many have come to me asking that I pray for them.

Q. About the case of the cripple from San Giovanni Rotondo.

A. I remember that this man asked that I pray for him:[1] I ignore the result that was obtained. He's a poor soul who still comes to the convent regularly to beg for alms. He came again a few times, saying: "The Lord started the grace and doesn't finish it."[2]

---

[1] To be precise, and given the oath, here Padre Pio notes: "The phrase they would usually employ was 'Grant me the grace', a phrase pronounced on account of their ignorance. And I would answer: 'I will recommend you to the Lord, to our Lady; it is not I who grant the graces.' "

[2] Here, too, Padre Pio notes: "The phrase used was: '*You* started granting to me etc.' And I said: '*The Lord*, etc.' "

Q. About the case of the chancellor of the magistrate's court in San Giovanni Rotondo.

A. I was downstairs hearing confessions; he would complain of his foot, and use a walking cane. So he, too, came to me to recommend himself.[3] As usual, I said more or less: "Trust in the Lord, I will recommend you, etc." This is what I know. I don't know anything about the rest.

Q. Do you know that much commotion was made over you? That photographs were being distributed? That certain women would wear them around their neck? That candles were lit before your image?
A. Yes, except for the candles.

Q. What was your attitude in the face of these displays?
A. The faithful coming to me, I tried to listen to everyone as best as I could. As for the use and abuse of photographs, I've always reproached and reproved. I know the superiors, too, acted at the same time.

Q. Didn't you see in the spreading of all this "fame" a danger to your virtue? Didn't it occur to you to ask to be transferred to a place where you could serve God out of sight?
A. I did desire solitude, because I have even been assaulted. I didn't ask anything because I have always followed the rule of deferring to my superiors, since they know everything.

Q. Is it true that once when you were unwell you were put in the guest quarters? And why?
A. Yes, indeed. The superior thought of putting me there because he was alone (it was during wartime), and he had to take care of the church, to teach in school—everything.

---

[3] See footnote 1.

Q. But couldn't the superior have attended to his duties if Your Paternity, sick, had stayed in his own cell?
A. No, on account of the assistance I needed.

Q. Who tended you in the guest quarters?
A. The benefactors: On that occasion, everyone offered to help. P. and a certain Vincenzino, etc.

Q. Women, too?
A. Yes. The sister of the Father Guardian (Father Paolino of Casacalenga) and other women.

Q. Whether they would only assist him during the day.
A. No, always—at night, too.

Q. What year was this?
A. In 1918, or at the beginning of 1919: I don't recall exactly.

Q. Before or after the episode of the "stigmata"?
A. Excellency, I do not remember.

Q. Is it true that there are currently some people from out of town who have been staying in San Giovanni Rotondo for several months now, to be able to come see you at the convent?
A. Yes, a couple of people. A sick woman from Trieste, who needs fresh air more than anything else—I actually think she is from the Trentino region. A woman from Turin whom I have been seeing since Christmas. They frequent the church, come to Mass, to vespers; they do their devotions.

Q. What do you think of all this coming and going of women—to offer help, to spread and maintain the fame of extraordinary events, or events that are thought to be so?
A. I wouldn't know.

Q. Do you think it regular for a religious to live outside the cloister, assisted by women, etc.?
A. Surely, it is not regular. But I acquiesced out of obedience, because I saw the necessity.

Q. About the behavior of these people.
A. Excellency, I was ill, what could I say?

Q. But did it seem that their behavior was discreet, proper, etc.?
A. This, yes.

Q. And what about all these women who spread, as I said before, the fame of extraordinary things?
A. I don't know about this, Excellency. After all, I would see people around me, and I couldn't understand why.

Q. About his spiritual situation.
A. Excellency, please do not ask, because when it comes to judging others, I can, but if I have to talk about myself I become altogether frightened.

Q. About his prayer life. Whether he practices mental prayer daily, and for how long.
A. Usually for a couple of hours, sometimes more, sometimes less.

Q. About the method he follows in his mental prayer.
A. To prepare, I fix my mind on a subject from the life of our Lord; I develop it, and I meditate over it. I do the petition, the resolution, etc.

Q. At what times he does this meditation.
A. Usually, for about an hour, an hour and a half, in the morning, then in the evening. In addition, the meditation with the Community for a half hour every evening.

Q. About the preparation for the Holy Mass, and the thanksgiving after it.

A. The preparation, depending on the opportunity, given by the model of the ministry; the thanksgiving prayer, fifteen minutes, half an hour, depending on the circumstances.

Q. What other specific devotions he practices.

A. The whole Rosary, my habitual prayer. Then the ejaculations, etc.

Q. Do you recite the Divine Office with the Community?

A. Yes, except for the hours when I'm usually not here.

Q. Which penitential practices, if any, besides the ones prescribed communally, he performs.

A. None: I take the ones the Lord sends. I have been forbidden penitential practices, on account of my poor health.

Q. Are you particularly dedicated to studying?

A. Excellency, I am always hearing confessions. For this reason I am always keeping up to date with the necessary studies.

Q. Along which way do you think souls must be directed?

A. Along the way of virtue and of the accomplishment of one's duties.

Q. Do you think souls should be directed along extraordinary ways?

A. Yes, but only when the Lord calls them to it.

Q. How do you feel and what do you think about the ways of the spirit, about mysticism?

A. That nobody goes along that path unless the Lord himself leads him that way, by an extraordinary manifestation of his grace.

Q. Are you aware of the doctrines of the Church on this matter? Have you fully accepted them, and still do?
A. Oh, for goodness' sake! I did accept them, and still do, in full.

Q. And with respect to any other matter, any other teaching, do you intend always to submit yourself to the authority of the Holy Church, which alone can, by Divine Assistance, illuminate, direct, govern, approve, and condemn?
A. Yes, Excellency. For the Holy Church, it is God himself who speaks.

All these things, with the pertinent notes, having been read and approved, Padre Pio was dismissed, upon the oath *de secreto servando* taken on the Holy Gospels. In confirmation of everything preceding, it was signed.

P. Pio of Pietrelcina
Capuchin

Acta sunt haec per me, Visitatorem Apostolicum

L.✠S.   Br. Raphael C., Episc. Volaterr. *Visit. Apost.*

NUMBER XXI

Examination of the "Stigmata" of Padre Pio of Pietrelcina *Capuchin*

June 17, 1921

Today, at 4:30 P.M., I went to the cell occupied by the Reverend Padre Pio of Pietrelcina, and, after the oath *de veritate dicenda* he took on the Holy Gospels, in the presence of the Reverend Father Lorenzo of San Marco in Lamis, superior of the convent of San Giovanni Rotondo, I proceeded to the *examination of the wounds* that are said to be on Padre Pio's hands, feet, and chest.

Padre Pio wears woolen half-gloves on his hands. Having asked him to please take them off, I start with an *examination of the right hand*. On the palm of the right hand a large round spot can be observed, two inches in diameter, covered with—or formed by—small scabs made of bloody matter, with the edges turned up on the same side, attesting therefore their tendency to fall off. These small scabs are divided into sections, according to the lines formed by the movements of the hand.

Q. Padre Pio, about the permanence of these scabs.
A. Once these fall off, others are found to be developing.

The examination goes on. All around the spot there is something like a rose of light-colored blood that adheres to the skin—blood that obviously must disappear when washed with water, as confirmed by Padre Pio.

It is obvious that there is no lesion of the skin, no hole, either central or lateral: From this, it seems possible to infer that the blood that is visible on the hand and that coagulates in these scabs comes out of the skin itself through exudation.

Q. Padre Pio, does the blood indeed come out of the hand itself?
A. Yes.

Q. Padre Pio, do you feel any pain?
A. My whole hand is aching; the pain is stronger in the middle, inside.

Asked to please close his hand, Padre Pio does, until he makes a fist, but not clenched.

Q. Whether his difficulty in clenching his hand comes from the scabs or from the pain.
A. From the pain, which intensifies when I clench it.

*

*   *

On the back of the right hand, in the middle, there is also a round spot, smaller, about 1.4 inches in diameter, also covered with scabs, but bigger, with the edges even more turned up—they look even closer to falling off.

But the epidermis under the scabs is tougher: One can see it's less tender than on the palm—it's like a scab-like sediment, bloodier, brighter, over which lay the denser scabs, drier and more black, that are about to fall off.

All around this spot there is not the bloody rose that is observable on the palm (which is superficial and easily washable with water, as I have already said).

Here, too, in the spot on the back of the hand, there is no lesion. In the middle the scab adheres more to the skin, as if more deeply, and is almost more concave.

Q. Padre Pio, about the pain you feel.
A. Just like on the palm.

Using two fingers like calipers, with Padre Pio's hand in the middle, it appears that the center of the sore on the palm corresponds with the upper edge of the sore on the back, in a straight line.

*

*   *

Examination of the left hand. The spot on the palm has a diameter of two inches; the one on the back 1.6 inches.

The characteristics are identical to those of the right hand, therefore it is not necessary to repeat a description: Only, the scab on the back is almost more adherent and recessed— not in the middle, but at the lower edge.

With the "calipers", the center of the sore on the palm coincides in a straight line with the upper edge of the sore on the back, as above.

*

*   *

Examination of the right foot. Padre Pio wears socks and shoes. Once the foot is uncovered, on the upper side there is something like a rosette, of about one inch in diameter, with no trace of blood, neither recently flowed, nor long ago. To clarify: Let's imagine a closed wound, fully healed, over which a more delicate and whiter skin has grown: Such is the sign that appears on the upper side of this right foot.

Q. Padre Pio, does blood drip out of this sign, and do scabs form on it?
A. Sometimes there are droplets of blood; sometimes there are very small scabs that have never even turned black.

On the sole, in the middle, a rosette is observed of a 0.6-inch diameter. Here, too, no trace of blood. Actually, it is covered with a thin layer of almost callous skin about to come off, since its edge is turned up all around. This rosette must have been slightly bigger in the past, because above the current upper edge, formed by the aforementioned callous skin, at a distance of about a fifth of an inch, there is a strip of a similarly callous skin: In the interstice, the skin is new, fresh, and white. Therefore, once that callous skin that is now visible falls off, it seems that there should remain no trace of special signs.

The "calipers" with two fingers cannot be done well, but it seems that the center of the rosette on the upper side of the foot corresponds directly to the center of the one on the sole.

Q. Padre Pio, about the pain.
A. Just like in the hands.

*
*   *

Examination of the left foot. On the upper side, there is a rosette just like on the right foot. It looks like a healed wound over which new skin has formed, slightly colored, under the epidermis, in a light shade of purple. This new skin is covered at some points with a superficial film that is falling off.

Under the sole, just like under the right foot, but the callous film is almost completely fallen off, so the outline isn't perfectly recognizable anymore; and, once it will have come off completely, it seems that no trace of special signs will remain.

The "calipers" examination yields the same results.

Q. Padre Pio, about the pain.
A. Just like in the hands and in the other foot.

Q. Whether he can walk easily.
A. I don't always experience the same fatigue. I cannot stand up for long because of the internal pain.

*
*   *

Examination of the chest. [In the original document, here on the side the Apostolic Visitor draws the image of the sore on the chest, as he saw it. (Brackets in Ital. ed.)] On the left side, 1.2 inches from the last rib, there is a triangular spot (like the one shown in the drawing), whose side measures about 0.8 inches, the color of red wine. There are no openings, cuts, wounds. About 2.8 inches above it, there are other small, scattered spots, as shown in the drawing, but small: the last one, on top, slightly bigger.

Q. Padre Pio, does blood come out of this sign?
A. From time to time, not always. When the bleeding is most intense it can soak a whole handkerchief.

Considering the absence of wounds, it can be justifiably supposed that the blood comes out through exudation.

Q. Padre Pio, has this sign always looked like this?
A. More or less the same, as far as I know: I've never really observed it.

Q. Whether anywhere on his person, on the chest, on the back he may have other similar signs, eczema, etc.
A. No, I never had.

Having read and approved all of this, Padre Pio took, on the Holy Gospel, the oath *de secreto servando* concerning this examination. In confirmation of everything preceding, it was signed.

P. Pio of Pietrelcina
Cap.

In turn, the Reverend Father Lorenzo of San Marco in Lamis, touching the Holy Gospel, swore on the truthfulness of this report, the result of the examination at which he was present, and on the faithfulness of the minutes, and under oath he bound himself *ad secretum servandum*. In confirmation of everything, it was signed.

Fr. Lorenzo of S. Marco in Lamis
Capuchin Superior

Acta sunt haec per me, Visitatorem Apostolicum

L.✠S.   Br. Raphael C., Episc. Volaterr. *Visit. Apost.*

NUMBER XXII

Fourth Deposition of Padre Pio of Pietrelcina *Capuchin*

June 17, 1921—7 P.M.

Following the examination of the sores that appear on the person of *Padre Pio of Pietrelcina*, before me, the undersigned Apostolic Visitor, has remained the said Padre, who, having taken the oath *de veritate dicenda* on the Holy Gospels, so stated, testified, and answered.

Q. Whether he needs to revise anything in his previous depositions.
A. No, neither to add nor to take out.

Q. You said you dedicate more than two hours to prayer. How is it possible, with so many audiences and confessions?
A. I try to do it in the morning, before leaving my room; then during the day, whenever I have time.

Q. What time he gets up.
A. I set the alarm clock for 4:30 A.M.

Q. Whether, while praying, he follows closely the structure of the meditation, or is inclined to change subjects, etc.
A. Ordinarily, I do follow the order, but sometimes it happens that something, some truth will strike me more, and I stay there, like someone who admires an object that is more striking than others.

Q. Whether, while praying, he keeps the notion of place, time, of his following duties, etc.
A. Usually yes—sometimes I don't have a perception of the place, the time, or of what is around me, all that could be defined as external.

Q. Is it easy for you to start praying, or do you need time to concentrate? Is it easy for you to stop praying, or do you need to make an effort, or does the time available for prayer fly?
A. Ordinarily I don't find it too hard to concentrate on the subject. I do stop gently, usually, but I sense the desire, a deep, spontaneous, genuine desire to stay.

Q. During your prayer, does anything mystical happen to you? E.g., visions . . .
A. Yes. Visions of heavenly persons.

Q. Whether they are intellectual visions, or physical.
A. Intellectual visions, through the eyes of the intellect.

Q. Do these things happen often during your prayer, ordinarily, or as isolated episodes?
A. As isolated episodes.

Q. During an earlier deposition you stated that since 1911–1912 you started feeling pain in the areas where the sores later appeared. From 1911–1912 until 1908 [1918], were these pains intermittent, continuous, or quasi-continuous?
A. They were intermittent, because there were breaks. They generally happened from Thursday evening through Saturday morning, and occasionally on Tuesdays, too.

Q. Did anyone know about these pains?
A. I believe the director did, but I certainly don't recall what precisely he knew explicitly. A few other people did, too, like the pastor of my hometown, who learned it from the director—and I think I confirmed it to him, if not explicitly. While I was home on account of my poor health, the pastor would ask for my help, e.g., for some funeral processions: The director informed him so that he refrained from asking for my help on the days I have said I was in pain.

Q. Is it true what they say, that one day, while you were hearing confessions in the sacristy, it was so crowded that you came out of the confessional stepping over everyone's heads?
A. It happened this way. I was hearing confessions in the sacristy, on a raised area; the sacristy was overcrowded with men; it was hot; we were suffocating: they screamed and squalled asking for help. I saw that the best thing to do was to leave, because once the confessor left, they, too, would come out. I finished the confession of the first one who happened to be there; I remember—I think I can say this with certainty—that I couldn't go down the steps, because they were occupied: I had to step over those men—at least the first ones—then I found myself outside, and I turned to send them away.

Q. The iodine that you used, did you use it to stop the bleeding or to disinfect?
A. To stop the bleeding.

Q. Did you use it on all of the sores?

A. Yes, and also on the feet and on my chest. I didn't even know whether it would work. I saw others use this medication, when they happened to cut themselves, to stop the bleeding.

Q. It appears that, when you requested the carbolic acid, you really requested it in secret, from your Brothers, too, to administer injections to the students.

A. I'll repeat what I have already testified—that the secret was requested to conceal from those who would transport it that it was a dangerous medicine: It didn't concern my Brothers. The purpose, yes, was to disinfect the syringe for the injections, which I, too, know how to administer. In a boarding school for boys there is often such necessity.

All these things having been read and approved, Padre Pio was dismissed upon the oath *de secreto servando* taken on the Holy Gospels. In confirmation of everything, it was signed.

P. Pio of Pietrelcina, Cap.

Acta sunt haec per me, Visitatorem Apostolicum

L.✠S.   Br. Raphael C., Episc. Volaterr. *Visit. Apost.*

NUMBER XXIII

Fifth Deposition of **Padre Pio of Pietrelcina** *Capuchin*

June 17, 1921—9 P.M.

Before me, the undersigned Apostolic Visitor, has again appeared, summoned, *the Reverend Padre Pio of Pietrelcina,* who, having taken the oath *de veritate dicenda* on the Holy Gospels, so testified and answered.

Q. Whether you need to revise anything in your previous deposition.
A. No.

Q. Whether you have ever suffered from nervous disorders, hysteria, etc.
A. By the grace of God, no.

Q. How long has it been, precisely, since you have put anything on the sores?
A. The iodine, two years; less for the starch glycerolate: Once it was applied by the Father Provincial himself, because I was bleeding.

Q. Why, in some letters, he has addressed women, even religious, as *tu.*
A. Always the same: I hardly ever use *lei*: I use *tu* and *voi* indifferently.

Q. When news of extraordinary things concerning Your Paternity started spreading, some women, who seemed to know, when asked for information would answer that they couldn't talk, since *silence* had been imposed on them. By whom? Why?
A. I might have done it myself, because it would have been humiliating for me if they had talked—at least this has always been my feeling.

Q. Is it true that, despite the Father Provincial forbidding private conversations in the guest quarters, they went on nonetheless?

A. Yes, because I spoke to the Father Provincial, who said: "For now you can continue them." Nevertheless, I've tried to eliminate them as far as possible.

At this point I, the undersigned Visitor, despite the oath already taken by the Reverend Padre Pio, again remind him of the sanctity of such religious act. I call to his attention the gravity of the matter, and I ask him what he thinks of the oath itself. And he answers: "It's the most solemn act a man may perform, since it means to call upon God to be witness of the truth."

That said, I invite him to answer, under the sanctity of a special oath, the following questions, one at a time, with him kneeling down and keeping his hands on the Holy Gospel:

— Does Your Paternity swear on the Holy Gospel that he has never made use of perfumes, and that he is not using them now on your person?

And Padre Pio swears, adding that, even regardless of his being a religious, he has always found their use revolting.

— Does Your Paternity swear on the Holy Gospel that he has not, directly or indirectly, produced, nurtured, cultivated, grown, preserved the signs he bears on the hands, his feet, and his chest?

A. I swear.

— Does Your Paternity swear on the Holy Gospel that he has never made use of dermatography on his person, that is, that he has never, on account of a sort of autosuggestion, made signs that could then appear visible depending on fixations or obsessions?

A. I swear, for goodness' sake, for goodness' sake! Quite the contrary, if the Lord relieved me of them, how grateful I would be!

Q. Do you confirm your faith in everything the Holy Church believes and teaches, do you condemn everything the Holy Church condemns, and do you intend to be always a devout son, obedient to the Church?
A. Yes, everything. I mean to swear it, and I do.

And Padre Pio swears this on the Holy Gospel, by his own explicit request.

All these things having been read and approved, Padre Pio was dismissed, upon the oath *de secreto servando* taken on the Holy Gospels. In confirmation of everything, it was signed.

P. Pio of Pietrelcina, Cap.

Acta sunt haec per me, Visitatorem Apostolicum

L.✠S.   Br. Raphael C., Episc. Volaterr. *Visit. Apost.*

NUMBER XXIV

Sixth Deposition of **Padre Pio of Pietrelcina** *Capuchin*

June 20, 1921—4:30 P.M.

Before me, the undersigned Apostolic Visitor, has appeared, summoned, the *Reverend Padre Pio of Pietrelcina*, who, having taken the oath *de veritate dicenda* on the Holy Gospels, so testified and stated.

Q. Whether he needs to revise anything in his previous deposition.
A. No.

Q. Whether he confirms the episode he has already testified about, of having found himself with Mrs. Massa of San Giovanni Rotondo, who was ill, though remaining in the convent.
A. Yes, I confirm it.

Q. But it appears that this episode should rather be ascribed to a hallucinatory state of said lady, in the agitation caused by her illness.
A. I won't discuss of the state of this lady. I'm only saying I was there.

Q. Is it true that, in a similar case, while you were in the convent, you found yourself one day in Foggia, with the lieutenant general commanding the military division?
A. Excellency, I don't think so—I don't have any memory of this.

Q. It was also alleged that you went to see this general to complain that some soldiers were disturbing a convent, or because they had been stationed in a convent.
A. Excellency, I do not remember.

Q. So how do you explain that one of your Brothers of that time allegedly said: "This is positive, since Padre Pio himself told a devout woman: 'I took a trip', but didn't want to say where."
A. Excellency, I don't know anything about this. There has been recklessness on the part of some who wanted to use my name for things I would have never dreamed of either saying or revealing. It was crazy, and I have to thank the Lord that the greatest grace I know I received concerning this matter, was indeed the grace not to lose my mind and my health, so numerous were the lies that were told.

Q. But didn't you try to counter this "recklessness" and clarify the truth?

A. Some cases may have been true—but I wouldn't have wanted to see them talked about—and strangers learn about them. Whenever I did know of something, I never failed to raise my voice, as far as it was possible for me to do so: After all, of many of these things that were said to be true, or even made up, the last one to know, or the one who knew the least, was myself.

Q. Do you confirm that you happened to find yourself with some sick people far away, and to have heard their confession, all while staying in the convent?

A. I don't recall this at all.

Q. Is it true that one time you assured a young Brother that he would never again fall out of God's grace?

A. I don't remember this specific episode, but I wouldn't rule it out, since similar cases have happened to me many, many times. But my words should be intended not in the sense of a moral certainty, but in the sense of using the means, and of taking advantage of the graces, thanks to which we can stay away from sin. If I have used similar words with someone, they weren't isolated, but I used them as consequence of other assumptions.

[Here, in the original document the text of the question is missing. Padre Pio's answer follows.]

A. Yes—[and here Padre Pio has a good laugh]—at times something crosses my mind, and to express it I think that way, and the words just come to my lips.

Q. Do you know Greek?

A. I studied it a little, but now I don't even remember how to read it.

Q. Is it true that, without knowing this language sufficiently well, you once wrote a letter using it?

A. A letter, I don't think so: at most, some greetings, fruit of the kind of knowledge I had.

Q. And is it true that you received a letter all stained? And that the crucifix was put on it?

A. Yes—I was home—a letter written in French by my then-director. And it was the pastor of my hometown who put the crucifix on it.

Q. There has been much talk about many healings that happened through and were implored by Your Paternity with your prayers. But actually, it appears they don't hold true. Can Your Paternity recall some true, certain, complete healings?

A. I have prayed, yes: They know the outcome, not I.

Q. Is it true that in the case of two mute young women you promised them a grace for a certain day—Holy Saturday— then, since it wasn't obtained that day, you promised it for another day, and on like this for several times?

A. No, no, no: It was they, those involved, who at that time tried to say one thing and then the opposite. But who ever made them this promise? Even from a human point of view, who would want to make such a promise without any certainty?

Q. But did Your Paternity hear what was said about you? And what did you do? What did you say?

A. I only said: "Pray." They said: "On such and such day you must grant us the grace—we'll be waiting for it." I would add: "You can't give God deadlines."

Q. And did you ever say anything about your dying at age thirty-three, etc.?
A. Not in the slightest. Thank goodness that it's not up to man to decide about his death—after all, who knows where I should be now!! . . .

Q. But what did Your Paternity think when hundreds and thousands of people would flood in? What was your attitude?
A. I was terrified. I tried to listen to everyone as far as possible, and to work. Even in the Community we were invaded. We had to resort to the *Carabinieri*.

Q. But what did these people say? For what reason did they come?
A. "We need to go to confession."

Q. When the Community was gradually changed, was Your Paternity sorry?
A. A little sadness between Brothers is indeed felt—finding yourself in a new environment—but then, of course, I resigned myself to the will of God. I would say: "Lord, if this is best for me and the others."

Q. Regarding the women assisting you while you were ill in the infirmary, do you confirm what you have already testified? Did it seem to you that sometimes they would fail to be prudent, truthful, discreet?
A. Yes, I confirm. That they failed, oh no, this no.

Q. Regarding the celebration [of the Holy Mass] at 10 A.M.. Why not celebrate earlier?
A. There is also a physical reason, which it would be inconvenient for me to state. But it's obvious that if the superior wants to arrange things differently. . .

Q. Why do you take so much time for the Consecration, especially of the chalice? Do you repeat the words?
A. I try to enter deeply into the mystery, to recollect myself, but I do not repeat the words of the formula at all.

Q. Could Your Paternity explain to me why there is a difference between the signs he has on his hands and those on his feet, which seem cicatrized.
A. They don't always keep the same appearance: At times they are more noticeable, at times less so; sometimes they look like they are about to disappear, but they don't, and then come back, flourishing again. And this happens to all the signs, including the one on the side.

Q. Some say that other signs appear on your forehead, too.
A. (laughing) Oh, for the love of God! What do you want me to answer! Sometimes I've found some small blisters on my forehead or my head, but I never gave them any thought, and I certainly never dreamed of telling anyone! . . .

Q. In conclusion, do you confirm once more, under the sanctity of the oath, all and each of the depositions taken during these past few days, especially with regard to the so-called scent and the signs on your person?
A. Yes, Excellency.

All of this having been read and approved, Padre Pio was dismissed upon the oath *de secreto servando* taken on the Holy Gospels. In confirmation of everything, it was signed.

P. Pio of Pietrelcina

Acta sunt haec per me, Visitatorem Apostolicum

L.✠S.   Br. Raphael C., Episc. Volaterr. *Visit. Apost.*

NUMBER XXV

Chronological Order of the Sessions

Number	Date	Time	Deposition of:	Order in the Compendium
1	June 14, 1921	9 P.M.	Canon Archpriest Prencipe	1
2	June 15, 1921	8:30 A.M.	Same as above	2
3	June 15, 1921	5 P.M.	Padre Pio	18
4	June 15, 1921	7 P.M.	Same as above	19
5	June 16, 1921	9 A.M.	Fr. Lorenzo, Superior	6
6	June 16, 1921	10 A.M.	Fr. Ignazio	9
7	June 16, 1921	4:30 P.M.	Padre Pio	20
8	June 17, 1921	8 A.M.	Fr. Luigi	11
9	June 17, 1921	10 A.M.	Fr. Lorenzo, Superior	7
10	June 17, 1921	11:30 A.M.	Fr. Ignazio	10
11	June 17, 1921	4:30 P.M.	Examination of the Stigmata	21
12	June 17, 1921	7 P.M.	Padre Pio	22
13	June 17, 1921	9 P.M.	Same as above	23
14	June 18, 1921	7:30 A.M.	Fr. Romolo	13
15	June 18, 1921	11 A.M.	Fr. Lodovico	15
16	June 18, 1921	4:30 P.M.	Can. Archpr. Prencipe	3
17	June 18, 1921	7 P.M.	Can. Palladino	4
18	June 19, 1921	8 A.M.	Fr. Luigi	12
19	June 19, 1921	10 A.M.	Fr. Pietro, Provincial	16
20	June 19, 1921	5 P.M.	Can. Palladino	5
21	June 20, 1921	7:30 A.M.	Fr. Romolo	14
22	June 20, 1921	8:30 A.M.	Fr. Cherubino	17
23	June 20, 1921	11 A.M.	Fr. Lorenzo, Superior	8
24	June 20, 1921	4:30 P.M.	Padre Pio	24

NUMBER XXVI

Letter of Padre Pio to the Religious **Sister Giovanna Longo** *Brigittine Nun,* **Via delle Isole, Roma**

1-26-20[4]

My ever-dearest daughter,

May Jesus always be all yours, may he look upon you with benevolent eyes, may he assist you always and in everything with his vigilant grace, and may he make you more and more dear to his Divine Heart. With these most sincere wishes that I express to you assiduously before Jesus, I'll now come to answer your latest, which pleased me exceedingly, on account of the divine operation in you. For this I give much thanks to God, and I beg him to continue *his divine operations.* In the meantime, do not be afraid of what is happening in you. *The one and only cause is God*; nothing evil will happen to you if you will continue to submit yourself humbly, patiently and confidently to his divine operations. Be reassured *about the strange phenomenon that occurred to you on the night of the eleventh of this month. The cause was indeed the one you yourself have imagined.* Admire, marvel, and give God the due thanksgiving.

You would like to know who is causing you to suffer joyfully so much, and to complain about what you ardently desire; to feel intoxicated in your suffering and to endure it with utmost distress! Don't you know that God alone can reconcile the opposites in a soul, and make *in pace amaritudo tua amarissima?* Therefore, let Love exercise his sublime and terrible eccentricities. Also, I urge you to confer every once in a while with the Most Reverend Father Benedetto about your spiritual life. *I want it, and that's it, and nothing*

---

[4] It must be 21 (1921), as shown by the postmark.

bad will happen to you. This suggestion must not create in you the suspicion that I didn't want to give you always a full and total spiritual direction, or that I had doubts about the divine operations in your spirit: On the contrary, it must generate and confirm in you the just conviction that your spirit will be much benefited by such advice. Did I make myself clear? If I didn't know the goodness and the sound doctrine of the aforementioned Father, I would have never advised you to do what I have so far described. As for what you say *in your letter* regarding me, I'd like to be convinced, but in vain. Pray to Jesus that he give me some reflected light and lift me from this extreme *suffering*, which I am bearing for him—as long as this is the best for me. To tell you the truth, my dear daughter, I cannot breathe with this *tremendous burden* oppressing me. And I also realize that this enormous burden falling heavily upon my soul is a great annoyance in the spiritual direction of souls—and may it not be the will of God that I am an obstacle to the advancement of these souls.

After all, if from all I feel I must infer that I should refrain from spiritual direction, he should let me know, and I will bow before the divine will.

My respects to the Reverend Mother Superior, the Reverend Mistress of the Novices, and to all the other religious, and tell them to recommend me to the Divine Mercy—I always do the same for them. Give my regards to my sister, and I impart my fatherly blessing on you and her.

P. Pio Cap.

Acta sunt haec per me, Visitatorem Apostolicum

L.✠S.   Br. Raphael C., Episc. Volaterr. *Visit. Apost.*

NUMBER XXVII

Questions Posed to Padre Pio in Relation to the Preceding Letter, and His Answers

1. Whether the Reverend Padre Pio of Pietrelcina acknowledges having written and sent the letter of which a copy is attached, transcribed word by word from the original, a letter starting with the words: "May Jesus always be, etc.", and ending: "I impart my fatherly blessing on you".

Ans.[hereafter *Answer*] Padre Pio of Pietrelcina acknowledges that he himself wrote and sent the letter, of which a copy was attached for him, transcribed from the original, starting with the words: "May Jesus always be, etc.", and ending: "I impart my fatherly blessing on you."

2. What are the so-called "divine operations" that were to happen or were happening in the person to whom the letter was addressed?

Answer. The aforementioned Padre doesn't remember what the so-called "divine operations" are that were to happen or were happening in the person to whom he addressed the letter, so much time having passed since he wrote such letter, and not knowing the letter the person had addressed to him.

3. On what does the Reverend Padre Pio base—or did he base—his assertion that of such "operations" the "one and only cause is God".

Answer. The aforementioned Padre, although he does not know the letter mentioned above and remembers neither the content nor the specific facts, answers in all good conscience that he rests his assertions on assured criteria inferred from truthful doctrines, approved by H[oly] M[other] Church, and from his personal knowledge of this soul, having guided, directed, and heard her confessions for several years.

4. What did "the strange phenomenon" that occurred on the night between January 11 and January 12, 1920, to

the person to whom the letter was addressed, consist of? Provide a precise and detailed explanation.

Answer. Padre Pio has absolutely no memory of what was told to him in the letter this person sent him; therefore he cannot give any explanation concerning what is asked to him.

5. What would have been the cause of this "strange phenomenon", according to the person to whom it allegedly happened.

Answer. Padre Pio answers as above, that is, that he does not remember anything.

6. How can the Reverend Padre Pio confirm that the cause "was indeed th[at]".

Answer. Padre Pio cannot answer this question, since in order to answer he would have to be able to recall the event that was related to him.

7. In urging the Religious, to whom the letter was addressed, to confer every once in a while with the Most Reverend Father Benedetto about her spiritual life, Padre Pio added: "I want it, and that's it, and nothing bad will happen to you." What "bad" things were feared might come from this direction?

Answer. Padre Pio, in urging the Religious, to whom the letter was addressed, to confer every once in a while with the Most Reverend Father Benedetto about her spiritual life, assuring the sister that nothing bad come to her from such direction, said this to remove from her heart the fear that she might be not well understood by that Father as far as her spiritual life was concerned. And Padre Pio told her not to fear anything in this regard, since that Father also had known her before she entered the cloister.

8. To what "suffering" and to what "tremendous burden" is the Most Rev. Padre Pio alluding toward the end of the letter?

Answer. At that time Padre Pio found himself in a great spiritual aridity, and under a tremendous temptation, coming from Satan, which advised him not to worry about the good of others.

9. Does the Most Reverend Padre Pio still keep the Religious' letter mentioned in the letter attached here as a copy? In case of affirmative answer, produce it.

Answer. Padre Pio does not keep the Religious' letter at all.

I swear on the Holy Gospels that everything I have said above in answering the questions fully conforms to the truth, and under the sanctity of the same oath I affirm and declare that I will maintain inviolable the secret of the Holy Office concerning everything.

San Giovanni Rotondo, August, 1921

P. Pio of Pietrelcina Cap.

The answers above and the final declaration are all written by the hand of Padre Pio.

Acta sunt haec per me, Visitatorem Apostolicum

L.✠S.   Br. Raphael C., Episc. Volaterr. *Visit. Apost.*

APPENDIX

Father Benedetto of San Marco in Lamis, Capuchin

1. It really is *per accidens*, and I am not sure whether it is part of my task, that I will make a very brief mention of this Father, who it is suspected had so much influence on Padre Pio's morale, that he even caused—through suggestion and unwittingly—the "stigmata"!

2. I have already discussed this suspicion elsewhere in this document, and I think I was able to dispel it, but I could not help noticing that perhaps Father Benedetto, for all his good will and his virtues—he was described to me as a superb religious—and for all his doctrine, is not the *ideal* [spiritual] director to instruct in the ways of mysticism.

3. Why? Just a very few words. I include in the compendium copies of letters Father Benedetto addressed to Padre Pio. Now, from these examples, to my own reserved judgment it appears that Father Benedetto's mysticism is the following:

    a. Too *elegiac*. It's all a sigh, a crying without cease. And mysticism, true mysticism, is not like that: It's more confident, more serene, more joyous, because it is more elevated.

    b. *Curious.* Father Benedetto wants the Lord to speak: He insists that Padre Pio ask him about public flagellations and about the special conditions of Father Benedetto's own soul; and then he must write back, and report Heaven's answers, but immediately, and thoroughly, by virtue of obedience. How much more reserved with the Lord are the ways of the true mystics!

c. *Intrusive.* With what anxiety did Father Benedetto seek in Rome the authorization *ad confessiones* for the religious! And how much he desired the appointment as extraordinary in the religious houses, where he would be able to find "mystical" souls to direct! And when he met a resisting soul (among the Brigittine nuns), how he begged Padre Pio that he use his authority to bring the daughters to the Father! And when, in the same convent, he was met by an energetic Mother Superior, how angry he was at this obstinate woman! . . .

Were the true mystics like this? Did they consider themselves mystics? Did they elevate themselves as teachers? Did they stubbornly want to be one at all costs? Did they seek souls to direct?

d. If to all of this is added what I was told during the Apostolic Visitation, and which turns out to be true anyway—that Father Benedetto, for all his science and experience, is too *credulous*, too *enthusiastic* before anything that appears to be extraordinary and supernatural—it may also be said that his "mysticism" *is not prudent*, and therefore is not good mysticism.

4. Given all this, whoever has the authority will be able to decide what is necessary to be done, and on a more informed basis. *It may be good to limit his activities, especially where, on account of his excessive zeal, he can lead to spiritual*

confusion (there are examples in monasteries in Rome); *to watch over his publications; to recall him from the heights of "mysticism" down to the more simple ways of asceticism, for his own good and for the souls he directs.* Also, if this can be suggested to him the right way, *he might also be told (but an explicit mention might be even more fruitful) which system he will adopt in the future in directing, in person or in writing, Padre Pio of Pietrelcina.*

† Br. R. C. *Bishop*

COMPENDIUM OF THE APPENDIX

Examples of Correspondence
of the Reverend Father Benedetto
of San Marco in Lamis, Capuchin,
Addressed to the Reverend Padre Pio
of Pietrelcina, Capuchin
(years 1913–1921)

1

San Marco, Feast of the Pardon of Assisi
[August 2] 1913

Breviter [In short]. Father Benedetto alludes to a soul who makes revelations regarding him [Father Benedetto]; he says he has many and serious proofs of the goodness of this soul. (N.B. Another letter also mentions this same soul.)

2

San Marco la Catola, March 9, 1916

My dearest son,

I wish I could say you are right, but I cannot, because I would insult the truth. As your superior and confessor, I would be under the strictest obligation to condemn you and admonish you, all or in part, if there were illusions, deceit, and faults. It is also my duty to discharge my conscience, to confirm to you God's abandonment, or the risk to deserve it when there would be reason to believe it so: This way I would set you on the road to repentance and to returning to him.

You certainly cannot think, therefore, that I, established as an external and internal judge of a soul, may want, in order to console it, to pronounce a sentence not consistent with the truth, and to lull it into a sleep that would be fatal for its eternal destiny. In this sense, charity would be nothing but deadly hate, and mercy heartless cruelty.

Unless, then, you think I am merciless, you must accept my assurances and consider them an oath. Neither are you allowed to suppose that I judge lightly, and without that deep conviction generated by an insight that the divine Goodness and Wisdom do not deny to the ministers who are called to act on their behalf on earth; otherwise, I would be a fool in guiding you without knowing the path God has in mind for you. Keep calm, therefore, and believe—at least with the tip of your spirit and as much as you can— what I told you and am repeating.

The night in which you are immersed and lost is a most painful trial, but supremely sweet because of its benefits to the spirit. Its purpose is to reduce the human will to silence, so that the divine will can take its place—and you, stripped of the common way of thinking and of an ordinary exercise of your mental faculties, may be able to ascend to the one that is purely supernatural and celestial.

Therefore it is easy to argue that you can not only hope that God's returning to the soul, but that he is already operating in you with an action whose strength and effectiveness equal his intense love for you.

To the exquisite purpose I just mentioned you must also ascribe the difficulty experienced in believing, which sometimes looks like infidelity in the matter of things revealed.

With this darkness God wants to prepare you for the most spiritual vision of his beauty and greatness.

The phenomenon experienced in your heart becomes a touch or a unitive embrace, and the Lord gave it to you as a gift to comfort you so you could face the subsequent storm you described to me.

The awareness of your indignity is a healthy insight, and we will have it perfect once in holy Paradise. But it does not come from actual guilt, rather, from the revelation you have of how miserable man is without grace. There is no guilt: If there were infirmities, you should take pride in them with the Apostle to the Gentiles, without distrust or fear of being abandoned.

Do not worry about distinguishing between good and evil—it's useless. Whenever you will act according to the rules, to your confessor's advice, and in obedience to the superior, be infallibly certain that you will do good, even if you are not able to recognize it as such.

3

San Marco, August 17, 1916

The impetus of wanting to be in eternal peace is a good thing, but must be moderated: It's better to do the divine will on earth than to enjoy Paradise. To suffer and not to die. Purgatory is sweet when we suffer for the love of God. As for the other trials, they are all signs of divine predilection and gems for the soul [...] Rest assured that internal battles are not a danger to fidelity, but an occasion for gaining precious merits, bearing the names of crown and laurel.*

---

* Bracketed ellipses indicate omissions of text. Suspension of thought points were in the original letters.

4

San Marco, December 2, 1916

The temptations of blasphemy, of despair, etc., are wares offered by the enemy, but they are rejected, therefore they're not an evil. If the devil makes a din, it's a very good sign: What is terrifying is peace and harmony within the human soul.

5

San Marco, August 6, 1917

In your conscience, from the moment you acquired the use of reason until now, there have never been mortal sins or grave ingratitude—and I'm telling you this with full authority and knowledge. If, therefore, you happen to have the vision of a sinful and ungrateful life, to the point of deserving at times the wrath of God and of having mortally offended him, this vision is false and therefore diabolical, and the suffering that it causes cannot be attributed to anything but the same cause: It must be despised and avoided.

If, on the other hand, the agony is produced by the awareness of failings and small, involuntary faults—so much so that they're not even venial—in your past life, and this on account of the understanding of the infinite fidelity that we owe to God, then the cause is the Holy Spirit. But even in this case the agony cannot be considered as an atoning suffering, but as a transfiguring suffering—that is, of delicate love.

6

San Marco, August 28, 1917

My dearest Piuccio,

Not much longer, and you will be consoled. Offer up to God this current trial, to spare me and many others similar martyrdoms. Sacrifice the crucified Love on the altar of the heart and you will find the comfort you desire. I can imagine your desolation, and I wish I could console you, but whoever could take a soul away from the Almighty's grip? As for your internal suffering, try to comfort yourself by thinking of my repeated assurances: Your Lord is not your enemy—the Lord's aim is toward making your spirit grow.

Is Heaven still quiet? Will he really break a bruised reed, or quench a smoldering wick? No, it's impossible, and in the name of obedience interrogate him again, and write his answer to me promptly.

Recommend this soul that cries over universal desolation, and especially the desolation of our poor province. I bless you.

7

San Marco, September 22, 1917

You cannot, you must not die as a soldier: You'll never have me ask this obedience of you [. . .]

Do not be troubled by the suffering of your spirit: It's a cross willed by Divine Love, and nothing else. Do not be frightened by the darkness. Have faith in what I often told you in person and in writing [. . .] Ah, how bitter my soul is! Don't you have a word or a ray of hope to offer me that will sustain me in such agony? How can you see a Father so afflicted, and not say at least that we're at the beginning of the end? Will Israel be destroyed? My dear son, dispel now this nightmare that is crushing me, and speak clearly, precisely, and positively.

8

San Marco la Catola,
October 14, 1917

My dearest Piuccio,

I've received your latest, in which you tell me you have a fever: I hope the Lord will soon free you from the hard trial he let happen for his own adorable purposes, and perhaps to save other Brothers [...] My dear son, how much I wish I could be by your side to comfort you. But I trust that at the end of the month we will see each other again in San Giovanni Rotondo. I order you, by virtue of holy obedience, to ask the Lord for this grace.

For now I'll tell you that moral depressions are a tool of the devil, while there's nothing that should make you afraid and discouraged: I assure you of this, in the fullness of my authority as a superior and director. Do not fear darkness, because in it God speaks to you—and do not fear the internal martyrdom, which is an effect of your love and a sign of love on the part of the Supreme Good. Be sure then of my assertion, and don't dither for anything ...

If the time is right, let me know about the end of the flagellation: I beg you with tears in my eyes.

9

June 7, 1918

[It is] not Justice, but the crucified Love that crucifies you
and wants to unite you with his most loving/bitter suffering, with no comfort and no other support than desolate
anxieties. Justice has nothing to vindicate in you, but in
others, and you, as a victim, owe on behalf of your brothers what is still lacking in Jesus Christ's Passion . . .

I'll repeat that the Lord is with you, and it is Him
who, for love, is hanging you on the harsh gallows of his
Cross.

10

San Marco, August 27, 1918

[N]o dereliction, no avenging justice, no unworthiness on
your part deserving of rejection and condemnation. All that
is happening in you is the consequence of love; it is a trial,
it is a vocation to co-redemption, and therefore it is a source
of glory. Once this is given for certain and undoubted, the
anxiety disappears, as well as the agitation that the enemy
causes for his evil delight in tormenting, and that the Supreme
Good permits, for the above-mentioned purpose.

To declare yourself *a thorn* tormenting our loving Lord,
and to acknowledge such unworthiness as a self-evident,
shining reality that leaves no room even to the shadow of
the opposite, is a solemn lie, a scene painted in vivid and
bright colors presented to you by the valiant artist of darkness, who is as nefarious as he is excellent at highlighting
his paintings with a strong chiaroscuro. It is *absolutely* not

true that you responded badly to grace, and that you caused with your infidelity a distancing from God, the rejection of his embrace, and an irreconcilable enmity. *Dominus tecum.* He—the patient love, suffering, restless, broken down, beaten and with his heart and insides wrenched, in the shadows of the night, and even more so in the desolation of the Gethsemane garden—is united with you in your pain, and unites you with his. That's all, this is the truth and only the truth. Yours isn't a purge, either, but a *painful union.*

The fact of the wound completes your passion just as it completed that of the Loved One on the Cross. Might the light and joy of the Resurrection follow? I hope so, if he so likes. Kiss the hand that transverberated you and most tenderly embrace this sore which is a mark of love.

11

San Marco, October 18, 1918

My dear son, tell me *everything* clearly and in detail. What is the operation of that person? Whence does the blood flow, and how many times a day or a week? What happened to your hands and feet, and how? I want to know everything with precision and in virtue of holy obedience.

On what do you base your laments? How can you say your spirit does not know God if your heart bleeds with love that is most strong in sweetness and most sweet in violence? And how can you call yourself abandoned if God torments you with love? [. . .]

Alas, I am in great fear for my soul. I think God is making calamities roar around me, and I am the cause for the most part [. . .]

12

San Marco, Feast of Saint Stephen, 1918

My dearest Piuccio, I didn't understand clearly which darkness you mean, which, as you say, enfolds you. While the Infinite Love in the immensity of its strength pouring itself in the small vase of your existence makes you experience the impossibility of containing it—so that you feel conquered and annulled—what does the darkness mean? Do you mean the darkness of not being able to understand or explain the operation going on in you, or a darkness that precedes and accompanies the operation itself? I believe it must be the confusion of your spirit fallen prey to the transports of the infinite Charity. Be precise then when writing to me, and do not veil the reality of those loving events with words that somehow hide their beauty.

The preparatory suffering is almost over in you, and all you have to do is subject yourself to the necessary martyrdom of feeling unable, while carrying it, to bear the weight of an immense love. Tell me then simply about the phases of this love, of its most sweet embraces and transports, since there's no point in talking about anything else. Always tell me everything, and often. What is the pain in your heart that pierces it like a lance? It's the completion of the crucifixion: Jesus was not only nailed, but transfixed by a lance. If blood should flow out of it, you will dip a white bandage in it, and you will send it to me by certified mail.

13

San Marco, November 13, 1919

The doubt assailing you sometimes that you are not in the grace of God, and therefore he doesn't listen to your wailing, has no ground, since it's impossible that the soul be in agony, tormented by zeal for the divine glory and the salvation of its brothers, without having charity as its cause, support, and life [. . .]

As I told you already, you are at the last stage, even though you are not yet perfectly out of the previous one. Take heart—a little longer, and the consummating baptism will come.

I recommend to you the utmost docility in obedience, to which everything must yield, even the dearest feelings and charity itself. I would also like to see more courage in warning the Brothers around you about their sometimes grave flaws. So much was wasted there, so many infractions to our holy customs, and you never spoke up: You didn't even report to me the things you noticed, which were certainly displeasing to God. In particular, do you think it is a good thing for Father Placido to stay there, against the orders given, leaving Father Paolino teaching alone, while the school is formally open? Sometimes I am tempted by the suspicion that you think anything close to you and showing affection for you is good. Tell me if I'm mistaken.

14

Rome, February 20, 1920

A prelate (tempted, in my opinion, by illusion) wishes to know why the Lord has always contradicted him in his every pious enterprise, and whether the Lord might have [. . .] a design on him: He's seventy years old! [. . .]

I am composing that correspondence that will be titled *The Ways of Divine Love*, which considers the soul from the beginnings of devotion until the highest grades of oration. I don't know, though, how well I shall do toward the end. I told you I simply couldn't, and you insisted that I try. We'll see. But one cannot write of some things if he doesn't experience them.

15

Rome, October 13, 1920

In a recent dream I was given a child, turned by smallpox into one sore—but he was recovering. What should I think of it? I took it for one of the usual tricks played by nocturnal imagination. The sense of pity it inspired in me was so profound that I am inclined to believe it may be a revelation. Alas, the Lord is covered with sores; but how to judge him to be on the way to recovery?

16

Rome, October 20, 1920

First of all I will repeat my idea on the contrasting forces that are battling you inside. The last to prevail will be the one that will make you regard dying for your brothers as sweet, and that will be the time for you to go to the Father. Before then, you have to rejoice in living and suffering for them.

The crisis cannot be near, unless the above-mentioned criterion and the prophecy of that spirit fail. More time is needed.

Here then Father Benedetto, who had to pass the examination to be granted the faculty to hear confessions in the vicariate, asks Padre Pio to recommend him to someone he may know in Rome.

17

Rome, November 8, 1920

Last night Monsignor Santopaolo came here: Thank you. Let's hope the recommendations truly help me. In the meantime, the devil makes me see things as obscure and difficult, based on the fact that the procedure for my authorization is taking a long time. Oh, tell Jesus to make haste, as he can do, and that he let not Satan tease me! Do me this favor promptly and ardently. As for me, I do not know which saint to turn to, anymore. I'm waiting for a nod for Monsignor Valbonesi and Monsignor Cani [. . .]

What I had predicted is coming true in your spirit, and until the very end you will see my predictions being fulfilled. Take heart, then, and keep going until you are all consummated for your brothers.

18

Rome, November 14, 1920

Yesterday I had my examination privately with a bishop, and *pro una vice* both for the faithful and for the sisters [. . .] Now pray to J.C. [Jesus Christ] that I may be assigned as

extraordinary to the Brigittine, for the sake of our crucified Sister Benedetta and Sister Giovanna [. . .]

This morning I went to see Monsignor Cerretti, having
being summoned by him, and he was so kind and pleasant
[. . .]

Monsignor [. . .], also courteous and gracious with me,
[. . .] desires prayers for the conversion of a priest and for a
friend who has lost the respect of his superiors, that he
may again be well-regarded.

He also wants to know *expressly* whether he should admit
among the Carmelites a young woman, opposed by her family, who wants to run away from home to carry out her
design [. . .] He is in charge of the sister in Rome, and if he
sees himself favored he may do me good.

Teresa tells me that the divine designs are being and will
be fulfilled in me, alluding to that vision I mentioned to
you. I, on the contrary, fear in the heart of my soul of
being treated as I deserve, and of being crushed by divine
and human sternness. Ask the Lord, and especially, beg him
to have mercy on me.

19

Rome, December 21, 1920

If I were more humble and had courageously denied myself,
his [Satan's] art would be frustrated. But as I desire it, I
cannot do it, so he keeps playing with my weakness. Why
don't you ask the Lord that he give me once and for all the
appropriate and absolute self-contempt, and the ability to
abandon completely myself in him? It's a kind of heroism
he knows I am not capable of, and for which heroic grace

is needed. He must therefore expect from me nothing but the always old, always new misery [. . .]

Pray that God may entrust to me a religious community where there are souls that can comfort me, and superiors are willing to let me freely exercise the apostolic ministry [. . .]

20

Rome, December 31, 1920

My dearest Piuccio,

I urge you to despise the torment caused by Satan's awful suggestions: They are baseless and ridiculous. I wish mine were so, too! [. . .] But might it be true this time, what my soul dreads? Tell me, for Heaven's sake, and at any rate, please obtain for me that peace you wish for yourself.

Once again, I am not on good terms with the Brigittine—or rather, with the superior; I would be sorry if I had to make the decision of not going anymore, on account of those dear creatures of ours, who are there and belong to us. Pray that God avoid the dreaded final break.

I also meant to let you know that Sister Giovanna, for reasons I do not know, did not come to confession: Perhaps she thinks she can do without it? If you write to her, urge her, without revealing in any way that I informed you, to seek as much enlightenment as possible, and show to her how the saints are not content with only one helping hand in the ways of the spirit, but sought one hundred—with the exception of some enlightened, and of sure competence, spiritual directors.

21

Rome, January 4, 1921

Listen, Piuccio, let's make a deal. Each time I write I want answers that at least acknowledge the reception, and I want my questions and recommendations satisfied *as soon as possible.* I've always had the habit of answering everyone, and from my dear sons—especially from them—I want affection translated into practice, preferential love, and unconditional obedience.

22

Rome, January 6, 1921

I find consolation in the abundant harvest, and may God increase the crop forever more: Amen. I always see my activity as limited, with a labored, meager success. May he not humiliate me and punish me as I deserve! You would like to know who is causing you to suffer joyfully so much, and to complain about what you ardently desire; to feel intoxicated in your suffering and to endure it with utmost distress! Don't you know that God alone can reconcile the two opposites in a soul, and make *in pace amaritudo tua amarissima?* Therefore, let Love exercise his sublime and terrible eccentricities.

You affectionately laugh at how God is treating me: I wish I, too, could laugh at myself, but I can't. I can't, because I must fear myself much, even though I know perfect love *expellit timorem.* And when will charity be victorious over the overbearing and tenacious self? Can I experience on my own a complete, or even an incomplete, triumph over myself, if he leaves me at the mercy of myself and lets me be myself? Since he knows what I am, may he let me know once and for all what it means [to abide] in him, or him in me, hastening, if possible, the light revealing my whole reality. Tell our Dear One straight out, that this slowness is no use: If he wants more patience from me and you, he should free you from your duty as son of mine, and free me from the duty of considering him as my only Good.

Now, two questions you will answer *immediately, distinctly, and exhaustively*: What are your thoughts, and all your thoughts, about Sister Foresti's new institution, and what do you think is necessary to do for its good functioning and its success? What do you think *in your heart* of the Brigittine, and what do you think should be done for their own good, and the subsequent glory of God? I'll repeat that you must be explicit, categorical: and all this by the merit of h[oly] obedience.

23

Rome, February 11, 1921

Needless to say, your worries are vexations from the usual forger, the old troublemaker; also, I don't think it necessary to repeat to you that the ardent desire to co-redeem must prevail until the end, and join you with the prolonged agony deserving the mercy that is implored for the lukewarm and the obstinate. It will be so, and in the inebriation of suffering you will always see joined the yearning for suffering and the glory of succeeding.

24

Rome, February 25, 1921

Know that Sister Maria Lilia has been here for twenty days, still convalescing. I only learned it on the twentieth, and I went to see her, but she resolutely refused to confide anything about her spirit. I was quite discomfited, fearing my frustrated insistence may be a punishment for my vanity and my lack of humility. Ask the Lord about this and let me know what is to be thought of this creature, and whether I must abide by my resolution never to offer a handout again to anyone, unless I am insistently requested to do so, since I think it displeases God to show it off.

I haven't told you yet that I haven't set my foot in the Brigittine convent since Christmas, very much disgusted by the Mother Superior.

25

Rome, March 18, 1921

May my heart rise and resurrect from any weariness, shadow, torment; may it be released from even the most tenuous bond, and may it rise freely toward its Good, its Everything. I'm getting to know better and better this terrible *I*, and it seems to me that it's not a light of knowledge that lights the night of one's heart and dispels its thick illusion, but an experiential glimmer of a dreadful reality that awakens again that usual fear, more deep and grounded [. . .]

I want to know everything since last year, *clearly* and *by virtue of obedience*; I want pains and joys to be described to

me in their details, when they occurred, how they pro-
gressed, even if it takes you a month to write the report.

26

Rome, March 26, 1921

I understand your cross and the resulting anxiety, but it is
the Cross of Jesus, crushing and yet loved [. . .] But you
should always reveal your heart to me, as I mentioned
in my next-to-last letter, this being one of your duties,
and one of my rights to know. At least every once in a
while a concise—but exhaustive and clear—report is necessary. Do not neglect the importance for a spiritual director to have a soul *explained* in front of him and to know
its subsequent *story*. What is not said is lost, and God is
not pleased.

27

Rome, April 20, 1921

Here the outside apostolic ministry is considered almost like
wandering: The greatest merit resides in being nailed to
the usual internal duties. Tell God out loud that he grant
me full and undisputed freedom of action. I want to see if
this time, this time only, you can fully please me. If I am
not granted this grace, I will be *seriously* annoyed, and I
will confide more in strangers than in my dear sons. I must
absolutely be contented.

28

Rome, April 24, 1921

The violent, turbulent storm was followed by the intimate, persuasive, persistent temptation of ambitions grounded in self-love, and of the sadness in seeing Providence condemn me to inaction—or to an action not corresponding to my zeal and interior strength. I hope I can truly, finally exclaim *Deus meus et omnia* [...]

Yours, as you yourself realize, is simply a foolish contradiction from Satan, who pushes you now toward presumption, now toward discouragement. One has to wait for it to pass. Keep trusting in the goodness of God, since we are forbidden to distrust.

29

Rome, June 4, 1921

I want the help of prayers, of words and information about your invisible self...

30

Undated

A soul from Barletta heard the Lord say he must place himself in the hands of his confessor and depend on him completely. He wants to know first, whether this might be an illusion; second, in what sense this should be understood; and third, whether such obedience rules out any other direction, so that this soul must think that others [confessors, directors] may not understand him well.

31

Undated

Also beg him [the Lord] that he tell you whether the events afflicting me are expiatory or simply a trial, and what he has in store for me in the future. *I want to know*, and he must tell me.

32

Undated

Don't be upset if you lose your temper—although you must never grow complacent. If the Lord doesn't grant you the grace of a permanent and enduring sweetness, it is to leave you with a base on which to practice holy humility. For penance, every time you lose your temper, immediately force yourself to be twice as amiable [. . .]

Here are the answers to your questions:

1st. It's absolutely licit to recommend the poor, especially those who are not known to be so, to the rich and generous.

2nd. It's licit to distribute to the poor the donations received for that purpose, since by doing it you are simply executing the will of the donors, and by no means exercising control.

3rd.   It would be objectionable to receive money without the donors expressing in any way the purpose; but when they establish its use, even if they [only] express alternatives, then it is not contrary to our duties, since we use it according to their wishes.

. . .

Now this is what I want from you. Pray that the Lord

1st.   console the afflicted and the sick who recommend themselves to me;

2nd.   break in our province the scourge of ambition and scatter the evil tongues;

3rd.   pray that a person, whose life turns out to be an evil for the people, may turn to God;

4th.   enlighten that obstinate woman, the Mother Superior of the Brigittine, and make poor Margherita free to receive my spiritual help.

This is a true copy of the original letters.

L.✠S.   Br. Raphael C. Episc. Volaterr. *Visit. Apost.*

PART THREE

Appendices

Monsignor Raffaello Carlo Rossi

Cardinal Raffaello Carlo Rossi,
the illustrious master of theology and mystics [. . .],
not only in his writings and his preaching
but also in the practice of a holy life
was a master of virtue and doctrine.

— Cardinal Augusto Ottaviani

Besides Padre Pio, the other main character of the Apostolic Visitation of 1921 concerning the stigmatic friar is undeniably the future Cardinal Raffaello Carlo Rossi.[1] Poise, culture, a holy life, managerial ability, perceptiveness, and wisdom were the characteristics of his life as well as of this inquiry. But who exactly was this bishop, who later would be elevated to positions of highest responsibility in the universal Church?

Carlo, the first of three sons, was born in Pisa on October 28, 1876, to Francesco Rossi and Maria Palamidessi. His was a well-to-do family that afforded him a good education, moral and intellectual. A dramatic event, however, rocked his childhood. Notorious for her beauty, his mother had a brief affair with a lawyer in Pisa, and when the husband found out, she was sent away from the family for good. It had been a grave incident, but not a stable relationship:

The husband, however, was inflexible and decided to suspend any contact with her. From then on, absent his wife, Francesco Rossi entrusted his sons to a young woman, Emma Negrini.

Carlo suffered enormously for what had happened. The incident would have not a small influence on his life. Gentle and sensitive, he was always close to his mother: He would go see her, counsel her, express his love for her, and he was close to her, suggesting that she accept trials as a way to purify her heart. He was already a consultor of the Holy Office when, in 1911, the news of his mother's illness—breast cancer—made him rush to her. Arriving in Pisa, he found she had died, and for her he decided to do all he could: celebrate, even before the funeral, the Holy Mass.

His vocational journey had started early. When he was fifteen he felt called by the Lord, and asked his father's permission to enter the seminary. When the father refused, he waited a few years. He enrolled in the Faculty of Literature and Philosophy at the University of Pisa, and there he met as a mentor Giuseppe Toniolo, a very famous sociologist and a man of remarkable Christian virtues.

After turning twenty-one, he was free to follow his vocation, and, after thinking over which religious family he should choose, he decided to enter the Order of the Discalced Carmelites, which he did on October 3, 1897, taking the name of Brother Raffaello. He put on the Carmelite habit on December 19, 1898, and on September 20, 1901, he made his perpetual profession, consecrating the promises with a special vow of perseverance until death. This is the text of his vow: "I, Brother Raffaello of Saint Joseph, Discalced Carmelite, of my own free will and in full conscience, *to the greater glory of God, and for the spiritual growth and the happy state of our Order*, I promise to God omnipotent, to the Most Holy Virgin of Mount Carmel and to our Holy

Mother Teresa [of Avila], firmness in my vocation, so that whatever in the future I may do, or even just think, against this firmness and perseverance (may God forbid it), will be my mortal sin until I die."[2]

Ordained as a priest on December 21, 1901, by Msgr. Ferdinando Capponi, Archbishop of Pisa, he was sent to Rome to complete his studies in dogmatic theology and moral theology at the Gregorian University. At that time, the prestigious theological faculty included exceptional masters, such as the future Cardinal Ludovico Billot. Carlo, now Brother Raffaello, had them as teachers; he also forged important friendships with some of his schoolmates, such as Eugenio Pacelli, the future Pius XII.

His studies completed, he was sent to Florence, to the Convent of Saint Paulinus. He distinguished himself with his orthodox doctrine and his radical choices in matters of faith. This induced his superiors to trust him with important assignments, and in 1909 he was called to Rome at the Holy Office, as a coadjutor with right of succession. Since then, the assignments came one after the other.

On August 6, 1910, he was nominated a consultor of the Sacred Congregation for the Seminaries and Universities, and on July 9, 1919, he was designated Apostolic Visitor of the Apulia Regional Seminary in Molfetta. In this capacity he stood out for his insightful observations and the wisdom of the advice and the measures he proposed regarding some issues. At the same time, Brother Raffaello took charge of the ordinary administration of the English College in Rome, a task that he carried out brilliantly.

Spiritually rich, gifted with leadership and managerial talents, on April 22, 1920, at age forty-four, he was elected Bishop of Volterra. Brother Raffaello was a humble man and asked not to be consecrated, but to no avail. Recalling this moment, he wrote to his brother: "I would have done without this burden, too heavy for my shoulders—you know I am not a colossus; but the H[oly] Father was so firm I had to bow my head and obey." [3]

Aware of the apostolic burden and of the responsibilities he was about to take on himself, during the spiritual exercises preceding the consecration he wrote: "As bishop, I will keep my eyes fixed on Jesus, eternal Shepherd of souls, and in the examples and teachings of the Divine Master I will seek and find the guide of the episcopal ministry. I will look to the apostles, of whom I am an undeserving successor, and it will encourage me to keep in mind their zeal and their evangelical strength, to the point of martyrdom. In carrying out my daily duties as bishop, my constant model will be the Holy Archbishop of Milan, Saint Charles [Borromeo], whose name I received in the holy baptism not without intention... After all, my life will be summed up in three words: prayer, mortification, and apostolate. My eyes will always be up toward the Lord: I want to live close to Jesus in the Sacrament, to consume myself before him in the silence of adoration and love. In everything and always I will deny myself in the big things as well as in the small ones: a duty and a necessity for a bishop more than for a religious... In my apostolate I will not rest: I will keep watch, I will assist, I will reprove. I will always preach, I will want my clergy educated in the apostolate: I will require of them a proactive attitude toward the quest and care for souls." [4]

In Volterra, Monsignor Rossi worked with great passion. He worked hard to promote universal education, he tried to improve parish life, he helped the Pontifical Missionary Works, and he revived the devotion to the Eucharist. He was the first one to show, through his own example, the importance of the visit to the Most Holy Sacrament. The seminary is where he channeled most of his energy. In the light of his experience [as Apostolic Visitor to seminaries], Monsignor Rossi closely followed the organization of the life in the seminary, the curriculum, the superiors, and the students themselves.

While he was engaged in the beginnings of his episcopal activities—and still busy with other "Roman" assignments—he was recalled to Rome to take on the prestigious role of assessor of the Consistorial Congregation, the current Congregation for the Bishops.[5] Monsignor Rossi, however, had developed a profound passion for the pastoral life; and upon receiving the news through a letter from Cardinal De Lai, he wrote back: "Most Reverend Eminence, conflicting feelings have arisen in me as a result of the venerated letter by Y. Most Rev. E. [hereafter Your Most Reverend Eminence]. First, I should dutifully mention the confusion felt upon the announcement and the gratitude for this new attestation of the Holy Father's deep benevolence and of Your Most Reverend Eminence's paternal esteem. I am aware I am undeserving of both [. . .]. But I need also to explain the other feelings I experienced. Eminence, although I would never desire anything but the will of God, which I know is made known through the will of the Holy Father, I was by now living the life of my ministry, which has for me the greatest and most holy appeal; I would also suffer, I won't deny it, the separation from the souls [in my care]. I do not mind the inconveniences and the burdens of the apostolate: It is a comfort and a consolation for me to practice it without rest, like the apostles, like Saint Charles.

Your Eminence will recall how I did not desire and seek the episcopate; now that, by the will of God, I am what I am, it would be my dream to consume myself in the ministry for souls. . . and consume myself right here amidst this clergy—who sincerely sides with me; amidst this flock—whom often, around the diocese, I have seen gather around me and listen to me; and amidst my dear and good seminarians (I am writing from that pious place, the seminary), who are such a big part of my soul.

"For the double reason of being a religious and a bishop, I must and want to obey the Holy Father; if he required of me personally this sacrifice, I would certainly offer it up to the Lord, but while I may humbly present at his feet my plea, I will beg him insistently to leave me with these my children, whom I see grow before my very eyes in number and in virtue. To leave them—why not say it in all candor?—would be for me a very painful rupture. And since this is the moment for the most humble and frank expressions, I believe I can truthfully say it would be for them, too. Once more, Eminence, please forgive me for this singular language." [6]

In this circumstance, too, the Holy Father was firm, and Monsignor Rossi had to assume the role of assessor until 1930. It was much work, on account of the poor health of Cardinal De Lai, his direct superior. The workload was such that, in his capacity of spiritual director of a few priests, he was forced to acknowledge that he couldn't write to them within reasonable time. During that period, he was responsible for many charges. In particular, he was involved in the preparatory phase of the signing of the concordat between the Holy See and the Italian state, and on account of the successful outcome of the negotiation reached on February 11, 1929, Pius XI, recognizing Monsignor Rossi's merits, nominated him "first representative of the Apostolic See for the implementation of the *Concordato.*"

For the high esteem he earned, on June 30, 1930, he was elevated to the dignity of cardinal, and became secretary of the Sacred Consistorial Congregation.

After that, he was entrusted with the *ponenza* in approximately a hundred causes of beatification and canonization. He then became president of the Commission of Cardinals for the Pontifical Sanctuaries of Pompeii, Bari, and Loreto: Regarding the first, he actively promoted the enlargement and the diffusion of its spirituality. He was among the promoters of the reform of the breviary. He also saved from certain demise the Pious Society of Saint Charles, founded by Monsignor Scalabrini. For this religious family he was akin to a second founder: He gave it a legal structure, he saved the struggling vocations, he promoted new ones, and from 1930 until his death he was sensibly elected superior general of the Scalabrini Institute. His work for this religious family is a shining example of his Christian prudence and his pastoral wisdom.[7]

He was sensitive to social issues, and in this area he distinguished himself with initiatives and interventions which earned him the praise of Rep. Giorgio La Pira.

Though covered with honors, Cardinal Rossi remained a humble and poor man. His bedroom in his apartment in the Palazzo della Cancelleria in Rome showed this in full: a bed resting on two stools, a modest desk, a chair, nothing else.

Laden with work, worn out by all his engagements, Monsignor Rossi started feeling ill at the beginning of 1947. On account of his circulatory problems, the pope's personal doctor, Dr. Galeazzi, prescribed complete rest. Apparently, his health improved. But on the night of September 16, he died suddenly in Crescano del Grappa, where he was for a period of rest.

On his table were the Gospels, the *Imitation of Christ*, and, opened, the *Proficiscere* (The Art of Dying Well) by Father Petazzi, S.J.

Cardinal Rossi's beatification process is currently underway, but it is certain that this quiet leading character in the life of Saint Pio of Pietrelcina and in the twentieth-century Church is destined to be rediscovered for his intellectual talents and for his high moral qualities. In truth, what is surprising, when reading the biographies and other works devoted to him, is the complete absence of any reference to his Apostolic Visitation to San Giovanni Rotondo in 1921. While his biographers show themselves knowledgeable about all of Cardinal Rossi's Apostolic Visitations and assignments, they are silent about the inquiry he conducted on Padre Pio. It almost seems as if they voluntarily pulled a veil of silence over this all-important page in the life of the future cardinal. Perhaps in the past talking about Padre Pio may have obfuscated or compromised something. In reality, as far as Cardinal Rossi is concerned, the inquiry on Padre Pio, rather than casting a shadow, sheds light on his enlightened prudence and his profound wisdom. This is for two reasons.

First, his positive and appreciative evaluation of the stigmatic friar has been confirmed by the facts: Monsignor Rossi, then, saw Padre Pio's holiness well before many others who would follow him.

Second, Padre Pio's Apostolic Visitor was the first to verify, on behalf of the Holy Office, the theological nature of the stigmata, concluding—accusations and doubts notwithstanding—in favor of their supernatural origin.

On Cardinal Rossi and Padre Pio, therefore, history is about to receive a new stream of studies.

II

Monsignor Rossi, Father Benedetto, and the *Chronicle of Padre Pio*

Introduction

In the last few lines of his report, Monsignor Rossi expresses a severe evaluation of Father Benedetto's spiritual direction, and asks that the *Chronicle of Padre Pio* he was writing be acquired.

On this subject, after a short biographical profile of the Religious, I will offer some thoughts about the attitude of Padre Pio's spiritual director, and I will publish in its entirety the document subsequently requested by the Holy Office.

1. Fr. Benedetto Nardella of San Marco in Lamis

Born on March 16, 1872, Father Benedetto, after putting on the Capuchin habit on December 11, 1890, is ordained as a priest on December 11, 1898.

Gifted with a brilliant intellect, he immediately distinguishes himself, and on account of his managerial skills, from February 1908 until July 1919 he is elected superior of the Province of Foggia.

He first meets Padre Pio in Morcone on April 25, 1903, and from then on their relations intensify, until they become regular the day Father Benedetto becomes his superior.

Their interactions stop in June 1922, when, following the Apostolic Visitation of 1921, the Holy Office orders him to discontinue his spiritual direction of Padre Pio. Without being able to see his disciple ever again, Father Benedetto dies in San Severo on July 22, 1942.[1]

2. Father Benedetto's spiritual direction

As we have seen, toward the end of his report Monsignor Rossi expresses a severe opinion on the quality of the spiritual direction of Padre Pio's spiritual father, but his evaluation needs to be downplayed. The Capuchin Religious, in fact, shows little enthusiasm for his disciple's mystical phenomena: He doesn't spread rumors about the extraordinary events; he refuses the money offered to buy photographs of the stigmatic; and he jots down notes but does not write a biography of Padre Pio, waiting—as he himself declares—for the Lord to pronounce the last word on the day of his spiritual son's death. Moreover, in a letter he declares that he never refuted the accusations made against his disciple, in order to prove his indifference toward Padre Pio's extraordinary fame.

Informed of the phenomenon of the invisible stigmata, he asks his spiritual son few questions, and after learning about it, he never goes back to the topic. Even after the visible stigmatization he does not immediately go to see Padre Pio. He lets four and a half months pass before he verifies in person what had happened. An attitude that is anything but inquisitive! Besides, showing real prudence, he doesn't naively believe the stigmata, but decides to subject them to a medical examination conducted by Dr. Romanelli.

It should be noted that Father Benedetto shows great humility when faced with the request, certainly very painful to him, of the Holy Office: In fact, until his death, not only did he choose never to go to San Giovanni Rotondo, accepting that he wouldn't see Padre Pio's dear face again, but he also never wrote to him again.

As for the questions he asked his disciple about his own future, according to my point of view they can be judged less severely when one examines the whole correspondence, which in fact shows with what moral integrity and prudence Father Benedetto guided Padre Pio. In the future, we will dedicate a comprehensive study to his wisdom and spiritual maturity.

3. The document

We are now at the chronicle requested by Monsignor Rossi for the Holy Office. The document is kept in the Archive of the Congregation for the Doctrine of the Faith (ACDF, Dev. Var., 1919, I, *Cappuccini*, Padre Pio da Pietrelcina, folder II, Padre Pio, 24b.) Thanks to a copy kept in the Padre Pio File, the text had been partially published, with some edits to the original, in the essay by R. Fabiano, *Una biografia di Padre Pio incompiuta e il suo autore*, in "Studi su Padre Pio", issue 3 (September–December), 2002, pp. 393–403.[2]

In the document that follows, though, we will publish for the first time as an integral part of the chronicle other notes found in the notebook where Father Benedetto jotted down Padre Pio's biographical notes. They are nine interesting observations by Padre Pio on the spiritual life, from which emerge some guidelines in the spiritual direction of the young Capuchin. In the future we will also dedicate a study to this source, which is in need of a historical analysis and of a theological interpretation of the mystical phenomena it mentions.[3]

III

Chronicle of Padre Pio

By Father Benedetto of San Marco in Lamis

1. Around age three—the Rosary, prayers, etc.
2. When he was about five years old, he felt a compelling need to give himself all to God.
3. When he was five or six, the Heart of Jesus [image of the Sacred Heart] appeared by the high altar, signaled him to come closer to the altar and put the hand on his head, attesting his pleasure in, and his confirmation of, the offering of self [the future Padre Pio] to him and of his consecration to his love.
4. He felt a firm intention and a growing intense desire to love [God] and to give his whole self to him.
5. The Rosary, morning prayers. He felt strongly drawn to going to church—to going to Mass, to services, to the other devotional practices—pleasure in staying in church. Diabolical vexations began around age four—the devil appears in figures rarely lewd, but often threatening, ominous, terrifying. It was a torment to see the light put out and *every night* invariably left at the mercy of these visions. He couldn't sleep—some of his rest was agitated, etc.

6. He has no memory of either dreams or visions. Usual illnesses—transitory.

7. The attachment to piety and to the Church was growing, and the fear of the devil made his desire of clinging to God stronger. His most tender devotion and his trust were for the Virgin and Saint Joseph.

8. From his early childhood, he kept insisting on being admitted to Communion: He would ask his grandfather to take him to the pastor. The pastor resisted, on account of the custom at that time to wait until age eleven to receive Communion. This refusal would make him cry.

9. Feasts or solemnities—back then, priests discouraged the frequent reception of Communion.

10. The trials from Satan began when he was ten.

11. Around the age of fourteen, he felt called to the [Capuchin] Order.

12. Swimming in joy—annulled and annihilated in himself, in all the powerful and perfect oblation and abnegation of self.

13–14. He starts the novitiate—great piety and admiration to the point of daily tears over the Passion of O.L. [hereafter our Lord]. During the year of the novitiate, the vexations suddenly ceased. Before entering, he worries he will suffer ... alone ... in his cell.

15. During the novitiate, and afterward, quiet and recollection were habitual. As a student, he always had the gift of daily tears.

16. Around age twenty the gift of rapture began.

17. [The visions were] never ocular—[rather] imaginary and very vivid; sometimes of the Passion and scenes; often, actually continually, of the Holy

Family, in fixed and moving figures: Jesus and Mary exchanging caresses, Jesus amusing himself as a young child, displays of affection among the three of them. In his second and third year of religious studies he experienced the spiritual presence of God in a regular way—it has continued since.

18. Satan's physical vexations around his first year of priesthood. Under the guise of horrid human and beastly shapes—insults, threats, beatings. Twisting of arms, of limbs, of internal organs. The noise in Foggia was [Satan's] irritation for not succeeding in his intent of turning him away from God, from prayer, etc. In Foggia, he kept his mental faculties alert when drowsy, and the union with God was continual. The body suffered from debilitating illness, food deprivation. Medications of Costellino—year 1916—he came back from the medical examination needed to enter military service, and in Foggia he experienced the aforementioned phenomenon.

19–23. After the novitiate he went to Sant'Elia [a Pianisi] (1904–1905). Afterward, in 1906, he was in San Marco [in Lamis]. In San Marco from November through May—afterward, he is back in Sant'Elia, to finish his philosophy studies. After that, he went to Serra [Serracapriola], where he started theology, and stayed about a year. The headache started on Good Friday and lasted the whole time he was in Serra—the persistent tears made his eyes fall ill: In Serra the tears ceased.

24. Around 1907—the chest pain appears.

25. Around 1909—he went home.

26. Around 1907—he left Serra by medical orders.
27. From Serra he went first home; second to Montefusco, and third to Morcone: He is ordained as a deacon [in 1909]; ordained as a priest on July 10, 1910.[1] In 1911 we went to Naples from Morcone—in Naples for three days—in Venafro for a couple of months we only retained the sacramental species.
28. He never took philosophy exams even though he covered it.
29. He went through dogmatics. He studied moral theology by himself, at home with a priest.
30. In 1911, he was approved as a confessor in Benevento.
31. Back from Venafro, he is granted the dispensation from saying the Divine Office, and from the Mass of Our Lady.
32. The wound in the side between August 5 and 6 [1918], around 8 A.M., while he was hearing the confessions of the religious. The sore at the extremities the morning of September 20, during the thanksgiving prayer after Mass. Words from our Lord with his arms stretched out, but without knowing whether he was on the Cross. Rays and wounds.
33. The lack of nutrition was not a habit, but according to necessity.
34. He experienced the torments of hell in seeing the suffering of the damned. About two years before (1919) he had such torment every ten to fifteen days. He experienced the pain of the senses and the pain of loss [that is, the pain of having lost God]. It was as if his body and soul were among the damned and the demons—to save

others and himself from the place he was destined to go, but for the help of grace.

35.   Several appearances of the Most Holy Trinity—admonitions to be more merciful than ever with souls—assurances regarding his anxieties, doubts, and trepidations—revelations about souls in need of being reproached, exhorted, etc.

36.   When talking [to Padre Pio], our Lord would reveal his disgust with certain souls by moving restlessly, etc., as well as his pleasure in other souls.

37.   This year on the Feast of the Pardon of Assisi, slightly fewer than a million indulgences were obtained.

Some of Padre Pio's sayings:

— Religion is the only board that will lead the castaway on life's stormy sea to salvation.

— Reason bears disgraces, courage fights them, and religion overcomes them.

— Always have the heart of a judge for yourself, the heart of a son for God, and the heart of a mother for your neighbor.

— You cannot escape self-love but with sincere love of God.

— To despise the world it is sufficient to listen to reason, but to despise yourself you need to listen to God.

— Human wisdom teaches us to conceal our pride; only Christ's religion can destroy it.

— Scruples are like shoes you can't walk in because they are too tight—despise them.

— If we can have true patience amid the trials of this life, we will be martyrs even without the executioner's sword.

IV

Padre Pio's Stigmatization:
History and Testimonies

The first news of Padre Pio's stigmata dates back to a letter of September 8, 1911, addressed to Father Benedetto of San Marco in Lamis. In it, Padre Pio writes: "Last night something happened to me which I cannot explain or understand. In the middle of the palms of my hands appeared a little red spot, almost the shape of a one-cent coin, also accompanied by a strong and acute pain in the middle of that red spot. The pain was worse in the middle of my left hand, so much that I can still feel it. Under my feet, too, I feel a little pain. This phenomenon has been going on for almost a year, but it hadn't happened in a while. But don't get upset if I am telling you about this now for the first time; it's because that damn shame always had the better of me. Even now, if you knew how hard it was to force myself to tell you."[1]

The phenomenon keeps recurring, and a few months later, on March 21, 1912, Padre Pio writes to Fr. Agostino Daniele of San Marco in Lamis: "Every Thursday night through Saturday, as well as every Tuesday, is a painful tragedy for me. My heart, my hands, and my feet feel to me as if they were being run through by a sword, so great is the pain I experience."[2]

Initially, his spiritual fathers don't delve into the matter. Then, on September 30, 1915, Father Agostino writes to Padre Pio: "Tell me: First, since when did Jesus start favoring you with his celestial visions? Second, has he granted you the ineffable gift of his holy stigmata, albeit invisible? Has he made you experience, and how many times, his crowning with thorns and his flagellation?"[3]

On October 4, Padre Pio sends his reply, but doesn't answer the questions. His self-effacement, and his need to keep the secret about what he is going through, prevail: "Forgive me if I don't answer the questions you asked in your last letter. To tell you the truth, it repulses me to write about those things. Wouldn't it be possible, O Father, for now to forgo providing an answer to your questions?"[4]

But Father Agostino is none too willing to see his initiative go nowhere, and after a few days, on October 7, he writes again: "Finally, you beg me to allow you to forgo answering my questions. Frankly, I feel in my heart that I should insist: I believe this insistence won't displease Jesus, and you shouldn't feel repugnance in answering, since—do not doubt this—everything will be for the glory of God and for our salvation. You can answer me with a strictly private letter: Jesus will make me keep the secret; you know I have never talked to anybody except to those souls whom Jesus wants me to, when Jesus wants it. Why then so much reluctance? You must be sincere and tell me everything: Actually, you should pray to Jesus that he makes you reveal to me other things I may not know or I may forget to ask you."[5]

Padre Pio will obey, but his letter, dated October 10, 1915, reveals the detachment and the revulsion with which he speaks. Here are his words: "In your resolute intention of knowing, or rather, of receiving an answer to those questions of yours, I cannot avoid recognizing the express will of God, so with a trembling hand and my heart overflowing with pain, of which I ignore the cause, I will now obey you. Your first question is that you want to know since when did Jesus start to favor his poor creature with his celestial visions. If I am not mistaken, they must have started not long after my novitiate [year 1903]. The second question is whether he has granted me the ineffable gift of his holy stigmata. To this I must answer positively, and the first time that Jesus willed to deign me with this favor, they were visible, especially in one of the hands, and since this soul was very much dumbstruck by such a phenomenon, I prayed to the Lord that he stop such a visible phenomenon. Since then, they didn't appear anymore; but although the wounds disappeared, the very sharp pain did not, and I still feel it, especially in certain circumstances and on certain days. Your third and last question is whether the Lord made me experience, and how many times, his crowning with thorns and his flagellation. The answer to this question is also positive: As for the number of times, I would not know, I will only say that it has been several years that this soul suffers, about once a week. I think I obeyed you, didn't I?" [6]

A long silence about this issue ensued in their letters.

The information relative to singular mystical gifts resumes in August 1918, toward the end of World War I.

Prior to the signs of the Passion, Padre Pio receives the transverberation. On August 21, writing to Father Benedetto, Padre Pio tells of his "supreme martyrdom": "In virtue of this [obedience] I am about to make known to you what happened to me on the evening of the fifth and throughout the sixth of this month. I cannot fully convey to you what happened during this period of supreme martyrdom. I was hearing the confessions of our boys on the evening of the fifth, when suddenly I was filled with an extreme terror at the sight of a celestial person who presented himself before the eyes of my mind. He was holding in his hand some sort of tool, like a very long iron blade, with a very sharp tip, from which it seemed fire was coming out. As soon as I saw this, I watched this person forcefully throw such a weapon into my soul. I barely let out a moan; I felt as if I were dying. I told the boy to leave, because I was not feeling well and I lacked the strength to go on. This martyrdom continued, without interruption, until the morning of the seventh. I cannot express what I suffered during such a sorrowful period. I even saw my insides being ripped and stretched behind that weapon, and everything was put to fire and sword. From that day on I have been wounded to death. I feel deep in my soul a wound that is always open, and makes me relentlessly suffer as if in agony."[7]

This mystical phenomenon does not conclude immediately. Padre Pio's agony goes on, and a few days later, on September 5, he writes to Father Benedetto: "I see myself overwhelmed by an ocean of fire: The wound is reopened and bleeds, and keeps bleeding. All by itself it would be enough to make me die a thousand times. O my God, why don't I die? Don't you see that life itself is a torment for the soul you yourself wounded? Are you so cruel as to remain deaf to the cries of the suffering, and you won't comfort him? But what am I saying? . . . Forgive me, Father, I am beside myself, I don't know what I'm talking about. The excessive pain caused by the ever-open wound drives me crazy and makes me delirious, and I feel incapable of bearing it up."[8]

We are at the peak of this mystical itinerary. On September 20 an event occurs that will mark forever the life of the stigmatic friar. Although what happened was truly dramatic, Padre Pio is reluctant to talk about it. So on October 17 he very vaguely writes to Father Benedetto: "Who will free me from myself? Who will take me out of this body, bearer of death? Who will stretch out his hand to help me, so that I may not be dragged and swallowed into the vast and deep ocean? Must I resign myself to being dragged into the fast-advancing storm? Must I pronounce the *fiat* as I gaze at this mysterious person who covered me with wounds, and who doesn't desist from this hard, harsh, acute, and penetrating operation, and who doesn't allow time to close the old wounds, but over these he opens new ones, with infinite agony for the poor victim? Oh, my Father, come to my help, for Heaven's sake! All my insides pour blood, and several times my eyes had to resign themselves to see it flow outside, too. Oh! Would that this agony, this punishment, this humiliation, this confusion leave me! My soul cannot, and knows not, how to bear this."[9]

Opened by the mysterious person, "new wounds" over "old wounds" are too unusual for Father Benedetto to learn without astonishment. Moreover, his spiritual son complains that his insides, and even the outside of his person, "pour blood". The punishment, the humiliation, the confusion these phenomena provoke in him give his spiritual director urgent reason to intervene.

So the next day, in a paternal but commanding tone, Father Benedetto writes: "My dear son, tell me everything, clearly and not just by allusions. What is the operation of this person? Out of where is the blood pouring, and how many times a day or a week? What happened to your hands and feet, and how? I want to know everything with precision and in virtue of holy obedience."[10]

On October 22, 1918, Padre Pio writes back to him: "What should I tell you about your question regarding how my crucifixion happened? My God, what confusion and what humiliation I feel in having to make known what you have done to this miserable creature of yours! It was the morning of the twentieth of last month, in the choir, after the celebration of the Holy Mass, when I was surprised by a kind of rest, similar to a sweet sleep. All the internal and external senses and the very faculties of my soul were in an indescribable state of calm. In all this, everything around me and inside me was absolute silence; then I was filled with great peace and I abandoned myself to this absolute deprivation, and there was a pause in the midst of devastation. All this happened in a flash. And while all this was unfolding, I saw before me a mysterious person, similar to the one I saw on the evening of August 5, with the only difference that his hands and feet and side were bleeding heavily. The sight of him terrified me; I could not describe to you what I felt at that moment. I felt I should die, and I would have died if the Lord had not intervened to relieve my heart, which was almost jumping out of my chest. The vision of this person faded away, and I realized that my hands, feet and side had been transfixed and were bleeding heavily. Imagine the agony I experienced then, and I now continue to experience almost every day. The wound close to the heart bleeds constantly, especially from Thursday night through Saturday. My dear father, the pain of this agony and the resulting confusion deep in my soul are killing me. I am afraid I shall bleed to death, if the Lord doesn't listen to the wailing of my poor heart and doesn't relieve me of this operation. Will Jesus, who is so good, grant me this grace? Will he at least free me of the confusion I experience on account of these outward signs? I will lift up my voice to him and I will not cease to implore him, that in his mercy he may free me not from the agony, not from the pain—which is impossible, and I feel I am inebriated with pain—but from these outward signs, which cause me indescribable and unbearable confusion and humiliation." [11]

Father Benedetto wants to understand what is going on. At the end of February, he goes "for several days" to see Padre Pio in San Giovanni Rotondo, and he personally verifies the event.[12] On March 3, 1919, Father Benedetto writes to Father Agostino and confides: "He doesn't have spots or marks, but real sores perforating his hands and feet. I observed the one he has on his side: a real tear that continually drips blood or bloody fluid. On Fridays it is blood. I found him barely capable of standing up; but I left him able to celebrate, and when he celebrates Mass the gift is visible to the public, since he has to keep his bare hands up."[13]

On April 24, 1919, Father Benedetto informs the order's minister general: "Most Reverend Father General, I had until now kept quiet on account of a certain feeling of reserve that naturally arises in such circumstances, and because of the delicate nature of the spiritual ministry, with both reasons advising to hide the gifts of the Great King. [. . .] At the beginning of March, I went personally to ascertain *de visu* what was there. It was a Friday evening, and as soon as I arrived, I comfortably examined his hands: They were pierced and bleeding; I saw a tear in his side, several inches long and wet with blood; the bandage applied on it, which I took, was drenched with water and blood."[14]

On November 1919, writing to the French Capuchin Fr. Edouard d'Alençon, a distinguished scholar of Franciscanism, the new minister of the Capuchin province, Father Pietro of Ischitella, offers a brief description of the stigmata: "In short. On the palm of each hand, a dark red, roundish scab can be observed, as big as a five-cent coin, with clear borders and partially detached from the skin. A corresponding identical scab, but slightly smaller, is found on the back of his hands. Similarly on the soles and on the upper side of his feet. On the left side of his thorax a sort of cross is observed, whose longer arm, laid obliquely, goes from the fifth to the ninth rib for about 2.4 inches, while the arm across is shorter by about half. The impression of these signs happened exactly on the afternoon of September 20, 1918,[15] and so far they have been almost unchanged."[16]

Among the testimonies belonging to this period one stands out, provided by Monsignor Costa, Bishop of Melfi and Rampolla, who in September 1919 writes to the province minister, Father Pietro of Ischitella: "Although I came here not with an inquiring spirit, but purely as a simple faithful, moved by the desire to edify myself and to implore graces for me, for my loved ones, for my dioceses, I could not, however, help observing, interrogating, and getting a sense of Padre Pio's personality. My impressions could be summed up in one: the impression, that is, that I spoke and talked with a saint. The stigmata, which I was able to kiss dearly, and which cannot be reasonably doubted, after the examinations conducted by experts, are very eloquent mouths, like those that represent the seal of love which God impresses upon those who are most dear to him, and to him most intimately united in virtue of their intense faith and their ardent charity."[17]

V

Chronology of the Life of Padre Pio

1887. May 25: Francesco Forgione is born in Pietrelcina (in the Province of Benevento), son of Grazio and Maria Giuseppa De Nunzio. He is baptized the following day.

1891. Vexations from the devil begin around age four. The devil appears to him in ominous figures, rarely lewd. "It was a torment to see the light being put out and every night invariably left at the mercy of these visions. He couldn't sleep. Some of his rest was agitated" (*Chronicle* by Father Benedetto).

1892. At age five he experiences the desire of consecrating himself to God. The following year he has a vision of the Sacred Heart of Jesus "[a]ttesting his pleasure in, and his confirmation of, the offering of self [the future Padre Pio] to him and of his consecration to his love" (*Chronicle* by Father Benedetto).

1899. He receives the sacrament of confirmation and, for the first time, he receives the Eucharist.

1903. He enters the Capuchins, in the novitiate of Morcone (in the Province of Benevento). He takes the name Brother Pio of Pietrelcina.

1904. He makes his simple profession, after his transfer to Sant'Elia a Pianisi.

1907. He is transferred to Serracapriola. He makes his solemn profession. "Around age twenty, the gift of rapture began."

1909. First days of July: He is transferred to Morcone. July 18: He is ordained as a deacon. For health reasons he begins a long period of residence in Pietrelcina, interrupted at times, until 1916. End of September: He goes to Montefusco. Mid-November: He goes to Gesualdo.

1910. August 10: After being granted a dispensation to anticipate his ordination, he is ordained as a priest in the cathedral of Benevento by Archbishop Paolo Schinosi. The first signs of the stigmata appear during this year.

1912. The phenomenon of the invisible stigmatization repeats itself every Thursday evening through Saturday. Diabolic vexations take place. "Satan's physical vexations around his first year of priesthood. Under the guise of horrid human and beastly shapes— insults, threats, beatings. Twisting of arms, of limbs, of internal organs. The noise in Foggia was [Satan's] irritation for not succeeding in his intent of turning him away from God, from prayer" (*Chronicle* by Father Benedetto).

1915. Asked by Father Agostino of San Marco in Lamis, Padre Pio admits to experiencing, almost every week for several years, the "crowning with thorns" and the "flagellation". Drafted in the army, he is granted a one-year convalescent leave.

1918. March 16: Declared unfit for military service on account of double bronchial pneumonia. May 30: He offers himself as a victim for the sinners, that the war may end. August 5–7: Phenomenon of the transverberation. September 20: Jesus Crucified appears to him, saying: "I unite you with my Passion", and gives him the stigmata.

1919. First medical examinations of the stigmata. In May, one by Dr. Luigi Romanelli, accompanied by the provincial, Father Benedetto of San Marco in Lamis; in June and July, new visits by Dr. Romanelli; in July, in consequence of an official order of the Holy Office given to Fr. Giuseppe Antonio of San Giovanni in Persiceto, examination performed by Professor Amerigo Bignami, tenured professor of medical pathology at the Royal University in Rome. With him is the new provincial, Father Pietro of Ischitella. Professor Bignami advises to seal Padre Pio's wounds with bandages for a few days. During the first eight days, a remarkable quantity of blood gushes out unexpectedly from the bandaged stigmata, and in the end it is decided to stop the experiment. After a few months, the order's minister general sends Dr. Giorgio Festa, a Roman doctor known to the General Curia of the order. Padre Pio consents to the request for a new medical visit, even though Bignami hurt him when he pushed a pin into the stigmatic's hand. First popular uproars on account of a threatened transfer of Padre Pio.

1920. April 18: Fr. Agostino Gemelli visits Padre Pio for a few minutes. Quickly dismissed by Padre Pio, the next day he sends to the Holy Office a harsh evaluation of the stigmatic. In the meantime, Padre Pio assures him that the Lord will bless the future Catholic university.

1921. June 14–21: The Holy Office orders the first first Apostolic Visitation concerning the stigmatic friar. The Bishop of Volterra, Raffaello Rossi, goes with great discretion to see Padre Pio, to investigate and interrogate the Capuchin. Until 1939 there won't be any other Apostolic Visitations directly ordered by the Holy Office to investigate Padre Pio. Until then, this is the only inquiry with Padre Pio's sworn statements.

1922. Once they receive the Apostolic Visitor's report, the cardinals of the Holy Office write to the minister general of the Capuchins: they don't adopt any disciplinary measures, but declare they will keep watching Padre Pio and order the following: that any "oddity and commotion" be avoided; that Padre Pio is "not to impart benedictions on the people"; that "for no reason is he to show the so-called stigmata"; that he stop "any communication, even by way of letter" with Father Benedetto of San Marco in Lamis; that the superiors of the order prepare to transfer Padre Pio, whenever the popular mood will make it possible; that Father Benedetto turn over the *Chronicle*. During this same time, the Holy Office receives new slanderous accusations from Monsignor Gagliardi, which will turn out to be groundless.

1923. The Holy Office declares that the supernatural nature of the phenomena attributed to Padre Pio does not hold true, and urges the faithful to conform to this declaration. Padre Pio is forbidden to celebrate Holy Mass in public. A crowd of three thousand people protests in front of the convent. Padre Pio is granted the faculty to celebrate in church. His transfer is urged: Some Fascists send death threats should the transfer occur.

1923–1926. The Holy Office receives a constant stream of accusations from Monsignor Gagliardi and some priests in San Giovanni Rotondo. They are responsible for the doubts and the anxiety of the Holy Office.

1929. New order to transfer Padre Pio. The Holy Office grants a delay because of riots.

1931. May 23: The Holy Office makes known that Padre Pio is forbidden to celebrate Mass in public, and his faculty to hear confessions is revoked. The Capuchin is deeply grieved.

1933. July 16: Padre Pio is authorized to celebrate in public again; the faculty to hear confessions is gradually restored.

1935. August 10: Twenty-fifth anniversary of Padre Pio's ordination; great influx of faithful.

1940. A committee is established for the funding of a clinic according to Padre Pio's intentions.

1941. The order's minister general asks for and is granted by Monsignor Ottaviani, assessor of the Holy Office, the faculty to let Padre Pio hear confessions in church also in the afternoons.

1942. Princess of Piedmont Marie José, together with the daughter of the king of Belgium and a large entourage, visit Padre Pio.

1943. The influx of faithful resumes. Heavy presence of soldiers of every rank and nationality.

1946. June 2: Padre Pio goes to town to vote. He will always vote in the following years.

1947. The construction begins for the House for the Relief of Suffering, which will be inaugurated on May 5, 1956.

1948. April: Father Karol Wojtyła meets Padre Pio, who hears his confession.

1954. February 19: His Most Reverend Excellency Monsignor Giovanni Montini writes on behalf of Pius XII: "The fervent concern of the Most Reverend Padre Pio of Pietrelcina for the health of His Holiness adds itself, with particular consolation, to the universal tokens of affection from the whole Catholic world. Thanking the good Padre for his filial charity and for the prayers he so kindly solicits from others, the August Pontiff offers warm wishes for his person and his sacred ministry, and sends to him his heartfelt Apostolic Benediction."

1956. July 2: Laying of the first stone of the new church to be built in San Giovanni Rotondo.

1959. Padre Pio recovers from pleurisy while the statue of Our Lady of Fatima stops in San Giovanni Rotondo.

1960. July 30–September 17: Apostolic Visitation of Msgr. Carlo Maccari, and his negative report.

1961. New orders from the Holy Office, also concerning the duration of Padre Pio's Holy Mass.

1962. Many bishops, while attending the Second Vatican Council, go and visit Padre Pio. Monsignor Wojtyła writes to Padre Pio. He asks for, and obtains, a grace for a doctor named Wanda Poltawska.

1963. Further exchange of letters between Monsignor Wojtyła and Padre Pio. For the first time, the Polish bishop asks for prayers for himself, and after fifteen days he becomes Archbishop of Krakow.

1964. Cardinal Ottaviani, head of the Holy Office, makes known Paul VI's will that "Padre Pio carry out his ministry in complete freedom".

1968. Padre Pio's health declines. Some of the stigmata start to close without leaving any trace—in July, it's the ones on the back of his hands; then, gradually, all the others. On September 23, at 2:30 A.M., Padre Pio, repeating "Jesus, Mary, Jesus, Mary", dies.

1983. March 20: The Cognition Process on the life and virtues of the Servant of God Pio of Pietrelcina is officially opened. An impressive array of documents is gathered.

1997. March 20: Padre Pio is proclaimed Venerable.

1999. June 2: Padre Pio is proclaimed Blessed.

2002. June 16: Before an overflowing crowd, John Paul II proclaims Padre Pio a Saint, and establishes his feast day as an obligatory memorial in the Church's liturgical year.

NOTES TO PART THREE

Notes to Appendix I

[1] For a bibliography on Msgr. Raffaello C. Rossi, please refer to note 20 to the Introduction to Part I, on page 65 of this book.

[2] Valentino and Vito Bondani, *Raffaello Carlo card. Rossi: A servizio della Chiesa* (Rome: OCD, 1977), pp. 18–19.

[3] Valentino and Vito Bondani, *Raffaello Carlo card. Rossi: A servizio della Chiesa* (Rome: OCD, 1977), p. 31.

[4] Valentino and Vito Bondani, eds. *Pastore e maestro* (Milan: Ancora, 1971), pp. 23–24.

[5] In fact, at that time the Consistorial Congregation had a wider competence than the current Congregation for the Bishops.

[6] Valentino and Vito Bondani (editors), *Pastore e maestro* (Milan: Ancora, 1971), pp. 334–335.

[7] With regard to this topic, we refer to the already-mentioned Valentino and Vito Bondani, *Paternità di servizio. Raffaello Carlo card. Rossi e gli Scalabriniani* (Rome: OCD, 1981).

Notes to Appendix II

[1] For further useful information, see *Epistolario*, pp. 51–54.

[2] I owe this kind bibliographical instruction to the friendship and the vast erudition of Prof. Luciano Lotti, whom I thank warmly here.

[3] The reader will easily observe that Father Benedetto laconically jotted down theological expressions that are imprecise. Anything but ignorant of theology and mystics, Father Benedetto surely meant with these notes to remind himself of events and phenomena he would have clarified personally in the future.

Notes to Appendix III

[1] Let's bear in mind that the exact date of Padre Pio's priestly ordination is August 10, 1910.

Notes to Appendix IV

[1] *Epistolario*, p. 234.
[2] Ibid., p. 266.
[3] Ibid., p. 659.
[4] Ibid., p. 663.
[5] Ibid., pp. 665–66.
[6] Ibid., p. 669.
[7] Ibid., p. 1065.
[8] Ibid., pp. 1072–73.
[9] Ibid., p. 1090.
[10] Ibid., p. 1091.
[11] Ibid., pp. 1093–95. Father Emilio of Matrice, at that time a fifteen-year-old seminarian in the boarding school of San Giovanni Rotondo, reminisces: "The morning of September 21, 1918, as soon as we approached dear Padre Pio, we realized he had a wound on the palms of his hands, that he was walking with a certain difficulty, and that his face was redder than usual. We began investigating the reason of all this, but we learned only from Father Paolino, a few days later, that our Padre Pio had received from the crucifix in the choir the Lord's wounds, that is, Jesus' stigmata on the chest, the hands, and the feet. Father Paolino finally urged us to keep quiet, to avoid talking about it with anybody, and to be really good with the Padre, who was suffering so much. Although he never talked about his sores, after a few days, Padre Pio let us reverently kiss the palms of his wounded hands. We boarders kept quiet; but—I don't know how it happened—not much time passed before the fact of Padre Pio's receiving the stigmata quickly became common knowledge. The newspapers sent to San Giovanni their best reporters, who for several days wrote whole pages about Padre Pio and San Giovanni Rotondo. Thus was quickly born the phenomenon of the 'Holy Friar of the Gargano'. The little church soon became the destination of pilgrimages from all over Italy and all over the world." Father Emilio of Matrice's memoir, titled *I ricordi del cuore*, is kept in

the Padre Pio Archive, section II (typewritten documents), no. 6, now published in *Le stigmate*, pp. 78–79.

[12] Ibid., letter 527, p. 1128ff.

[13] Agostino of San Marco in Lamis, p. 288.

[14] Diocesan Tribunal of Manfredonia, *Transumptum processus in Curia Sipontina constructi super vita et virtutibus Servi Dei Pii a Pietrelcina* (Manfredonia, 1989), vol. 26, pp. 711–12.

[15] This is a mistake on the part of Father Pietro of Ischitella. As Padre Pio says, the stigmatization occurred in the morning, after Holy Mass.

[16] *Le stigmate*, p. 61.

[17] Ibid., p. 67.

ACKNOWLEDGMENTS

I am indebted to many for the publication of this volume. Above all, to the Archbishop of Taranto, His Most Reverend Excellency Monsignor Benigno Papa, for his characteristic cultural sensibility and for the paternal attentiveness he demonstrated toward me since our first meeting. In the course of many years he has proved to be a real father to me, and an enlightened shepherd. For him and for his encouragement, always open and intelligent, I feel the gratitude of a son.

I am very grateful to Msgr. Pierino Galeone, founder of the Istituto Secolare "Servi della Sofferenza", who welcomed me as a son and disciple and helped me during my interior and intellectual journey. With regard to this volume, he offered me valuable indications and significant in-depth analysis of the spirituality and the personality of the Capuchin whom, for many years, he got to know closely, deeply absorbing his way of life and his teachings. To him, too, I express particularly deep gratitude and filial affection.

I want to express special gratitude and esteem to Dr. Vittorio Messori: his extensive foreword offers the opportunity to read, amidst the jumble of so many voices and questionable opinions, the insightful judgment of a master to whom I am indebted, also with regard to my own interior and intellectual journey.

Msgr. Emanuele Tagliente, vicar of the Istituto Secolare "Servi della Sofferenza" and professor of canon law at the Romano Guardini Institute for Religious Sciences, and

Msgr. Carmelo Pellegrino, official of the Sacred Congregation for the Cause of Saints and professor at the Pontifical Gregorian University, inspired this volume and tenaciously wanted it to be written. I sincerely thank them, too, with brotherly affection and profound esteem.

For his availability and his learned competence, Msgr. Alejandro Cifres, director of the Archive of the Sacred Congregation for the Doctrine of the Faith, deserves my heartfelt thanks. I am obligated to Dr. Daniel Ponziani, official of the aforementioned archive, for valuable bibliographical information and for his constant attention in offering clarifications and in suggesting paths of archival research. I wholeheartedly thank them both for their contribution.

I warmly thank Edizioni Ares, in particular Dr. Riccardo Caniato. Since our very first contact he demonstrated a lively intellectual sensibility toward my editorial proposal, accepting the invitation to publish it, and suggesting integrations and useful clarifications. For his constant, always timely, availability, and for his professional dedication to the success of this publication, I am sincerely grateful to him.

I also owe gratitude to Fr. Francesco Colacelli, editor of *Voce di Padre Pio*, for kindly granting the publication of the photographs kept in the journal's archives, showing himself open and attentive to my requests.

I sincerely thank Fr. Ildefonso Moriones, general postulator of the Discalced Carmelites, for his helpfulness in offering me the bibliography necessary to the study of Cardinal Rossi and for granting the copyright of the pictures of this Servant of God, whose beatification process is currently underway.

From the historical point of view, the draft of this volume was revised and critically examined by my brother, Prof. Emanuele Castelli, researcher in historical science and professor at the Pontifical Gregorian University. Our brotherly bond is for him my concrete thanksgiving.

From a stylistic point of view, the draft of this volume was patiently read by and enlightened by the help and suggestions of Dr. Alberto Fornaro, a chief radiologist and a writer. I am deeply tied to him by emotional bonds and, now, by an intellectual debt.

Moreover, I am grateful to my friend Fr. Luciano Lotti, editor of the journal *Studi su Padre Pio*, whom I often quote on account of his vast erudition on Padre Pio and of his valuable suggestions about specific problems and issues.

I thank the Romano Guardini Institute of Religious Sciences in Taranto for supporting the publication of this book.

For many different reasons and with profound gratitude I am grateful and indebted to some of my dearest friends: Dr. Gabriella De Donato, Giovanna D'Oronzo, Dr. Irene Errico, Giuseppe Gaeta, Sara Iaculli, Antonella Introcaso, Daniele Pulpito, Annunziato Russo, Luca Tenneriello. For their help and constant support I thank them all with deep affection and close friendship.

In particular, I have to express my affection and gratitude toward my mother, who, for long months, had the patience to see me immersed in this work, accepting my radical commitment to its publication and accompanying me with her active industriousness and her motherly love.

Finally, I want to thank him who from Heaven looks at me with undeserved love and accompanies me in each step of my priestly life.

Fr. Francesco Castelli

INDEX

Agostino Daniele, Father: in
investigation overview, 37, 41;
in stigmata history summary,
281–82; in text of report,
89–90; in witness depositions,
152, 181, 187, 193
amnesia hypothesis, 38–39
Apostolic Visitation, defined,
64n18
apparitions. *See* visions, Padre
Pio's
army service, Padre Pio's, 83,
152, 173, 200, 290

bandages: in stigmata history
summaries, 287, 291; in text
of report, 86, 129; witness
depositions, 149–50, 155,
168, 190, 191, 197
Barelli, Ms., 63n10
Bella, Monsignor, 63n7
Benedetto Nardella, Father:
overview, 273–75; *Chronicle*
document, 275–80;
correspondence copies,
241–62; in investigation
overview, 6, 24, 34, 38,
63n10; in Padre Pio's
depositions, 202, 207; in
Pio-Giovanna correspondence
copy, 233–34, 236; Rossi's
evaluation of, 132, 133,

238–40; in stigmata history
summaries, 281, 283–85, 290,
292; in text of report, 86,
89–90, 112–15, 130–32, 133
Benedetto Nardella, Father, in
witness depositions: Ignazio's,
168; Lorenzo's, 152, 154, 159,
160; Luigi's, 172; Pietro's,
196; Romolo's, 180
Benedict XV, 61n6
Benedict XVI, x, 4, 73n5
Bignami, Amico: in investigation
overview, 44, 46, 49, 72n52;
in stigmata history summary,
291; in text of report, 108,
109, 119–20, 121; witness
deposition, 193
bilocation phenomenon:
investigation overview, 19–20,
34–35; in Padre Pio's
depositions, 208–9, 227–28;
in text of report, 105–6,
130–31; witness depositions,
143–45, 156, 188
blind woman, healing rumor, 140
blood. *See* stigmata *entries*
Brigittine convent, in Benedetto's
correspondence, 253, 254,
257

cancer, healing rumor, 103
Cani, Monsignor, 252

303

Canonical Visitation, defined, 64n18

Capponi, Ferdinando, 267

carbolic acid, 24, 52, 116–17, 155, 204–5, 223

cell, Padre Pio's, 15–16, 34, 95, 125–26, 203–4

Cerretti, Monsignor, 253

changeability factor, Padre Pio's stigmata: in his deposition, 231; investigation overview, 46–47, 51, 53, 54–55; in text of report, 108, 119

chastity, Padre Pio's, 90, 98, 185, 187

Cherubino, Father, 32, 70n34, 89, 92, 155, 197–99

chest, examination of. *See* stigmata *entries*

choir, Padre Pio's presence: in Emilio of Matrice's memoir, 297n11; in his deposition, 202; investigation overview, 39; in stigmata history summary, 285; in text of report, 92, 126

choir, Padre Pio's presence, in witness depositions: Cherubino's, 198; Lorenzo's, 154, 158, 161; Luigi's, 174, 175, 177; Romolo's, 185

Christ. *See* Jesus, Padre Pio's visions/conversations

Chronicle of Padre Pio (Benedetto), 28, 159, 168, 172, 196, 275–80, 292

clerk's injury, healing rumor, 141–42, 173, 210

clothing, Padre Pio's, 56–58, 93–94

confessor role, Padre Pio's: in his depositions, 200–201, 222, 228, 230; John Paul II's testimony, 70n43; in stigmata history summary, 293; witness depositions, 180, 184, 186, 190, 198

consecration decisions, 31, 74n9

conversions, 31, 35, 73n5, 105, 140, 163–65, 199

correspondence, convent, 103–4, 138, 169, 198–99

correspondence, Padre Pio's: copies of, 233–37, 241–61; in his depositions, 207, 224, 229; investigation overview, 17–18, 19, 24, 75n28; Rossi's questions listed, 235–37; in stigmata history summary, 281–89; in text of report, 96–97, 112–14, 130–32

correspondence, Padre Pio's, in witness depositions: Ignazio's, 166–67, 168; Lorenzo's, 159–60; Luigi's, 172; Pietro's, 196; Romolo's, 181

Cozzi, Maria, 103

cracked bell story, 137

crippled man, healing rumor, 173, 209

crown of thorns, Padre Pio's, 124n143, 160, 231, 283

crucifix story, 181, 229

D'Addario, Raffaele, 40

daily habits, Padre Pio's, 14–15, 68n19, 161. *See also* Mass celebration, Padre Pio's; prayer life, Padre Pio's

d'Alençon, Edouard, 287

De Lai, Cardinal, 269–70
death prediction, 176, 230
demeanor, Padre Pio's. *See* nature
of Padre Pio
demon/devil encounters, Padre
Pio's: in Benedetto's *Chronicle*,
276–77, 278; in his
correspondence, 244; in his
deposition, 201; investigation
overview, 33; in stigmata
history summaries, 276–77,
289, 290; witness depositions,
135, 152–53, 181, 182–83,
193. *See also* diabolical origin
hypothesis
D'Enrico, Bambinella, 143–44
deposition transcripts, Padre Pio's,
199–231
Deskur, Cardinal, 57
devotees of Padre Pio's. *See*
religious enthusiasm
phenomenon
diabolical origin hypothesis, 23,
28, 110, 124
divine origin hypothesis, 23, 25,
26, 28, 110, 119–24
donations: in Benedetto's
correspondence copy, 260–61;
investigation overview, 16; in
text of report, 98–99; witness
depositions, 163, 178, 184–85,
192, 196

eating habits, Padre Pio's: in
Benedetto's *Chronicle*, 279; in
his deposition, 206;
investigation overview, 12–13;
nephew's story, 68n19; in text
of report, 88–89, 110;
unpublished testimony, 67n15

eating habits, Padre Pio's, in
witness depositions:
Lodovico's, 190; Lorenzo's,
157; Luigi's, 175; Pietro's,
194–95; Prencipe's, 138;
Romolo's, 182, 186
ecstasies, Padre Pio's, 122–23,
172, 187. *See also* visions,
Padre Pio's
Emilio of Matrice, Father, 297n11
Evangelista, Father, 187

Fabbrocini, Adelchi, 135
fanaticism. *See* religious
enthusiasm phenomenon
feet, examination of. *See* stigmata
entries
Festa, Dr.: in investigation
overview, 44, 49–50, 76n45;
in stigmata history summary,
291; in text of report, 108,
119–20; in witness
depositions, 153, 154, 190
fevers. *See* hyperthermia, Padre
Pio's
Foggia, Bishop of, 82
Foresti, Sister, 256
fragrance, Padre Pio's: in his
depositions, 203–4, 225; and
his mission, xxi–xxv;
investigation overview, 25–26,
31, 34, 36, 52; in text of
report, 123, 124–26; witness
depositions, 153–54, 174, 182,
191, 195, 197
Franc, D., 153
Francis, Saint, xxii, 22, 76n9,
123, 181, 201
French letters episode, 37, 75n28
furnace comparison, 34, 127, 204

Gaeta, Saverio, xi–xii
Gagliardi, Pasquale (Monsignor), xvii–xviii, 5, 64*n*14, 292
Galatians, xxii
Galeone, Pierino, 69*n*23
Gemelli, Agostino (Father), xvii–xviii, 5, 24, 63*nn*9–10, 82, 112, 123, 291
Gemma Galgani, Saint, 42
Gina, Antonio, 153
Giovanna Longo, Sister, 130–32, 233–37, 254
graces. *See* healing rumors
The Graces of Interior Prayer (Poulain), 111
Greek writing episode, 37, 75*n*28, 172, 229

hands, examination of. *See* stigmata *entries*
healing rumors: investigation overview, 19, 71*n*46, 75*n*23; in Padre Pio's depositions, 209–10, 229; in text of report, 100–104
healing rumors, witness depositions: Lorenzo's, 156, 163; Luigi's, 173, 177; Palladino's, 147–48; Prencipe's, 135, 139–43; Romolo's, 180
health, Padre Pio's: in Benedetto's *Chronicle*, 279–80; in his depositions, 200, 201, 210–11; in stigmata history summary, 290, 294; in text of report, 83; unpublished testimony, 67*n*15; witness depositions, 138, 151–52, 167, 170, 172, 176

heart reading, Padre Pio's, 34, 153, 180, 207
Holy Office, Sacred Congregation of, overview, 61*n*6, 291–93
humility, Padre Pio's: investigation overview, xiv, 17–18, 34, 54, 74*n*18, 75*n*23; in text of report, 90, 91–92, 95–96, 100; witness depositions, 158, 191, 194
hunchbacks, healing rumors, 101, 140–41, 142–43, 209
hyperthermia, Padre Pio's: in his depositions, 204, 206; and his mission, xxi–xxv; investigation overview, 26, 31, 34; in text of report, 126–27; witness depositions, 153, 167, 172–73

Ignazio, Father: depositions of, 165–71; in investigation overview, 32; in Padre Pio's deposition, 205; in text of report, 90–91, 92; in witness depositions, 156, 188
Ill Mattino, 86–87, 135, 141
interrogation testimony. *See* deposition transcripts, Padre Pio's; witness depositions
Intrigillo, Gaetano, 56, 77*n*14
iodine: investigation overview, 36; Padre Pio's depositions, 202, 222–23, 224; in text of report, 117–18, 121; witness depositions, 155, 176, 197

Jesus, Padre Pio's visions/ conversations: in Benedetto's *Chronicle*, 280; in his

deposition, 202; and his mission, xxiv–xxv; investigation overview, xiii–xiv, 21, 33, 38–41, 76*n*38; in stigmata history summaries, 281–84, 286, 290–91; in text of report, 109
John Paul II, xvi, 57, 70*n*43, 293, 294, 295

Lemius, Father Joseph, 5–6, 23, 64*n*15, 82, 110, 115–16, 117
letters. *See* correspondence *entries*
Lodovico, Father, 32, 70*n*34, 91, 98, 155, 189–92
Lorenzo, Father: depositions of, 151–65; in investigation overview, 30–31, 70*n*34, 74*n*9; at Rossi's stigmata examination, 215, 219–20; in text of report, 90, 98, 115, 124*n*143, 126–27
Lorgna, Giocondo, 67*n*15
Lotti, Luciano, 73*nn*3–4
Luigi, Father, 32, 88, 91, 92, 171–79
Luzzatto, Sergio, x–xii, 62*n*7, 63*n*9

Maccari, Carlo, 294
magistrate's chancellor, healing rumor, 141–42, 173, 210
mail. *See* correspondence *entries*
Manfredonia, Archbishop, 82
Maria Lilia, Sister, 257
Maria (sick woman), bilocation phenomenon, 35, 208
Marie José, Princess, 293
Mario (nephew), 68*n*19
Martinis, Cardinal Saraiva, 69*n*23
Mary, Padre Pio's vision, 201

Mass celebration, Padre Pio's: in his depostion, 230–31; investigation overview, 18–19; in stigmata history summary, 292–93; in text of report, 86, 99–100, 129–30
Mass celebration, Padre Pio's, in witness depositions: Lorenzo's, 157–58, 161; Luigi's, 173–74, 178; Romolo's, 184, 187–88, 189
Massa, Giuseppe, 147
Massa, Luigi, 143–44
Massa, Mrs., 227
medical examinations, Padre Pio's stigmata: in his depositions, 206, 207; in history summary, 291; investigation overview, 44, 46, 48–50, 53, 72*nn*51–52, 76*n*9, *n*45; in text of report, 96, 108–9, 119–20, 121; in witness depositions, 153, 154, 190, 193
medicines: investigation overview, 24–25, 32, 36, 52; Padre Pio's depositions, 204–5, 206–7, 222–23; pharmacists depositions, xi, 63*n*7; in text of report, 116–17; witness depositions, 155, 168, 170, 176, 197
Melfi, Bishop of, 124, 191, 288
Menghini, Monsignor, 127
Merla, Angelo M., 153
Merry Del Val, Cardinal Rafael, 64*n*15
miracle rumors, cracked bell story, 137. *See also* bilocation phenomenon; conversions; healing rumors
Montefusco, 151

Montini, Giovanni, 293–94
moral portrait of Padre Pio. *See*
nature of Padre Pio
Morcaldi, Cleonice, 57
Morelli, Gaetano, 165
Morselli, Mrs., 128
mutes, healing rumors, 101,
135–36, 140, 229
mysterious person. *See* Jesus, Padre
Pio's visions/conversations
mysticism: Benedetto's, 238–40;
Padre Pio's deposition, in
213–14

nature of Padre Pio: investigation
overview, xiv–xv, 12, 14, 15,
27, 30, 36, 67*n*14; in text of
report, 87–88, 89–100. *See
also* chastity; humility;
obedience
nature of Padre Pio, witness depositions: Cherubino's, 198; Ignazio's, 170, 175; Lodovico's,
191–92; Lorenzo's, 158, 161;
Pietro's, 193, 194; Prencipe's,
138; Romolo's, 182–83
Nazareno, Father, 50, 152–53
Negrini, Emma, 266
noises: in Benedetto's *Chronicle*,
278; Padre Pio's deposition,
201; witness depositions, 135,
152–53, 172, 177, 181
Notte, Father Eusebio, 50

obedience, Padre Pio's: in his
deposition, 226; investigation
overview, 17–18, 21, 54; in
text of report, 90–91, 96–97,
107; witness depositions, 161,
162, 184, 194

Orlando, Giuseppe, 39
Ottaviani, Cardinal, xvi, 293, 294

pain, Padre Pio's: in Benedetto's
Chronicle, 279; in Emilio of
Matrice's memoir, 297*n*11; in
his depositions, 204, 206,
215–16, 218, 222;
investigation overview, 34, 36,
57; in stigmata history
summaries, 281, 283–86, 290;
in text of report, 45, 48, 122;
witness depositions, 183, 188
Palagi, Arthuro, 165
Palladino, Canon Domenico, 30,
73*n*1, *n*3, 90, 146–50
Paolino, Father Domenico: in
Benedetto's correspondence,
250; in Emilio of Matrice's
memoir, 297*n*11; in
investigation overview, 49,
66*n*6; in text of report,
84–85; in witness depositions,
154, 172–73
Passion of Christ. *See* Jesus, Padre
Pio's visions/conversations
Paul VI, xvi, 294
Pellegrino, Carmelo, 62*n*7
perfumes, 36, 126, 225. *See also*
fragrance, Padre Pio's
Perna, Michele, 146–47
petroleum jelly, 118, 202, 207
photographs of Padre Pio, 149,
157, 210. *See also* religious
enthusiasm phenomenon
physical appearance, Padre Pio's,
12, 67*n*12, 87–88
Pietro, Father: deposition of,
192–97; in investigation
overview, 32, 36, 63*n*10,

64n13; in Padre Pio's depositions, 224–25; in stigmata history summaries, 287–88, 291; in text of report, 89, 91–92, 93, 98, 128–29; in witness depositions, 154, 163
Pio, Padre (overviews): background, 83–84, 200–201; beatification/sainthood, xix–xx, 69n23; in Benedetto's *Chronicle*, 276–80; chronology of, 289–96; investigation origins, 4–6, 62n7, 63n7; mission of, xxi–xxv; opposition origins, xvii–xviii, 4–5, 81–82; Rossi's assessment summarized, 27–28, 132–33; scholarly arguments about, ix–xii, 62n7. *See also specific topics, e.g.*, Benedetto Nardella, Father; humility, Padre Pio's; stigmata *entries*
Pious Society of Saint Charles, 271
Pius X, 61n6
Pius XI, 65n20, 270
Pius XII, 293–94
Placido, Father, 84, 250
Poltawska, Wanda, 294
Poulain, Father, 111, 119, 120–23
poverty style, Padre Pio's: investigation overview, 15–16; in text of report, 98–99; witness depositions, 163, 184–85, 191–92, 196
prayer life, Padre Pio's: in his depositions, 208, 209, 212–13, 220–21; investigation overview,

17–18, 32, 35–36; in text of report, 99, 129; witness depositions, 161, 185, 191
Prencipe, Giuseppe (Archpriest): depositions of, 134–46; investigation overview, 29–30, 66n6, 73n2; in report text, 88, 90, 100–101, 126; in witness depositions, 150

Raffaele, Father, 84
religious enthusiasm phenomenon: overview, xi, xiv, xx–xxi; in Emilio of Matrice's memoir, 297n11; investigation overview, 27, 30, 32, 68n19, 73n2; in Padre Pio's depositions, 210, 230; and Padre Pio's mission, xxii–xxv; in stigmata history summary, 292–93; in text of report, 81–82, 84–87, 95–96, 127–30; witness depositions, 135, 150, 173–74, 193–94, 199. *See also* healing rumors
religious portrait of Padre Pio. *See* nature of Padre Pio
Ribola, Professor, 155
Ricci, Pasquale, 146–47
Roberto of Nove, Father, 67nn14–15, 68n19
Romanelli, Luigi: in investigation overview, 44, 46, 48–49, 72n51, 76n9; in Padre Pio's deposition, 207; in stigmata history summary, 291; in text of report, 96, 108, 119–20; in witness depositions, 154
Romolo, Father, 70n34, 88–89, 91, 92, 98, 179–89

Rossi, Raffaello Carlo:
    background, 65*n*20, 265–71;
    death/beatification process,
    271–72; inquiry approach,
    3–4, 11–23, 29–30;
    investigation directive, 6,
    9–11, 67*n*8, 291
Sacred Congregation of Holy
    Office, overview, 61*n*6
Saldutto, Gerardo, 66*n*21
Sales, Saint Francis de, 94–95
Santariello, healing rumor, 101,
    140, 142–43, 148
Santopaolo, Monsignor, 252
Schmucki, Ottaviano, 38, 39
self-stigmatization hypotheses:
    investigation overview, 23,
    24–25, 28, 51–54, 72*n*54; in
    Padre Pio's deposition, 225; in
    text of report, 109–18, 124
shirts, Padre Pio's, 56–58, 93–94
shoulder sores, in text of report,
    55–59
sick woman, bilocation phenom-
    enon, 35, 143–44, 156, 208
side, examination of. *See* stigmata
    entries
simplicity trait, Padre Pio's:
    overview, xiv–xv; investigation
    overview, 32; in text of
    report, 91, 92; witness
    depositions, 158, 161, 174,
    175, 182–83, 185, 198
soldier's story, bilocation
    phenomenon, 144–45, 227
spiritual nature, Padre Pio's. *See*
    nature of Padre Pio
stigmata, Padre Pio's: in
    Benedetto's *Chronicle*, 279; in

Emilio of Matrice's memoir,
    297*n*11; in his
    correspondence, 248, 281–82;
    in his depositions, 202,
    206–7, 225, 231; and his
    mission, xxi–xxv; history
    summarized, 281–89, 290–91,
    294; investigation overview,
    xiv, 20–25, 37–40, 44–59,
    72*n*54, 76*n*9, *n*45; Rossi's
    examination transcript,
    214–19. *See also* pain, Padre
    Pio's
stigmata, Padre Pio's, in text of
    report: overview, 107–9;
    diabolical origin hypothesis,
    110, 124; divine origin
    hypothesis, 119–24;
    self-induced hypotheses,
    109–18, 124
stigmata, Padre Pio's, in witness
    depositions: Cherubino's, 197;
    Ignazio's, 167–68; Lodovico's,
    190; Lorenzo's, 153, 154–55;
    Luigi's, 174–75; Pietro's, 195;
    Prencipe's, 138; Romolo's,
    180, 181–82
stigmata, Saint Francis', 22, 76*n*9
students, Padre Pio's, 167, 186,
    278, 279
studies, Padre Pio's, 200, 213
suffering, Padre Pio's: in
    Benedetto's *Chronicle*, 279–80;
    correspondence about, 234,
    236–37, 243–50, 258; and his
    mission, xxi–xxv; investigation
    overview, 21, 24, 53–54; in
    text of report, 107; witness
    depositions, 194, 198. *See also*
    hyperthermia, Padre Pio's

Tangero, Professor, 141
temperature, Padre Pio's. *See*
hyperthermia, Padre Pio's
Teresa, Saint, 94
theosophy, defined, 73*n*7
tidiness, Padre Pio's, 95
tobacco, 24, 156, 168
Toniolo, Giuseppe, 266
Tornielli, Andrea, xi–xii
Torre Maggiore man, bilocation
phenomenon, 208
transfers, Padre Pio's: in
Benedetto's *Chronicle*, 278–79;
in his deposition, 210;
investigation overview, 10–11,
27, 66*n*6; in stigmata history
summaries, 290, 291, 292; in
text of report, 83–84, 128,
132; witness depositions, 135,
151–52, 172
Trevisani, Mr., 141
tuberculosis patient, healing
rumor, 103–4

Valbonesi, Monsignor, 252
veratridine: investigation
overview, 24–25, 32; in Padre
Pio's deposition, 205; in text
of report, 116–17; witness
depositions, 155, 156, 168
virtues, Padre Pio's. *See* nature of
Padre Pio; women and Padre
Pio
visions, Padre Pio's: in
Benedetto's *Chronicle*, 276–78,
280; in his depositions,
201–2, 221; investigation
overview, 33; in text of

report, 99, 106–7, 109, 123;
witness depositions, 177. *See
also* demon/devil encounters,
Padre Pio's; Jesus, Padre Pio's
visions/conversations
Vives y Tuto, Cardinal Calasanz,
64*n*15
Votum, overview, xii–xxii, 3–4,
7–8, 61*n*1. *See also specific
topics, e.g.*, Benedetto Nardella,
Father; humility, Padre Pio's;
stigmata *entries*

witness depositions: overview,
xiv–xv, 13–14, 29–32, 232;
Cherubino's, 197–99;
Ignazio's, 165–71; Lodovico's,
189–92; Lorenzo's, 151–65;
Luigi's, 171–79; Palladino's,
146–50; Pietro's, 192–97;
Prencipe's, 134–46; Romolo's,
179–89
Wojtiła, Father Karol. *See* John
Paul II
women and Padre Pio: in his
depositions, 211–12, 224–25,
227, 230; investigation
overview, 16–17, 35, 70*n*34;
in text of report, 86, 97–98,
128
women and Padre Pio, witness
depositions: Cherubino's, 198;
Lodovico's, 192; Lorenzo's,
157, 160–61; Luigi's, 177–78,
183–85; Palladino's, 147,
148–50; Pietro's, 195;
Prencipe's, 135
wounds. *See* stigmata *entries*